Java Security

JAVA SECURITY

Preeti Jain

CENTRUM PRESS
NEW DELHI-110002 (INDIA)

CENTRUM PRESS

H.O.: 4360/4, Ansari Road, Daryaganj,
New Delhi-110002 (India)
Tel: 23278000, 23261597, 23255577, 23286875

B.O.: No. 1015, Ist Main Road, BSK IIIrd Stage,
IIIrd Phase, IIIrd Block, Bangalore-560085 (INDIA)
Tel: 080-41723429

Email: centrumpress@gmail.com
Visit us at: www.centrumpress.com

Java Security

First Edition, 2011

PRINTED IN INDIA

Printed at Tarun Offset Printers, Delhi-110053

Contents

Preface vii

1. Java Application Security 1
2. Need of Security 20
3. Java Network 83
4. Loading and Linking 107
5. Security on JBoss 146
6. Web Applications 250

Bibliography 277
Index 279

Preface

Java is a new programming language from Sun Microsystems. The Java language has a number of interesting properties. One property is that it is intended to be portable, even to the extent that programs can be dynamically loaded over the network and run locally. In particular, small programs called applets can be loaded and run by a user's WWW browser while the user is ``surfing" the Web. This idea is very powerful and is also an invitation to security problems. The Java language and runtime system attempt to address these security issues, with the result that Sun claims Java will be secure.

The Java approach to providing executable content is to have Web Browsers with an embedded Java interpreter and runtime library. These Web Browsers can download Java programs called applets, and have the Java interpreter execute the program. With this model, there are three fundamental layers: the Java language itself, the standard set of Java libraries, and the Web Browser itself. The security of the system depends fundamentally on the security of each of these three layers.

Author

1

Java Application Security

INTRODUCTION

When Java was first released by Sun Microsystems, it attracted the attention of programmers throughout the world. These developers were attracted to Java for different reasons: some were drawn to Java because of its cross-platform capabilities, some because of its ease of programming (especially compared to object-oriented languages like C++), some because of its robustness and memory management, some because of Java's security, and some for still other reasons.

Just as different developers came to Java with different expectations, so too did they bring different expectations as to what was meant by the ubiquitous phrase "Java is secure." Security means different things to different people, and many developers who had certain expectations about the word "security" were surprised to find that their expectations were not necessarily shared by the designers of Java.

This book discusses the features of Java that make it secure. In this book, we'll discuss why Java is said to be secure, what that security means (and doesn't mean), and—most importantly—how to use the security features of the Java platform within your own programs.

This last point is actually the focus of this book: while some of Java's security features are automatically a part of all Java programs, many of them are not. In this book, we'll learn about all those features, and how to utilize them in our own Java applications.

JAVA SECURITY

The first thing that we must do to facilitate our discussion of Java security is to discuss just what Java's security goals are. The term "security" is somewhat vague unless it is discussed in some context; different expectations of the term "security" might lead us to expect that Java programs would be:

- *Safe from malevolent programs*: Programs should not be allowed to harm a user's computing environment. This includes Trojan horses as well as harmful programs that can replicate themselves—computer viruses.
- *Non-intrusive*: Programs should be prevented from discovering private information on the host computer or the host computer's network.
- *Authenticated*: The identity of parties involved in the programme should be verified.
- *Encrypted*: Data that the programme sends and receives should be encrypted.
- *Audited*: Potentially sensitive operations should always be logged.
- *Well-defined*: A well-defined security specification would be followed.
- *Verified*: Rules of operation should be set and verified.
- Well-behaved: Programs should be prevented from consuming too many system resources.
- *C2 or B1 certified*: Programs should have certification from the U.S. government that certain security procedures are included.

In fact, while all of these features could be part of a secure system, only the first two were within the province of Java's 1.0 default security model. Other items in the list have been introduced in later versions of Java: authentication was added in 1.1, encryption is available as an extension to 1.2, and auditing can be added to any Java programme by providing an auditing security manager. Still others of these items will be added in the future. But the basic premise remains that Java security was originally and fundamentally designed to protect the information on a computer from being accessed or modified (including a modification that would introduce a virus) while still allowing the Java programme to run on that computer.

The point driving this notion of security is the new distribution model for Java programs. One of the driving forces behind Java, of course, is its ability to download programs over a network and run those programs on another machine within the context of a Java-enabled browser (or within the context of other Java applications). Coupled with the widespread growth of Internet use—and the public-access nature of the Internet—Java's ability to bring programs to a user on an as-needed, just-in-time basis has been a strong reason for its rapid deployment and acceptance.

The nature of the Internet created a new and largely unprecedented requirement for programs to be free of viruses and Trojan horses. Computer users had always been used to purchasing shrink-wrapped software. Many soon began downloading software via ftp or other means and then running that software on their machines. But widespread downloading also led to a pervasive problem of malevolent attributes both in free and (ironically) in commercial software (a problem which continues unabated). The introduction of Java into this equation had the potential to multiply this problem by orders of magnitude, as computer users now download programs automatically and frequently.

For Java to succeed, it needed to circumvent the virus/trojan horse problems that plagued other models of software distribution. Hence, the early work on Java focused on just that issue: Java programs are considered safe because they cannot install, run, or propagate viruses, and because the programme itself cannot perform any action that is harmful to the user's computing environment. And in this context, safety means security. This is not to say that the other issues in the above list are not important—each has its place and its importance (in fact, we'll spend a great deal of time in this book on the third and fourth topics in that list). But the issues of protecting information and preventing viruses were considered most important; hence, features to provide that level of security were the first to be adopted. Like all parts of Java, its security model is evolving (and has evolved through its various releases); many of the notions about security in our list will eventually make their way into Java.

One of the primary goals of this book, then, is to explain Java's security model and its evolution through releases. In the final analysis, whether or not Java is secure is a subjective judgment that individual users will have to make based on their own requirements. If all you want from Java is freedom from viruses, any release of Java should meet your needs. If you need to introduce authentication or encryption into your programme, you'll need to use a 1.1 or later release of Java. If you have a requirement that all operations be audited, you'll need to build that auditing into your applications. If you really need conformance with a U.S. government-approved definition of security, Java is not the platform for you. We take a very pragmatic view of security in this book: the issue is not whether a system that lacks a particular feature qualifies as "secure" according to someone's definition of security. The issue is whether Java possesses the features that meet your needs.

When Java security is discussed, the discussion typically centers around Java's applet-based security model—the security model that is embodied by Java-enabled browsers. This model is designed for the Internet. For many users, this is not necessarily the most appropriate model: it is somewhat restrictive, and the security concerns on a private, corporate network are not the same as those on the Internet.

In this book, we take a different tack: the goal of this book is to show how to use the security model and how to write your own secure Java applications. While some of the information we present will be applicable to a browser environment, the security of any particular browser is ultimately up to the provider of the browser. Some browsers allow us to change the security policy the browser uses, but many do not. Hence, reading about the security manager in this book may help you understand how a particular browser works (and why it works that way), but that won't necessarily allow you to change the security model provided by that browser.

THE JAVA SANDBOX

Discussions of Java's security model often center around the idea of a sandbox model. The idea behind this model is that when you allow a programme to be hosted on your computer, you want to provide an environment where the programme can play (*I.e.*, run), but you want to confine the program's play area within certain bounds. You may decide to give the programme certain toys to play with (*I.e.*, you may decide to let it have access to certain system resources), but in general, you want to make sure that the programme is confined to its sandbox.

This analogy works better when you consider it from the view of a close relative rather than from the view of a parent. If you're a parent, you probably consider the purpose of a sandbox to be to provide a safe environment for your child to play in. When my niece Rachel visits me, however, I consider the purpose of a sandbox not (only) to be to protect her, but also to protect my grandmother's china *from* her. I love my niece, but I can't give her leave to run through my house; I enjoy running the latest cool applet on the Internet, but I can't give it leave to run through my filesystem.

The Java sandbox is responsible for protecting a number of resources, and it does so at a number of levels. Consider the resources of a typical machine as shown in Figure. The user's machine has access to many things:

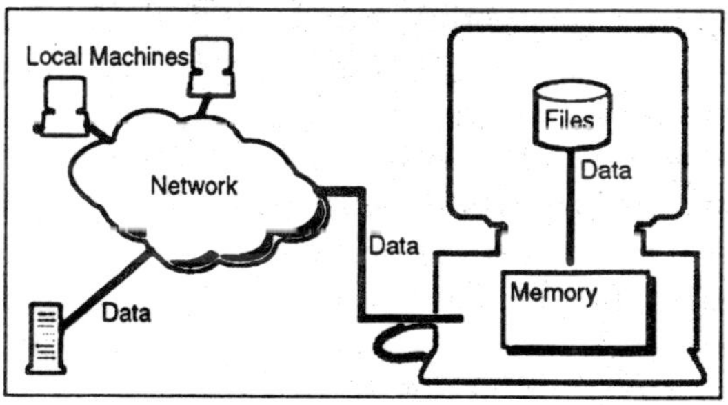

Fig. A Machine has Access to many Resources

- Internally, it has access to its local memory (the computer's RAM).
- Externally, it has access to its filesystem and to other machines on the local network.
- For running applets, it also has access to a web server, which may be on its local (private) net, or may be on the Internet.
- Data flows through this entire model, from the user's machine through the network and (possibly) to disk.

Each of these resources needs to be protected, and those protections form the basis of Java's security model.

We can imagine a number of different-sized sandboxes in which a Java programme might run:

- A sandbox in which the programme has access to the CPU, the screen, keyboard, and mouse, and to its own memory. This is the minimal sandbox—it contains just enough resources for a programme to run.
- A sandbox in which the programme has access to the CPU and its own memory as well as access to the web server from which it was loaded. This is often thought of as the default state for the sandbox.
- A sandbox in which the programme has access to the CPU, its memory, its web server, and to a set of programme-specific resources (local files, local machines, etc.). A word-processing programme, for example, might have access to the *docs* directory on the local filesystem, but not to any other files.
- An open sandbox, in which the programme has access to whatever resources the host machine normally has access to.

The sandbox, then, is not a one-size-fits-all model. Expanding the boundaries of the sandbox is always based on the notion of trust: when my one-year-old niece comes to visit, there's very little in the sandbox for her to play with, but when my six-year-old godchild comes to visit, I trust that I might give her more things to play with. In the hands of some visitors, a toy with small removable parts would be dangerous, but when I trust the recipient, it's perfectly reasonable to include that item in the sandbox. And so it is with Java programs: in some cases, I might trust them to access my filesystem; in other cases, I might trust them to access only part of my filesystem; and in still other cases, I might not trust them to access my filesystem at all.

APPLICATIONS, APPLETS, AND PROGRAMS

It's no accident that this chapter has the word "application" in its title, because the Java security model is solely at the discretion of a Java application. When an applet runs inside the HotJava browser, HotJava*TM* is the Java application that has determined the security policy for that applet. And although other popular browsers are not written in Java, they play the role of a Java application: it is still the case that the choice of security model is up to the browser and cannot be changed by the applet.

This makes the distinction between applications and applets a crucial one: applications can establish and modify their security policies while applets (generally) cannot. However, this distinction has diminished over time. Beginning with Java 1.2, users of Java applications have the opportunity to run an application within a sandbox that the user or system administrator has constructed. In the next section, we'll see how the same functionality can be achieved with Java 1.1 as well. Under these scenarios, the Java security model for applications is solely at the discretion of the user or system administrator.

This is a major change of perception for many users and developers of Java, who are used to considering the security differences between applets and applications as a significant differentiator between the two types of programs.

There will, of course, always be particular programming differences between applets and applications: an applet extends the *java.applet.Applet* class and is written as a series of callbacks, while an application can be any class that has a static method called *main()*. When this programming distinction is important, we'll use the terms "applet" and "application" as appropriate. But we'll typically use the term "programme" to refer to the Java code that we're running.

ANATOMY OF A JAVA APPLICATION

The anatomy of a typical Java application is shown in Figure. Each of the features of the Java platform that appears in a rectangle plays a role in the development of the Java sandbox. In particular, the elements of the Java sandbox are comprised of:

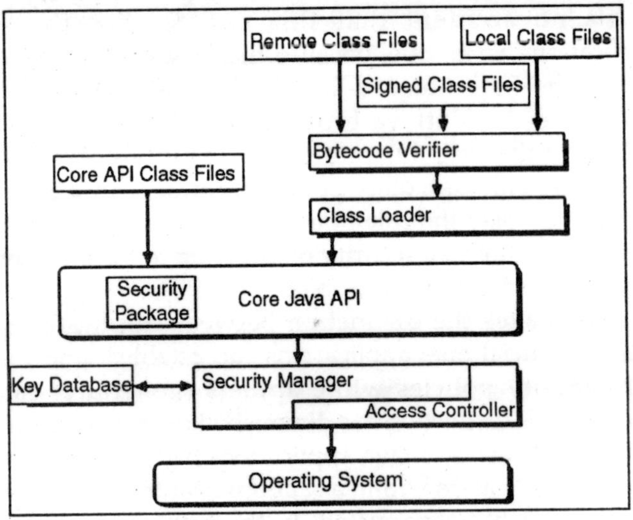

Fig. Anatomy of a Java Application

- *The bytecode verifier*: The bytecode verifier ensures that Java class files follow the rules of the Java language. In terms of resources, the bytecode verifier helps enforce memory protections for all Java programs. As the figure implies, not all files are subject to bytecode verification.
- *The class loader*: One or more class loaders load classes that are not found on the *CLASSPATH*. In 1.2, class loaders are responsible for loading classes that are found on the *CLASSPATH* as well.
- *The access controller*: In Java 1.2, the access controller allows (or prevents) most access from the core API to the operating system.

- *The security manager*: The security manager is the primary interface between the core API and the operating system; it has the ultimate responsibility for allowing or preventing access to all system resources. In 1.2, the security manager uses the access controller for most (but not all) of those decisions; in 1.0 and 1.1, the security manager is solely responsible for those decisions.
- *The security package*: The security package (that is, classes in the *java.security* package) forms the basis for authenticating signed Java classes. Although it is only a small box in this diagram, the security package is a complex API, and discussion of it is broken into several chapters of this book.

  This includes discussions of:
  - The security provider interface—the means by which different security implementations may be plugged into the security package
  - Message digests
  - Keys and certificates
  - Digital signatures
  - Encryption (an optional extension to the security package)

    The security package was initially available in Java 1.1.
- *The key database*: The key database is a set of keys used by the security manager and access controller to verify the digital signature that accompanies a signed class file. In the Java architecture, it is part of the security package, though it may be manifested as an external file or database.

The last two items in this list have broad applicability beyond expanding the Java sandbox. With respect to the sandbox, digital signatures play an important role, because they provide authentication of who actually provided the Java class. As we'll see, this provides the ability for end users and system administrators to grant very specific privileges to individual classes or signers. But a digital signature might be used for other applications. Let's say that you're deploying a payroll application throughout a large corporation. When an employee sends a request to view his payroll information, you really want to make sure that the request came from that employee rather than from someone else in the corporation. Often, this type of application is secured by a simple password, but a more secure system could require a digitially signed request before it sent out the payroll information. We'll discuss security concerns in both these contexts in this book.

In particular, two different examples will form the theme of the examples that are developed through this book:

1. A browser-type programme (called *JavaRunner*) that we'll use to explore the sandbox aspects of Java's security model
2. The payroll application of a large company (XYZ Corporation) that we'll use to explore how the features of Java's security model can be used for purposes other than the sandbox (*e.g.*, to sign a payroll request)

We'll develop a full implementation of the first of these examples; while we won't provide a complete payroll application, we will provide a number of examples of the security features required for such an application.

RUNNING A JAVA APPLICATION

The parameters of the Java sandbox that we've outlined are possible elements of a Java application, but they are not required elements of an application. The remainder of this book will show us how and when those elements can be introduced into a Java application. First, however, we're going to discuss the techniques by which Java applications can be run. There are two techniques that we'll introduce in this section: the *JavaRunner* technique and the *Launcher* technique. While both allow you to run an application securely, the examples in this chapter do not provide any security. We'll fill in the security pieces bit by bit, while we flesh out the security story. At that point, we'll show how to run Java applications securely. Typically, we're used to running Java applications simply by specifying on the command line the name of a class that contains a *main()* method. Consider this application that reads the file specified by a command-line argument:

```
public class Cat {
  public static void main(String args[]) {
    try {
      String s;
      FileReader fr = newFileReader(args[0]);
      BufferedReader br = new BufferedReader(fr);
      while ((s = br.readLine()) != null)
        System.out.println(s);
    } catch (Exception e) {
        System.out.println(e);
    }
  }
}
```

This is a regular Java application; if we wanted to run it and print out the contents of the password file on a Unix system, we could run the command:

```
piccolo% java Cat/etc/passwd
root:x:0:1:0000-Admin(0000):/:/usr/bin/csh
daemon:x:1:1:0000-Admin(0000):/:
bin:x:2:2:0000-Admin(0000):/usr/bin:
...
```

From a security point of view, this is a very rudimentary programme. It contains none of the elements of the sandbox that we just listed; it has the default (wide-open) sandbox given by default to every Java application. This application can perform any operation it wants.

SECURITY AND THE OPERATING SYSTEM

The security policy imposed by Java is augmented by the security features of the operating system on which Java is running. A Java application with a wide-open security policy may attempt to read the password file, but if the user running the application does not normally have permission to read the password file, the Java application will not succeed. The actual security policy that is in effect for a Java application will be the intersection of the security policy built into the application and the security policy of the operating system when the application is run. For the purposes of this book, we ignore the security features that the operating system may provide.

There are two ways in which we can add security features to this application. One way is to add to the application a class loader, a security manager, use of the access controller, and so on. This additional programming would set the bounds of the sandbox for this particular application.

The other route we can take is to run this application under the auspices of another application that we'll call *JavaRunner*. This is completely analogous to the way in which we typically run applets: *appletviewer* is a Java application that runs applets, and *JavaRunner* is a Java application that runs other applications. *Java-Runner* is responsible for establishing the parameters of the Java sandbox (that is, it ensures that appropriate class loaders, a security manager, and the like are all in place) before it invokes the target application, just as *appletviewer* establishes the parameters of the Java sandbox before it invokes the target applet.

This technique removes the difference (in terms of security) between an applet and an application: both types of programs are now subject to the Java sandbox.

There are a number of circumstances in which this is useful:

- If you download (or purchase) Java applications and want them to run in a sandbox.
- If you want to ensure that your internally developed applications all run in the desired sandbox (without having to include that code in every application).
- If you have a corporate or campus network and need to distribute Java applications under a new security model. Perhaps the new model will:
- Give different security permissions to programs downloaded from within the corporate firewall than those from outside the corporate firewall (without requiring internal classes to be signed)
- Authenticate users on the corporate network before

allowing sensitive payroll data to be sent (even over the corporate network)

- Encrypt that payroll data, so internal spies can't decipher it
- Allow the user greater discretion over the resources granted to a particular programme

Although the *JavaRunner* programme is designed to run other applications, there is no reason why it cannot be modified to run applets as well. Such a modification would require some extra code to parse the HTML containing the applet tag and set up an instance of the *AppletStub* and*AppletContext* classes for the applet itself. We're not showing the code to do that only because it's not really relevant to the discussion of Java security—but the *JavaRunner* could easily be extended to become an *appletviewer* (or, with an appropriate Java bean that interprets HTML, a full-fledged browser). The advantage, of course, is that as author of the browser you would have full control over the security model the browser employs.

OUTLINE OF THE JAVARUNNER APPLICATION

Here's the basic implementation of the JavaRunner application:

```
public class JavaRunner implements Runnable {
  final static int numArgs = 1;
  private Object args[];
  private String className;

  JavaRunner(String className, Object args[]) {
    this.className = className;
    this.args = args;
  }

  void invokeMain(Class clazz) {
    Class argList[] = new Class[] { String[].class
      };
    Method mainMethod = null;
    try {
      mainMethod = clazz.getMethod("main",
          argList);
```

```
     } catch (NoSuchMethodException nsme) {
            System.out.println("No main method in
" + clazz.getName());
            System.out.println.exit(-1);
     }

     try {
           mainMethod.invoke(null, args);
     } catch (Exception e) {
           Throwable t;
           if (e instanceof
            InvocationTargetException)
           t = ((InvocationTargetException) e)
          .getTargetException();
          else t = e;
          System.out.println("Procedure  exited
with exception " + t);
          t.printStackTrace();
    }
 }

   public void run() {
           Class target = null;
           try {
                  target =
                     Class.forName(className);
                   invokeMain(target);
           } catch (ClassNotFoundException cnfe)
              {
                System.out.println("Can't load "
                   + className);
           }
   }

   static Object[] getArgs(String args[]) {
         String passArgs[] = new
            String[args.length - numArgs];
         for (int i = numArgs; i < args.length;
```

```
            i++)
               passArgs[i - numArgs] = args[i];

         Object wrapArgs[] = new Object[1];
         wrapArgs[0] = passArgs;
         return wrapArgs;
   }
  public static void main(String args[]) {

         if (args.length < 1) {
             System.err.println("usage: JavaRunner
classfile");
              System.exit(-1);
         }
         ThreadGroup tg = new
ThreadGroup("JavaRunner Threadgroup");
         Thread t = new Thread(tg,
             new JavaRunner(args[0],
               getArgs(args)));
      t.start();
      try {
             t.join();
      } catch (InterruptedException ie) {
          System.out.println("Thread was
             interrupted");
      }
   }
}
```

This is a fully functional (if not full-featured) version of the *JavaRunner* programme; we can use it to run our *Cat* application like this:

```
piccolo% java JavaRunner Cat/etc/passwd
root:x:0:1:0000-Admin(0000):/:/usr/bin/csh
daemon:x:1:1:0000-Admin(0000):/:
bin:x:2:2:0000-Admin(0000):/usr/bin:
...
```

This will give us exactly the same results as when we ran the programme by hand. The *invokeMain()* method will use the Java reflection API to find the static *main()* method of the *Cat* class and then construct an appropriate argument list to pass to that method.

Note that the use of the reflection API introduces a dependency on Java for this programme. You can write a similar programme under Java 1.0, but not without using the native (C) interface to Java. Note also that we construct a new thread group and thread, and run the *main()* method under control of that thread. The primary reason we do that will become clear in Chapter when we discuss thread security policies. But there's no reason why you couldn't expand this example to run multiple targets simultaneously, in which case each target should have its own thread and thread group anyway.

We've cheated a little bit here by using the *forName()* method of the *Class* class to find our target application class—we'll hear more about that in Chapter when we discuss class loaders. For now, it will suffice to know that this will load our target class (assuming that the target class is found on the *CLASSPATH*).

In addition, we still haven't done anything to set up a security manager or to enable the access controller. As a result, the sandbox for an application run under this programme is non-existent: the bytecodes will not be verified, and there will be no restriction on any actions that the application may perform. But this is the example that we'll expand upon during the rest of this book as we add security features to it.

Don't think that the only function of a programme like this is to run Java applications (or even Java applets). Consider the Java web server—it must dynamically invoke servlets for different web requests as those requests come in. An RMI server might operate similarly, perhaps even loading the code to perform its operations from a client machine. Although we stick with this example throughout the book, the need for security in server applications parallels the need for security in end-user applications.

BUILT-IN JAVA APPLICATION SECURITY

Beginning in Java 1.2, the Java platform itself comes with

a security model built into applications it runs. This model is based upon information in the user's *CLASSPATH*. Setting the *CLASSPATH* is the same operation in Java 1.1 and Java 1.2, but in Java 1.2, classes that are found on the*CLASSPATH* may optionally be subject to a security model. This allows you to run the application code in a user- or administrator-defined sandbox: in particular, it uses the access controller of Java 1.2 to provide the same security environment for the target application as a Java-enabled browser provides for an applet.

The successful use of this facility depends upon the class loader that the built-in application runner will use, as well as depending upon the environment set up by the access controller and security manager. We'll examine how these facilities interact with this method of running applications in the next few chapters. For now, we'll just outline how this method operates.

As always, Java applications are run on the command line as follows:

```
piccolo% java Cat/etc/passwd
root:x:0:1:0000-Admin(0000):/:/usr/bin/csh
daemon:x:1:1:0000-Admin(0000):/:
bin:x:2:2:0000-Admin(0000):/usr/bin:
...
```

This example loads the *Cat.class* file from the user's *CLASSPATH* and runs the application with the single argument*/etc/passwd*. As always, when an application is run in this manner, the sandbox in which the application runs is unlimited: the application can perform any activity it wants to. There is a very important difference between running these examples in Java 1.1 and running them in 1.2: in 1.2, classes that are loaded from the*CLASSPATH* will be loaded by a class loader. The addition of the class loader to the *CLASSPATH* allows us to build a sandbox for the application. However, none of these examples actually builds a sandbox yet. In order to build a sandbox for these examples, we must specify the -Djava.security.manager flag on the command line. This flag enables a security manager and access controller to be installed; we'll discuss the details of this option in Chapter.

The -Djava.security.manager flag is only available in Java 1.2. Without it, Java applications in 1.2 behave exactly as they do in 1.1: they have a wide-open sandbox. For historical reasons (and because it makes describing this facility easier), we'll refer to the ability to run applications with an optional argument to specify a sandbox as the *Launcher*. Given that the *Launcher* is a standard part of Java, you might ask why we're going to the trouble of implementing our own *JavaRunner*. One reason is simply to make our discussion clearer: it is easiest to understand the architecture of Java's security policy in the context of *JavaRunner*. Other reasons have to do with certain limitations that we'll discover about the *Launcher*:

SECURE APPLICATIONS IN 1.2 AND 1.2 BETA 2

In releases of 1.2 up through beta 2, running a secure application requires use of a special class: the *Launcher* class (*sun.misc.Launcher*). To run an application under control of the *Launcher*, you would execute this command:

```
piccolo% java sun.misc.Launcher Cat/etc/passwd
```

In 1.2 beta, classes that are loaded from the *CLASSPATH* are not subject to the sandbox. In order to load those classes through a class loader and subject them to the sandbox, you must specify an alternate classpath for the classes that make up the application:

```
piccolo% java -Djava.app.class.path=/classes
sun.misc.Launcher \
```

Cat/etc/passwd

If the *Cat* class is found in/*classes*, it will be subject to the sandbox. If it is found in the *CLASSPATH*, it will not.

Beginning in 1.2 beta 3, the *Launcher* class was incorporated into the virtual machine itself, but the syntax to use it changed in the last few beta releases. In FCS, the correct syntax is:

```
piccolo% java -Djava.security.manager Cat/etc/
passwd
```

- The *Launcher* comes only with Java 1.2 and later releases; if you're still using 1.1, you'll have to use the *JavaRunner* programme.

- The *Launcher* can only run classes from the *CLASSPATH*—it cannot load classes from the network or from another location. However, simply because the programme in question is an application does not mean we won't want to load its classes from a server—but we'll need*JavaRunner* to do that.
- The security manager used by the *Launcher* does not have all the features we might desire. While most of its features are configurable through the access controller (also a feature of Java 1.2), there are certain advanced policies that we cannot configure in that way. These features can only be achieved with some programming on our part.

Hence, both the *Launcher* and *JavaRunner* are useful mechanisms for running Java applications; which one you use depends on your particular requirements.

2

Need of Security

INTRODUCTION

Java's security model is one of the key architectural features that makes it an appropriate technology for networked environments. Security is important because networks represent a potential avenue of attack to any computer hooked to them. This concern becomes especially strong in an environment in which software is downloaded across the network and executed locally, as is done, for example, with Java applets and Jini service objects.

Because the class files for an applet are automatically downloaded when a user goes to the containing web page in a browser, it is likely that a user will encounter applets from untrusted sources. Similarly, the class files for a Jini service object are downloaded from a code base specified by the service provider when it registers its service with the Jini lookup service.

Because Jini enables spontaneous networking in which users entering a new environment look up and access locally available services, users of Jini services will likely encounter service objects from untrusted sources. Without any security, these automatic code download schemes would be a convenient way to distribute malicious code. Thus, Java's security mechanisms help make Java suitable for networks because they establish a needed trust in the safety of executing network-mobile code.

Java's security model is focused on protecting end-users from hostile programs (and bugs in otherwise benevolent programs) downloaded across a network from untrusted sources. To accomplish this goal, Java provides a customizable "sandbox" in which untrusted Java programs can be placed. The sandbox restricts the activities of the untrusted programme. The programme can do anything within the boundaries of its sandbox, but can't take any action outside those boundaries.

For example, the original sandbox for untrusted Java applets in version 1.0 prohibited many activities, including:

- Reading or writing to the local disk,
- Making a network connection to any but the host from which the applet came,
- Creating a new process, and
- Loading a new dynamic library

By making it impossible for downloaded code to perform certain actions, Java's security model protects the end-user from the threats of hostile and buggy code.

Because the sandbox security model imposes strict controls on what untrusted code can and cannot do, users are able to run untrusted code with relative safety. Unfortunately for the programmers and users of 1.0 systems, however, the original sandbox was so restrictive, that well-meaning (but untrusted) code was often unable to do useful work. In version 1.1, the original sandbox model was augmented with a trust model based on code signing and authentication.

The signing and authentication capability enables the receiving system to verify that a set of class files (in a JAR file) has been digitally signed (in effect, blessed as trustworthy) by some entity, and that the class files have not been altered since they were signed. This enables end users and system administrators to ease the restrictions of the sandbox for code that has been digitally signed by trusted parties.

Although the security APIs released with version 1.1 include support for authentication, they don't offer much help in establishing anything more than an all-or-nothing trust policy (in other words, either code is completely trusted or completely untrusted). Java's next major release, version 1.2, provided APIs to assist in establishing fine-grained security policies based on authentication of digitally signed code. The remainder of this chapter will trace the evolution of Java's security model from the basic sandbox of 1.0, through the code signing and authentication of 1.1, to the fine-grained access control of 1.2.

BASIC SANDBOX

In the world of personal computers, you have traditionally had to trust software before you ran it. You achieved security by being careful only to use software from trusted sources, and by regularly scanning for viruses just to make sure. Once some software got access to your system, it had full reign. If it was malicious, it could do a great deal of damage because there were no restrictions placed on it by the runtime environment of your computer. So in the traditional security scheme, you tried to prevent malicious code from ever gaining access to your computer in the first place.

The sandbox security model makes it easier to work with software that comes from sources you don't fully trust. Instead of approaching security by requiring you to prevent any code you don't trust from ever making its way onto your computer, the sandbox model allows you to welcome code from any source. But as code from an untrusted source runs, the sandbox restricts the code from taking any actions that could possibly harm your system. You don't need to figure out what code you can and can't trust. You don't need to scan for viruses. The sandbox itself prevents any viruses or other malicious or buggy code you may invite into your computer from doing any damage.

If you have a properly skeptical mind, you'll need to be convinced a sandbox has no leaks before you trust it to protect you. To make sure the sandbox has no leaks, Java's security model involves every aspect of its architecture. If there were areas in Java's architecture where security was not considered, a malicious programmer (a "cracker") could likely exploit those areas to "go around" the sandbox. To understand the sandbox, therefore, you must look at several different parts of Java's architecture, and understand how they work together.

The fundamental components responsible for Java's sandbox are:

- The class loader architecture
- The class file verifier
- Safety features built into the Java virtual machine (and the language)
- The security manager and the Java API

One of the greatest strengths of Java's sandbox security model is that two of these components, the class loader and security manager, are customizable. By customizing these components, you can create a customised security policy for a Java application. Unfortunately, this customizability doesn't come for free, because the very flexibility of the architecture creates some risks of its own. Class loaders and security managers are complicated enough that the mere act of customization can potentially produce errors that open up security holes.

In each major release of the Java API, changes were made to make the task of creating a custom security policy less prone to error. The most significant change occurred in version 1.2, which introduced a new and more elaborate architecture for access control. In version 1.0 and 1.1, access control, which involves both the specification of a security policy and the enforcement of that policy at run time, is the responsibility of an object called the security manager. To establish a custom policy in 1.0 and 1.1, you have to write your own custom security manager. In 1.2, you can take advantage of a security manager supplied with the Java 2 Platform.

This ready made security manager allows you to specify a security policy in an ASCII *policy file* separate from the programme. At runtime, the ready made security manager enlists the help of a class called the access controller to enforce the security policy specified in the policy file. The access control infrastructure introduced in 1.2 provides a flexible and easily customised default implementation of the security manager that should suffice for the majority of security needs. For backwards compatibility, and to enable parties with special security needs to override the default functionality provided by the ready made security manager, version 1.2 applications can still install their own security manager. Using the ready made made security manager, and the extensive access control infrastructure that comes with it, is optional.

LOADER ARCHITECTURE

In Java's sandbox, the class loader architecture is the first line of defence. It is the class loader, after all, that brings code into the Java virtual machine—code that could be hostile or buggy.

The class loader architecture contributes to Java's sandbox in three ways:

1. It prevents malicious code from interfering with benevolent code,
2. It guards the borders of the trusted class libraries, and
3. It places code into categories (called *protection domains*) that will determine which actions the code will be allowed to take.

The class loader architecture prevents malicious code from interfering with benevolent code by providing separate name-spaces for classes loaded by different class loaders. A *name-space* is a set of unique names — one name for each loaded class — that the Java virtual machine maintains for each class loader. Once a Java virtual machine has loaded a class named Volcano into a particular name-space, for example, it is impossible to load a different class named Volcano into that same name-space. You can load multiple Volcano classes into a Java virtual machine, however, because you can create multiple name-spaces inside a Java application by creating multiple class loaders. If you create three separate name-spaces (one for each of three class loaders) in a running Java application, then, by loading one Volcano class into each name-space, your programme could load three different Volcano classes into your application.

Name-spaces contribute to security because you can in effect place a shield between classes loaded into different name-spaces. Inside the Java virtual machine, classes in the same name-space can interact with one another directly.

Classes in different name-spaces, however, can't even detect each other's presence unless you explicitly provide a mechanism that allows them to interact. If a malicious class, once loaded, had guaranteed access to every other class currently loaded by the virtual machine, that class could potentially learn things it shouldn't know or interfere with the proper execution of your programme.

Figure shows the name-spaces associated with two class loaders, both of which have loaded a type named Volcano. Each name in a name space is associated with the type data in the method area that defines the type with that name. Figure 3-1 shows arrows from the names in the name- spaces to the types in the method area that define the type. The class loader on the left, which is shown dark gray, has loaded the two dark gray types named Climber and Volcano. They class loader on the right, which is shown light gray, has loaded the two light gray types named BakingSoda and Volcano. Because of the nature of name-spaces, when the Climber class mentions the Volcano class, it refers to the dark grayVolcano, the Volcano loaded in the same name space. It has no way to know that the other Volcano, which is sitting in the same virtual machine, even exists

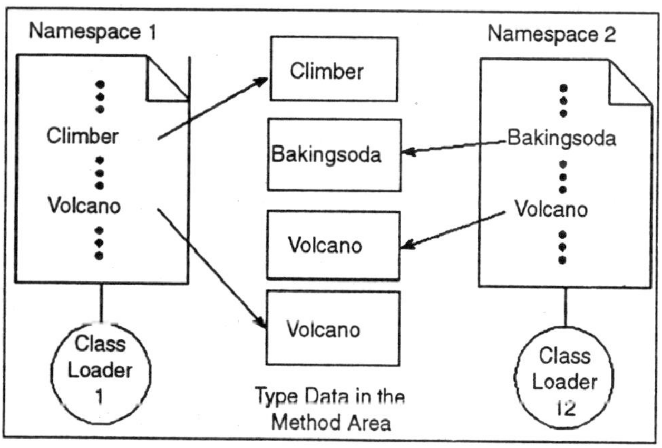

Fig. Class Loaders and Name-spaces.

The class loader architecture guards the borders of the trusted class libraries by making it possible for trusted packages to be loaded with different class loaders than untrusted packages. Although you can grant special access privileges between types belonging to the same package by giving members protected or package access, this special access is granted to members of the same package at runtime only if they were loaded by the same class loader.

Often, a user-defined class loader relies on other class loaders—at the very least, upon the class loaders created at virtual machine startup—to help it fulfill some of the class load requests that come its way. Prior to 1.2, class loaders had to explicitly ask for the help of other class loaders. A class loader could ask another user-defined class loader to load a class by invoking loadClass() on a reference to that user-defined class loader. Or, a class loader could ask the bootstrap class loader to attempt to load a class by invoking findSystemClass(), a static method defined in class ClassLoader.

In version 1.2, the process by which one class loader asks another class loader to try and load a type was formalized into a parent-delegation model. Starting with 1.2, each class loader except the bootstrap class loader has a "parent" class loader. Before a particular class loader attempts to load a type in its custom way, it by default "delegates" the job to its parent — it asks its parent to try and load the type. The parent, in turn, asks its parent to try and load the type. The delegation process continues all the way up to the bootstrap class loader, which is in general the last class loader in the delegation chain. If a class loader's parent class loader is able to load a type, the class loader returns that type. Else, the class loader attempts to load the type itself.

In most Java virtual machine implementations prior to 1.2, the built-in class loader (which was then called the primordial class loader) was responsible for loading locally available class files. Such class files usually included the class files that made up the Java application being executed plus any libraries needed by the application, including the class files of the Java API. Although the manner in which the class files for requested types were located was implementation specific, many implementations searched directories and JAR files in an order specified by a class path. In 1.2, the job of loading locally available class files was parceled out to multiple class loaders. The built-in class loader, previously called the primordial class loader, was renamed the "bootstrap" class loader to indicate that it was now responsible for loading *only* the class files of the core Java API. The name bootstrap class loader comes from the idea that the class files of the core Java API are the class files required to "bootstrap" the Java virtual machine.

Responsibility for loading other class files, such as the class files for the application being executed, class files for installed or downloaded standard extensions, class files for libraries discovered in the class path, and so on, was given in 1.2 to user-defined class loaders. When a 1.2 Java virtual machine starts execution, therefore, it creates at least one and probably more user-defined class loaders before the application even starts. All of these class loaders are connected in one chain of parent-child relationships. At the top of the chain is the bootstrap class loader.

At the bottom of the chain is what came in 1.2 to be called the "system class loader." Prior to 1.2, the name "system class loader" was sometimes used to refer to the built-in class loader, which was also called the primordial class loader. In 1.2, the name system class loader was more formally defined to mean the default delegation parent for new user-defined class loaders created by a Java application. This default delegation parent is usually going to be the user-defined class loader that loaded the initial class of the application, but may be any user-defined class loader decided upon by the designers of the Java Platform implementation.

For example, imagine you write a Java application that installs a class loader whose particular manner of loading class files is by downloading them across a network. Imagine you run this application on a virtual machine that instantiates two user-defined class loaders on startup: an "installed extensions" class loader and a "class path" class loader.

These class loaders are connected in a parent-child relationship chain along with the bootstrap class loader as shown in Figure. The class path's class loader's parent is the installed extensions class loader, whose parent is the bootstrap class loader. As shown in Figure 3-2, the class path class loader is designated as the system class loader, the default delegation parent for new user-defined class loaders instantiated by the application. Assume that when you application instantiates its network class loader, it specifies the system class loader as its parent.

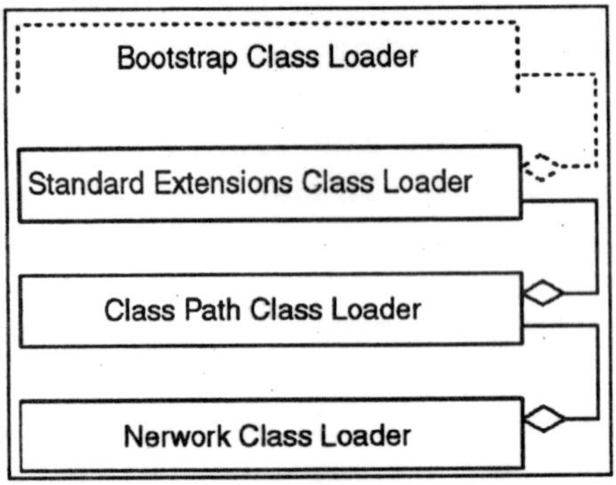

Fig. A Parent-child Class Loader Delegation Chain.

Imagine that during the course of running the Java application, a request is made of your class loader to load a class named Volcano. Your class loader would first ask its parent, the class path class loader, to find and load the class. The class path class loader, in turn, would make the same request of its parent, the installed extensions class loader. This class loader, would also first delegate the request to its parent, the bootstrap class loader.

Assuming that class Volcano is not a part of the Java API, an installed extension, or on the class path, all of these class loaders would return without supplying a loaded class named Volcano. When the class path class loader responds that neither it nor any of its parents can load the class, your class loader could then attempt to load the Volcano class in its custom manner, by downloading it across the network. Assuming your class loader was able to download class Volcano, that Volcano class could then play a role in the application's future course of execution. To continue with the same example, assume that at some time later a method of class Volcano is invoked for the first time, and that method references class java.util.HashMap from the Java API. Because it is the first time the reference was used by the running programme, the virtual machine asks your class loader (the one that loaded Volcano) to loadjava.util.HashMap. As before, your class loader first passes the request to its parent class loader, and the request gets delegated all the way up to the bootstrap class loader. But in this case, the bootstrap class loader is able to return ajava.util.Hashmap class back to your class loader.

Since the bootstrap class loader was able to find the class, the installed extensions class loader doesn't attempt to look for the type in the installed extensions. The class path class loader doesn't attempt to look for the type on the class path. And your class loader doesn't attempt to download it across the network. All of these class loaders merely return the java.util.HashMap class returned by the bootstrap class loader. From that point forward, the virtual machine uses that java.util.HashMap class whenever class Volcano references a class named java.util.HashMap.

Given this background into how class loaders work, you are ready to look at how class loaders can be used to protect trusted libraries. The class loader architecture guards the borders of the trusted class libraries by preventing untrusted classes from pretending to be trusted. If a malicious class could successfully trick the Java virtual machine into believing it was a trusted class from the Java API, that malicious class could potentially break through the sandbox barrier. By preventing untrusted classes from impersonating trusted classes, the class loader architecture blocks one potential approach to compromising the security of the Java runtime.

Given the parent-delegation model, the bootstrap class loader is able to attempt to load types before the standard extensions class loader, which is able to attempt to load types before the class path class loader, which is able to attempt to load types before your network class loader. Thus, given the manner in which the parent-child delegation chain is built, the most trusted library, the core Java API, is checked first for each type. After that, the standard extensions are checked. After that, local class files that are sitting on the class path are checked. So if some mobile code loaded by your network class loader wants to download a type across the network with the same name as something in the Java API, such asjava.lang. Integer, it won't be able to do it. If a class file for java.lang.Integer exists in the Java API, it will be loaded by the bootstrap class loader. The network class loader will not attempt to download and define a class namedjava. lang.Integer. It will just use the type returned by its parent, the one loaded by the bootstrap class loader. In this way, the class loader architecture prevents untrusted code from replacing trusted classes with their own versions.

But what if the mobile code, rather than trying to replace a trusted type, wants to insert a brand new type into a trusted package? Imagine what would happen if your network class loader from the previous example was requested to load a class named java.lang.Virus. As before, this request would first be delegated all the way up the parent-child chain to the bootstrap class loader.

Although the bootstrap class loader is responsible for loading the class files of the core Java API, which includes a package named, java.lang, it is unable to find a member of the java.lang package with the name, Virus. Assuming this class was also not found among the installed extensions or on the local class path, your class loader would proceed to attempt to download the type across the network.

Assume your class loader is successful in the download attempt and defines the type named java.lang.Virus. Java allows classes in the same package to grant each other special access privileges that aren't granted to classes outside the package. So, since your class loader has loaded a class that by its name (java.lang.Virus) brazenly declares itself to be part of the Java API, you might expect it could gain special access to the trusted classes of java.lang and could possibly use that special access for devious purposes.

The class loader mechanism thwarts this code from gaining special access to the trusted types in the java.lang package, because the Java virtual machine only grants that special package access between types loaded into the same package by the same class loader. Since the trusted class files of the Java API's java.lang package were loaded by the bootstrap class loader, and the malicious java.lang.Virus class was loaded by your network class loader, these types do not belong to the same *runtime package.* The term runtime package, which first appeared in the second edition of the Java Virtual Machine Specification, refers to a set of types that belong to the same package and that were all loaded by the same class loader.

Before allowing access to package- visible members (members declared with protected or package access) between two types, the virtual machine makes sure not only that the two types belong to the same package, but that they belong to the same runtime package — that they were loaded by the same class loader. Thus, because java.lang.Virus and the members of java.lang from the core Java API don't belong to the same runtime package, java.lang.Virus can't access the package-visible members and types of the Java API's java.lang package.

This concept of a runtime package is one motivation for using different class loaders to load different kinds of classes. The bootstrap class loader loads the class files of the core Java API. These class files are the most trusted. An installed extensions class loader loads class files from any installed extensions. Installed extensions are quite trusted, but need not be trusted to the extent that they are allowed to gain access to package-visible members of the Java API by simply inserting new types into those packages. Because installed extensions are loaded with a different class loader than the core API, they can't. Likewise, code found on the class path by the class path class loader can't gain access to package-visible members of the installed extensions or the Java API.

Another way class loaders can be used to protect the borders of trusted class libraries is by simply disallowing the loading of certain forbidden types. For example, you may have installed some packages that contain classes you want your application to be able to load through your network class loader's parent, the class path class loader, but not through your own network class loader. Assume you have created a package named absolutepower and installed it somewhere on the local class path, where it is accessible by the class path class loader. Assume also that you don't want classes loaded by your class loader to be able to load any class from the absolutepower package.

In this case, you would write your class loader such that the very first thing it does is make sure the requested class doesn't declare itself as a member of theabsolutepower package. If such a class is requested, your class loader, rather than passing the class name to its parent class loader, would throw a security exception. The only way a class loader can know whether or not a class is from a forbidden package, such as absolutepower, is by the class's name. Thus a class loader must have a list of the names of forbidden packages. Because the name of classabsolutepower.FancyClassLoader indicates it is part of the absolutepower package, and the absolute powerpackage is on the list of forbidden packages, your class loader should throw a security exception absolutely.

Besides shielding classes in different namespaces and protecting the borders of trusted class libraries, class loaders play one other security role. Class loaders must place each loaded class into a protection domain, which defines what permissions the code is going to be given as it runs. More information about this vitally important security job of class loaders will be given later in this chapter.

CLASS FILE VERIFIER

Working in conjunction with the class loader, the class file verifier ensures that loaded class files have a proper internal structure and that they are consistent with each other. If the class file verifier discovers a problem with a class file, it throws an exception. Although compliant Java compilers should not generate malformed class files, a Java virtual machine can't tell how a particular class file was created. Because a class file is just a sequence of bytes, a virtual machine can't know whether a particular class file was generated by a well-meaning Java compiler or by shady crackers bent on compromising the integrity of the virtual machine. As a consequence, all Java virtual machine implementations have a class file verifier that can be invoked on class files, to make sure the types they define are safe to use.

One of the security goals that the class file verifier helps achieve is programme robustness. If a buggy compiler or savvy cracker generated a class file that contained a method whose bytecodes included an instruction to jump beyond the end of the method, that method could, if it were invoked, cause the virtual machine to crash. Thus, for the sake of robustness, it is important that the virtual machine verify the integrity of the bytecodes it imports.

The class file verifier of the Java virtual machine does most checking before bytecodes are executed. Rather than checking every time it encounters a jump instruction as it executes bytecodes, for example, it analyses bytecodes (and verifies their integrity) once, before they are ever executed. As part of its verification of bytecodes, the Java virtual machine makes sure all jump instructions cause a jump to another valid instruction in the bytecode stream of the method. In most cases, checking all bytecodes once, before they are executed, is a more efficient way to guarantee robustness than checking every bytecode instruction every time it is executed.

The class file verifier operates in four distinct passes. During pass one, which takes place as a class is loaded, the class file verifier checks the internal structure of the class file to make sure it is safe to parse. During passes two and three, which take place during linking, the class file verifier makes sure the type data obeys the semantics of the Java programming language, including verifying the integrity of any bytecodes it contains. During pass four, which takes place as symbolic references are resolved in the process of dynamic linking, the class file verifier confirms the existence of symbolically referenced classes, fields, and methods.

PASS ONE: STRUCTURAL CHECKS ON THE CLASS FILE

During pass one, the class file verifier makes certain that

the sequence of bytes it is about to attempt to import as a type conforms to the basic structure of a Java class file. The verifier performs many checks during this pass. For example, every class file must start with the same four bytes, the magic number: 0xCAFEBABE.

The purpose of the magic number is to make it easy for the class file parser to reject files that were either damaged or were never intended to be class files in the first place. Thus, the first thing a class file verifier likely checks is that the imported file does indeed begin with 0xCAFEBABE. The verifier also makes sure the major and minor version numbers declared in the class file are within the range supported by that implementation of the Java virtual machine.

Also during pass one, the class file verifier checks to make sure the class file is neither truncated nor enhanced with extra trailing bytes. Although different class files can be different lengths, each individual component contained inside a class file indicates its length as well as its type. The verifier can use the component types and lengths to determine the correct total length for each individual class file. In this way, it can verify that the imported file has a length consistent with its internal contents.

The point of pass one is to ensure the sequence of bytes that supposedly define a new type adheres sufficiently to the Java class file format to enable it to be parsed into implementation-specific internal data structures in the method area. Passes two, three, and four take place not on the binary data in the class file format, but on the implementation-specific data structures in the method area.

PASS TWO: SEMANTIC CHECKS ON THE TYPE DATA

Pass two of the class file verifier performs checking that can be done without looking at the bytecodes and without looking at (or loading) any other types. During this pass, the verifier looks at individual components, to make sure they are well-formed instances of their type of component. For example, a method descriptor (its return type and the number and types of its parameters) is stored in the class file as a string that must adhere to a certain context-free grammar. One check the verifier performs on individual components is to make sure each method descriptor is a well-formed string of the appropriate grammar.

In addition, the class file verifier checks that the class itself adheres to certain constraints placed upon it by the specification of the Java programming language. For example, the verifier enforces the rule that all classes, except class Object, must have a superclass. Also during pass two, the verifier makes sure that final classes are not subclassed and final methods are not overridden.

In addition, it checks that constant pool entries are valid, and that all indexes into the constant pool refer to the correct type of constant pool entry. Thus, the class file verifier checks at run-time some of the Java language rules that should have been enforced at compile-time. Because the verifier has no way of knowing if the class file was generated by a benevolent, bug-free compiler, it checks each class file to make sure the rules are followed.

PASS THREE: BYTECODE VERIFICATION

Once the class file verifier has successfully completed the pass two checks, it turns its attention to the bytecodes. During this pass, which is commonly called the "bytecode verifier," the Java virtual machine performs a data-flow analysis on the streams of bytecodes that represent the methods of the class. To understand the bytecode verifier, you need to understand a bit about bytecodes and frames.

The bytecode streams that represent Java methods are a series of one-byte instructions, called *opcodes*, each of which may be followed by one o" more*operands*. The operands supply extra data needed by the Java virtual machine to execute the opcode instruction. The activity of executing bytecodes, one opcode after another, constitutes a thread of execution inside the Java virtual machine. Each thread is awarded its own *Java Stack*, which is made up of discrete *frames*. Each method invocation gets its own frame, a section of memory where it stores, among other things, local variables and intermediate results of computation. The part of the frame in which a method stores intermediate results is called the method's *operand stack*. An opcode and its (optional) operands may refer to the data stored on the operand stack or in the local variables of the method's frame. Thus, the virtual machine may use data on the operand stack, in the local variables, or both, in addition to any data stored as operands following an opcode when it executes the opcode.

The bytecode verifier does a great deal of checking. It checks to make sure that no matter what path of execution is taken to get to a certain opcode in the bytecode stream, the operand stack always contains the same number and types of items. It checks to make sure no local variable is accessed before it is known to contain a proper value. It checks that fields of the class are always assigned values of the proper type, and that methods of the class are always invoked with the correct number and types of arguments.

The bytecode verifier also checks to make sure that each opcode is valid, that each opcode has valid operands, and that for each opcode, values of the proper type are in the local variables and on the operand stack. These are just a few of the many checks performed by the bytecode verifier, which is able, through all its checking, to verify that a stream of bytecodes is safe for the Java virtual machine to execute.

The bytecode verifier doesn't attempt to detect all safe programs. If it tried to do that, it would run up against the Halting Problem. The Halting Problem, a well-known theorem in computer science, states that you can't write a programme that can determine whether any programme fed to it as input will halt when it is executed. Whether or not a programme will halt is called an "undecidable" property of the programme, because you can't write a programme that can tell you 100% of the time whether or not any given programme has the property. The undecideability of the Halting Problem extends to many properties of computer programs, including whether or not a set of Java bytecodes would be safe for a Java virtual machine to execute.

The way the bytecode verifier gets around the Halting Problem is by not attempting to pass all safe programs. Although you can't write a programme that can determine whether or not any given programme will halt, you can write a programme that recognizes some programs that will halt. For example, if the first instruction of a programme is halt, that programme will halt. If a programme has no loops in it, it will halt, and so on. Similarly, although you can't write a verifier that will pass all bytecode streams that are safe for the virtual machine to execute, you can write a verifier that will pass some of them.

And that's just what Java's bytecode verifier does. The verifier checks to make sure a certain set of rules are followed by each set of bytecodes its fed. If a set of bytecodes obeys all the rules, the verifier knows the bytecodes are safe for the virtual machine to execute. If not, the bytecodes may or may not be safe for the virtual machine to execute. Thus, the verifier gets around the Halting Problem by recognizing some, but not all, safe bytecode streams.

Given the nature of the constraints checked by the bytecode verifier, any programme that can be written in the Java programming language can be compiled to bytecodes that will pass the verifier. Some programs that could not possibly be expressed in the Java programming language will pass the verifier. And some programs (also not expressible in Java source code) that would otherwise be safe for the virtual machine to execute, will not pass the verifier.

Passes one, two, and three of the class file verifier make sure the imported class file is properly formed, internally consistent, adheres to the constraints of the Java programming language, and contains bytecodes that will be safe for the Java virtual machine to execute. If the class file verifier finds that any of these are not true, it throws an error, and the class file is never used by the programme.

PASS FOUR: VERIFICATION OF SYMBOLIC REFERENCES

Pass four of the class file verifier takes place when the

symbolic references contained in a class file are resolved in the process of dynamic linking. During pass four, the Java virtual machine follows the references from the class file being verified to the referenced class files, to make sure the references are correct. Because pass four has to look at other classes external to the class file being checked, pass four may require that new classes be loaded.

Most Java virtual machine implementations will likely delay loading classes until they are actually used by the programme. If an implementation does load classes earlier, perhaps in an attempt to speed up the loading process, then it must still give the impression that it is loading classes as late as possible. If, for example, a Java virtual machine discovers during early loading that it can't find a certain referenced class, it doesn't throw a NoClassDefFoundError error until (and unless) the referenced class is used for the first time by the running programme.

Thus, if a Java virtual machine performs early linking, pass four could happen shortly after pass three. But in Java virtual machines that resolve each symbolic reference the first time it is used, pass four will happen much later than pass three, as bytecodes are executed.

Pass four of class file verification is really just part of the process of dynamic linking. When a class file is loaded, it contains symbolic references to other classes and their fields and methods. A symbolic reference is a character string that gives the name and possibly other information about the referenced item- -enough information to uniquely identify a class, field, or method. Thus, symbolic references to other classes give the full name of the class; symbolic references to the fields of other classes give the class name, field name, and field descriptor; symbolic references to the methods of other classes give the class name, method name, and method descriptor. Dynamic linking is the process of *resolving* symbolic references into direct references. As the Java virtual machine executes bytecodes and encounters an opcode that, for the first time, uses a symbolic reference to another class, the virtual machine must resolve the symbolic reference.

The virtual machine performs two basic tasks during resolution:

1. Finds the class being referenced (loading it if necessary)
2. Replaces the symbolic reference with a direct reference, such as a pointer or offset, to the class, field, or method

The virtual machine remembers the direct reference so that if it encounters the same reference again later, it can immediately use the direct reference without needing to spend time resolving the symbolic reference again.

When the Java virtual machine resolves a symbolic reference, pass four of the class file verifier makes sure the reference is valid. If the reference is not valid—for instance, if the class cannot be loaded or if the class exists but doesn't contain the referenced field or method—the class file verifier throws an error.

As an example, consider again the Volcano class. If a method of class Volcano invokes a method in a class named Lava, the name and descriptor of the method in Lava are included as part of the binary data in the class file for Volcano. WhenVolcano's method first invokes Lava's method during the course of execution, the Java virtual machine makes sure a method exists in class Lava that has a name and descriptor that matches those expected by class Volcano.

If the symbolic reference (class name, method name and descriptor) is correct, the virtual machine replaces it with a direct reference, such as a pointer, which it will use from then on. But if the symbolic reference from class Volcano doesn't match any method in class Lava, pass four verification fails, and the Java virtual machine throws a NoSuchMethodError.

BINARY COMPATIBILITY

The reason pass four of the class file verifier must look at classes that refer to one another to make sure they are compatible is because Java programs are dynamically linked. Java compilers will often recompile classes that depend on a class you have changed, and in so doing, detect any incompatibility at compile- time. But there may be times when your compiler doesn't recompile a dependent class. For example, if you are developing a large system, you will likely partition the various parts of the system into packages. If you compile each package separately, then a change to one class in a package would likely cause a recompilation of affected classes within that same package, but not necessarily in any other package.

Moreover, if you are using someone else's packages, especially if your programme downloads class files from someone else's package across a network as it runs, it may be impossible for you to check for compatibility at compile-time. That's why pass four of the class file verifier must check for compatibility at run-time. As an example of incompatible changes, imagine you compiled class Volcano (from the previous example) with a Java compiler. Because a method in Volcano invokes a method in another class named Lava, the Java compiler would look for a class file or a source file for class Lava to make sure there was a method in Lava with the appropriate name, return type, and number and types of arguments.

If the compiler couldn't find any Lava class, or if it encountered a Lava class that didn't contain the desired method, the compiler would generate an error and would not create a class file for Volcano. Otherwise, the Java compiler would produce a class file for Volcano that is compatible with the class file for Lava. In this case, the Java compiler refused to generate a class file for Volcano that wasn't already compatible with class Lava.

The converse, however, is not necessarily true. The Java compiler could conceivably generate a class file for Lava that isn't compatible with Volcano. If the Lava class doesn't refer to Volcano, you could potentially change the name of the methodVolcano invokes from the Lava class, and then recompile only the Lava class.

If you tried to run your programme using the new version of Lava, but still using the old version of Volcano that wasn't recompiled since you made your change to Lava, the Java virtual machine would, as a result of pass four class file verification, throw a NoSuchMethodError when Volcano attempted to invoke the now non-existent method in Lava. In this case, the change to class Lava broke *binary compatibility* with the pre-existing class file for Volcano.

In practice, this situation may arise when you update a library you have been using, and your existing code isn't compatible with the new version of the library. To make it easier to alter the code for libraries, the Java programming language was designed to allow you to make many kinds of changes to a class that don't require recompilation of classes that depend upon it. The changes you are allowed to make, which are listed in the Java Language Specification, are called the rules of binary compatibility.

These rules clearly define what can be changed, added, or deleted in a class without breaking binary compatibility with pre-existing class files that depend on the changed class. For example, it is always a binary compatible change to add a new method to a class, but never to delete a method that other classes are using. So in the case of Lava, you violated the rules of binary compatibility when you changed the name of the method used by Volcano, because you in effect deleted the old method and added a new. If you had, instead, added the new method and then rewritten the old method so it calls the new, that change would have been binary compatible with any pre-existing class file that already usedLava, including Volcano.

SAFETY FEATURES

Once the Java virtual machine has loaded a class and performed passes one through three of class file verification, the bytecodes are ready to be executed. Besides the verification of symbolic references (pass four of class file verification), the Java virtual machine has several other built-in security mechanisms operating as bytecodes are executed. These mechanisms, most of which are elements of Java's type safety, are listed in Chapter as features of the Java programming language that make Java programs robust.

They are, not surprisingly, also features of the Java virtual machine:

- Type-safe reference casting

- Structured memory access (no pointer arithmetic)
- Automatic garbage collection (can't explicitly free allocated memory)
- Array bounds checking
- Checking references for null

By granting a Java programme only type-safe, structured ways to access memory, the Java virtual machine makes Java programs more robust, but it also makes their execution more secure. A programme that corrupts memory, crashes, and possibly causes other programs to crash represents one kind of security breach. If you are running a mission critical server process, for example, it is critical that the process doesn't crash. This level of robustness is also important in embedded systems, such as a cell phone, which people don't usually expect to have to reboot.

Another reason unrestrained memory access would be a security risk is because a wily cracker could potentially use it to subvert the security system. If, for example, a cracker could learn where in memory a class loader is stored, it could assign a pointer to that memory and manipulate the class loader's data. By enforcing structured access to memory, the Java virtual machine yields programs that are robust, but also frustrates crackers who dream of harnessing the internal memory of the Java virtual machine for their own devious plots.

Another safety feature built into the Java virtual machine—one that serves as a backup to structured memory access—is the unspecified manner in which the runtime data areas are laid out inside the Java virtual machine. The *runtime data areas*are the memory areas in which the Java virtual machine stores the data it needs to execute a Java application: Java stacks (one for each thread), a *method area*, where bytecodes are stored, and a *garbage-collected heap*, where the objects created by the running programme are stored. If you peer into a class file, you won't find any memory addresses. When the Java virtual machine loads a class file, it decides where in its internal memory to put the bytecodes and other data it parses from the class file. When the Java virtual machine starts a thread, it decides where to put the Java stack it creates for the thread. When it creates a new object, it decides where in memory to put the object.

Thus, a cracker cannot predict by looking at a class file where in memory the data representing that class, or objects instantiated from that class, will be kept. What's worse (for the cracker) is the cracker can't tell anything about memory layout by reading the Java virtual machine specification either. The manner in which a Java virtual machine lays out its internal data is not part of the specification. The designers of each Java virtual machine implementation decide which data structures their implementation will use to represent the runtime data areas, and where in memory their implementation will place them. As a result, even if a cracker were somehow able to break through the Java virtual machine's memory access restrictions, they would next be faced with the difficult task of finding something to subvert by looking around.

The prohibition on unstructured memory access is not something the Java virtual machine must actively enforce on a running programme; rather, it is intrinsic to the bytecode instruction set itself. Just as there is no way to express an unstructured memory access in the Java programming language, there is also no way to express it in bytecodes—even if you write the bytecodes by hand. Thus, the prohibition on unstructured memory access is a firm barrier against the malicious manipulation of memory.

There is, however, a way to penetrate the security barriers erected by the mechanisms that support type safety in a Java virtual machine. Although the bytecode instruction set doesn't give you an unsafe, unstructured way to access memory, there is a way you can go around bytecodes: native methods. Basically, when you call a native method, Java's security sandbox becomes dust in the wind. First of all, the robustness guarantees don't hold for native methods. Although you can't corrupt memory from a Java method, you can from a native method. But most importantly, native methods don't go through the Java API (they are how you go around the Java

API) so the security manager isn't checked before a native method attempts to do something that could be potentially damaging. (This is, of course, often how the Java API itself gets anything done. But the native methods used by the Java API are "trusted.") Thus, once a thread gets into a native method, no matter what security policy was established inside the Java virtual machine, it doesn't apply anymore to that thread, so long as that thread continues to execute the native method.

This is why the security manager includes a method that establishes whether or not a programme can load dynamic libraries, which are necessary for invoking native methods. Untrusted applets, for example, aren't allowed to load a new dynamic library, therefore they can't install their own new native methods. They can, however, call methods in the Java API, methods which may be native, but which are always trusted. When a thread invokes a native method, that thread leaps outside the sandbox. The security model for native methods is, therefore, the same security model described earlier as the traditional approach to computer security: you have to trust a native method before you call it.

One final mechanism built into the Java virtual machine that contributes to security is structured error handling with exceptions. Because of its support for exceptions, the Java virtual machine has something structured to do when a security violation occurs. Instead of crashing, the Java virtual machine can throw an exception or an error, which may result in the death of the offending thread, but shouldn't crash the system. Throwing an error (as opposed to throwing an exception) almost always results in the death of the thread in which the error was thrown.

This is usually a major inconvenience to a running Java programme, but won't necessarily result in termination of the entire programme. If the programme has other threads doing useful things, those threads may be able to carry on without their recently departed colleague. Throwing an exception, on the other hand, may result in the death of the thread, but is often just used as a way to transfer control from the point in the programme where the exception condition arose to the point in the programme where the exception condition is handled.

SECURITY MANAGER AND THE JAVA API

The first three prongs of Java's security model — the class loader architecture, class file verifier, and safety features built into Java — all work together to achieve a common goal: to protect the internal integrity of a Java virtual machine instance and the application it is running from malicious or buggy code it may load. By contrast, the fourth prong of the security model, the security manager, is geared towards protecting assets external to the virtual machine from malicious or buggy code running within the virtual machine. The security manager is a single object that serves as the central point for access control — the controlling of access to external assets — within a running Java virtual machine.

The security manager defines the outer boundaries of the sandbox. Because it is customizable, the security manager allows a custom security policy to be established for an application. The Java API enforces the custom security policy by asking the security manager for permission before it takes any action that is potentially unsafe. To ask the security manager for permission, the methods of the Java API invoke "check methods" on the security manager object.

These methods are called check methods because their names all begin with the substring "check." For example, the security manager's checkRead() method determines whether or not a thread is allowed to read to a specified file. The checkWrite() method determines whether or not a thread is allowed to write to a specified file. The implementation of these methods is what defines the custom security policy of the application.

Because the Java API always checks with the security manager before it performs a potentially unsafe action, the Java API will not perform any action forbidden under the security policy established by the security manager. If the security manager forbids an action, the Java API won't perform that action. When a Java application starts, it has no security manager, but the application can install one at its option by passing a reference to an instance of java.lang.SecurityManager or one of its subclasses to setSecurityManager(), a static method of class java.lang.System.

If an application does not install a security manager, there are no restrictions placed on any activities requested of the Java API—the Java API will do whatever it is asked. (This is why Java applications, by default, do not have any security restrictions such as those that limit the activities of untrusted applets.) If the application does install a security manager, then in 1.0 or 1.1 that security manager will be in charge for the entire remainder of the lifetime of that application. It can't be replaced, extended, or changed. From that point on, the Java API will only fulfill those requests that are sanctioned by the security manager. In 1.2, however, the currently installed security manager can be replaced by code that has permission to replace it by invoking System.setSecurityManager() with a reference to a different security manager object.

In general, a "check" method of the security manager throws a security exception if the checked upon activity is forbidden, and simply returns if the activity is permitted. Therefore, the procedure a Java API method generally follows when it is about to perform a potentially unsafe activity involves two steps. First, the Java API code checks whether a security manager has been installed. If not, it skips step two and goes ahead with the potentially unsafe action. Otherwise, as step two, it calls the appropriate "check" method in the security manager. If the action is forbidden, the "check" method will throw a security exception, which will cause the Java API method to immediately abort. The potentially unsafe action will never be taken. If, on the other hand, the action is permitted, the "check" method will simply return. In this case, the Java API method carries on and performs the potentially unsafe action.

As mentioned earlier in this chapter, the security manager is responsible for two things: for specifying a security policy and for enforcing that policy. The security policy, which states what kind of code will be allowed to take what kind of actions, is defined by the code of the security manager's check methods. The policy is enforced by the behaviour of the check methods when they are invoked.

Prior to 1.2, java.lang.SecurityManager was an abstract class. To establish a custom security policy in 1.0 or 1.1, you had to write your own security manager by subclassing SecurityManager and implementing its check methods. Your application would instantiate and install the security manager, which from that point forward for the remainder of the life of the application would enforce the security policy you defined in the code of its check methods. Although the customizability of the security manager was one of the greatest strengths of Java's security model, it was also a potential point of weakness. Writing a security manager is a complicated and error prone task. Any mistakes made when implementing the check methods of a security manager could potentially translate into security holes at runtime. To help make it easier and less error prone for developers and end-users to establish fine-grained security policies based on signed code, the java.lang. SecurityManager class in the version 1.2 is a concrete class that provides a default implementation of the security manager.

(In the remainder of this book, this default implementation of the security manager provided with version 1.2 will be called the "concrete SecurityManager.") Your application can instantiate and install this security manager explicitly, or allow it to be installed automatically. In Sun's Java 2 SDK version 1.2, for example, you can specify that the concrete SecurityManager be installed by using the -Djava.security. manager option on the command line.

The concrete SecurityManager class allows you to define your custom policy not in Java code, but in an ASCII file called a *policy file*. In the policy file, you grant *permissions* to *code sources*. Permissions are defined in terms of classes that are subclasses of java.security.Permission. For example, java.io. FilePermission represents permission to read, write, execute, or delete a file. Code sources are composed of a codebase URL from which the code was loaded and a set of signers that vouched for the code. When the security manager is created, it parses the policy file and createsCodeSource and Permission objects. These objects are encapsulated in a single Policy object that expresses the policy at runtime. Only one Policy object can be installed at any one time. Class loaders place types into protection domains, which encapsulate all the permissions granted to the code source represented by the loaded type. Each type loaded into a 1.2 virtual machine belongs to one and only one protection domain. The protection domain is remembered and is used when deciding whether or not the code will be allowed to take potentially unsafe actions.

When the check methods of the concrete SecurityManager are invoked, most of them pass the request on to a class called the AccessController. The AccessController, using the information contained in the protection domain objects of the classes whose methods are on the call stack, performs stack inspection to determine whether the action should be allowed.

The security manager has undergone quite a bit of change in 1.2. In versions 1.0 and 1.1, each check method indicates what is being checked in its method name. To check whether or not it is OK to read a certain file, the Java API invokes thecheckRead() method on the security manager and passes and the path name of the file to read as a parameter. For example, before attempting to read a file named/tmp/finances.dat, the security manager invokescheckRead("/tmp/finances.dat") on the security manager. The security manager declares 28 of these check methods, which in the remainder of this chapter will be referred to as "legacy check methods." Although new methods were added to the security manager in 1.2 that would otherwise render these legacy check methods obsolete, to maintain backwards compatibility the Java API continues to call the legacy check methods just as it did in prior releases.

The 27 legacy check methods are listed here along with the potentially unsafe action that trigger's their invocation by the code of the Java API:

1. *CheckConnect(String host, int port)*: Open a socket connection to the specified host and port number

2. *CheckConnect(String host, int port, Object context)*: Open a socket connection to the specified host and port number under the passed security context
3. *CheckAccept(String host, int port)*: Accept a socket connection from the specified host and port number
4. *CheckCreateClassLoader()*: Create a new class loader
5. *CheckAccess(Thread t)*: Modify a thread (change its priority, stop it, etc...)
6. *CheckAccess(ThreadGroup t)*: Modify a thread group (add a new thread, set deamonness, etc...)
7. *CheckExit()*: Cause the application to exit
8. *CheckLink()*: Load a dynamic library that contains native methods
9. *CheckRead(FileDescriptor fd)*: Read from the specified file
10. *CheckRead(String file)*: Read from the specified file
11. *CheckRead(String file, Object context)*: Read from the specified file under the passed security context
12. *CheckWrite(FileDescriptor fd)*: Write to the specified file
13. *CheckWrite(String file)*: Write to the specified file
14. *CheckDelete(String file)*: Delete the specified file
15. *checkListen(int port)*: Wait for a connection on the specified local port number
16. *CheckMulticast(InedAddress maddr)*: Join, leave, send, or receive IP multicast
17. *CheckMulticast(InedAddress maddr, byte ttl)*: Join, leave, send, or receive IP multicast
18. *CheckPropertiesAccess()*: Access or modify system properties in general
19. *CheckPropertiesAccess(String key)*: Access or modify the specified system property
20. *CheckTopLevelWindow(Object Window)*: Bring up the specified window without any warning
21. *CheckPrintJobAccess()*: Initiate a print job request
22. *CheckSystemClipboardAccess()*: Access the system clipboard
23. *CheckAWTEventQueueAccess()*: Access the AWT event queue

24. *CheckPackageAccess(String pkg)*: Access types from the specified package (used by class loaders)
25. *CheckPackageDefinition(String pkg)*: Add a new class to the specified package (used by class loaders)
26. *CheckSetFactory()*: Set the socket factory used by ServerSocket or Socket or set the URL stream handler used by URL
27. *CheckMemberAccess()*: Access class information via the reflection API

In 1.2, a set of permission classes was defined whose instances represent actions code is allowed to take. A new pair of check methods were added in 1.2 to class java.lang. SecurityManager, both named checkPermission():

- *CheckPermission(Permission perm)*: Take an action that requires the specified permission
- *CheckPermission(Permission perm, Object context)*: Take an action that requires the specified permission under the passed security context

The checkPermission() methods accept a reference to a Permission object, which indicates the action that is being requested. Thus, this method provides an alternative way to ask the security manager if it is OK to perform a potentially unsafe action. For example, to determine whether it is OK to read file/tmp/finances.dat, the Java API in 1.2 could take either of two approaches.

The Java API could take the old fashioned approach, and invoke the legacy methodcheckRead() passing the String "/ tmp/finances.dat" as a parameter. Or, the Java API could take the fresh new approach. It could create a java.io.FilePermission object, passing Strings "/tmp/finances.dat" and "read" to the FilePermission constructor. The Java API could then pass this Permission object to the security manager'scheckPermission() method.

Both the old fashioned approach of invoking a legacy check method and the fresh new approach of creating a permission object and invoking checkPermission() should yield the same result. To maintain backwards compatibility with security managers that were written for 1.0 or 1.1, however, the 1.2 Java API continues to take the old fashioned approach. The 1.2 Java API continues to call the 28 legacy check methods. Nevertheless, in the concrete SecurityManager class, the legacy methods are for the most part implemented in terms of the new checkPermission() method.

So by invoking the legacy method on the concrete SecurityManager, the Java API is indirectly invoking the checkPermission() method anyway. For example, the checkRead() method implementation in the concrete SecurityManager simply instantiates a newFile Permission object, passing the pathname String passed to it to the FilePermission's constructor, along with theString "read". The checkRead() method then invokes check Permission(), passing a reference to theFilePermission object.

The Java API may at times also invoke checkPermission() directly. For new concepts of potentially unsafe actions introduced in 1.2 and later versions, no legacy check methods exist. Thus, in some situations, the Java API may create a new Permission object for which no relevant check methods exists, and pass that Permission object directly to the security manager's checkPermission() method.

In the concrete SecurityManager class, the check Permission() method also delegates the job of deciding whether or not to allow the action to another method. The concrete SecurityManager's checkPermission() method simply invokes the static checkPermission() method of class java.security. AccessController, passing along the permission object. The AccessController class, therefore, is the actual entity responsible for enforcing the security policy when you use the concrete SecurityManager.

All of these changes in 1.2 are backwards compatible with 1.1 and 1.0. If you created a security manager for 1.1, it should still work as expected in 1.2. You can still create a custom security manager in 1.2 as well, which allows anyone with special security needs that aren't adequately addressed by the concrete Security Manager implementation to create a different kind of security infrastructure. Most people's security needs, however, will be likely met by taking advantage of the flexibility and extensibility built into the concrete Security Manager.

CODE SIGNING AND AUTHENTICATION

A critical piece of Java's security model is the support for authentication introduced in Java 1.1 in the java.security package and its subpackages. The authentication capabilities expand your ability to establish multiple security policies by enabling you to implement a sandbox that varies depending upon who vouched for the code.

Authentication allows you to verify that a set of class files was blessed as trustworthy by some party, and that the class files were not altered en route to your virtual machine. Thus, to the extent you trust the party who vouched for the code, you can ease the restrictions placed on the code by the sandbox. You can establish different security restrictions for code that is signed by different parties.

To vouch for, or sign, a piece of code, you must first generate a public/private key pair. You should keep the private key private, but can make the public key public. At the very least, you must somehow get the public key to anyone who wants to establish a security policy based on your signature. (As will be illustrated later in this section, distributing public keys is not necessarily as easy as it may seem.) Once you have a public/private key pair, you must place the class files and any other files you want to sign into a JAR file.

You then use a tool, such as jarsignerfrom the 1.2 SDK, to sign the entire JAR file. The signer tool will first perform a one-way hash calculation on the contents of the JAR file to generate a hash. The tool will then sign the hash with your private key, and add the signed hash to the JAR file. The signed hash represents your digital signature of the contents of the JAR file. When you distribute the JAR file that contains the signed hash, anyone with your public key can verify two things about the JAR file: the JAR file was indeed signed by you, and the contents of the JAR file were not in any way altered since you attached your signature. The first step in the digital signing process is the one-way hash calculation, which takes a big number as input and generates a small number, called the hash. In the case of a JAR file, the big-number input to the calculation is the stream of bytes that make up the contents of the JAR file.

The one-way hash calculation is called "one-way" because given just the hash (the small number), it is impossible to calculate the input (the big number). In other words, the hash value doesn't contain enough information about the input to enable the input to be regenerated from the hash. The calculation goes just one way, from big to small, from input to hash.

The hash, which is also called a message digest, serves as a kind of "fingerprint" for the input. Although different inputs can produce the same hash, the hash is considered unique enough in practice to represent the input from which it was generated. Much like a fingerprint can be used to identify the individual who made the fingerprint, a hash can be used to identify the input that caused the one-way hash algorithm to produce the hash. The hash is used during the authentication process to verify that the input is identical to the input that produced the original hash, in other words, that the input was not changed en route to its destination.

Given that it is impossible to reconstruct the input given just the hash, a hash is only useful if the input is also available. Thus, you normally transmit both input and hash together. By themselves, the combination of an input and its hash is not secure, however, because even an extremely unimaginative cracker could simply replace both the input and the hash. To prevent this scenario, you encrypt the hash with your private key before sending it.

The reason you encrypt the hash rather than simply encrypting the entire JAR file is that private key encryption is a time-consuming process. It is in general much faster to calculate a one-way hash from the JAR file contents and encrypt the hash with a private key than it is to encrypt the entire JAR file with the private key. A cracker will only be able to replace both an input and encrypted hash if the cracker has your private key, which you are supposed to keep secret. Thus, the combination of input and encrypted hash is more frustrating to a potential cracker than the mere combination of input and hash because, in theory, the cracker doesn't have your private key.

Anything encrypted with your private key can be decrypted with your public key. Public/private key pairs have the characteristic that it is prohibitively difficult given just the public key to generate the private key. If you can keep your private key out the hands of crackers, therefore, their best option is to try and replace the input with a different input that yields the same hash value. If the cracker wishes to replace one class file in your JAR file with a different class file that performs some devious act, for example, the odds are extremely high that the revised JAR file (the one that contains the devious class file) will produce a different hash.

But the cracker could add random data to the JAR file until the one-way hash calculation on the altered JAR file produces the same hash value as the original. If the cracker can produce such an alternative input — one that both helps the cracker achieve his or her nefarious goals and generates the same hash as your original input — the cracker would not need your private key. Because the cracker's input generates the same hash value as your original input, and you have already signed that hash value with your private key, the cracker can simply place your signed hash in a JAR file with his or her input. What's to prevent a cracker from taking this approach? Unfortunately for the cracker, such an approach would likely take too much time to be feasible.

Because one-way hash algorithms generate a small number (the message digest or hash) from a big number (the input), different inputs can produce the same hash. One-way hash algorithms tend to spread out the inputs that produce the same hash sufficiently randomly that the likelihood of getting the same hash value depends primarily on the size of the hash. For example, if you use a hash value that is 8 bits wide, your one-way hash algorithm will have only 256 unique hash values from which to choose. If you have a JAR file that produces the hash value 100 and you start calculating the 8 bit hash with this algorithm on other JAR files, you shouldn't be surprised if every 256 times or so you get the hash value 100. The more bits contained in the hash, of course, the less often the algorithm will produce the same hash.

In practice, 64- and 128-bit hash values are common, which are considered large enough to render the process of finding a different input that produces the same hash computationally infeasible. The main barrier preventing a cracker from replacing your benevolent input with a malicious input that serves the cracker's evil purposes *and* produces the same hash, therefore, is the time and resources the cracker would have to devote to searching for that malicious input.

The last step in the digital signing process, after you have generated the hash value and encrypted it with your private key, is to add the encrypted hash value to the same JAR file that contains the files from which you generated the hash value originally. A signed JAR file, therefore, contains the input — the class and data files you wanted to vouch for — plus the hash value (generated from the input) encrypted with your private key. The encrypted hash represents your digital signature of the class and data files contained in the same JAR file. The process of signing a JAR file is shown graphically in Figure.

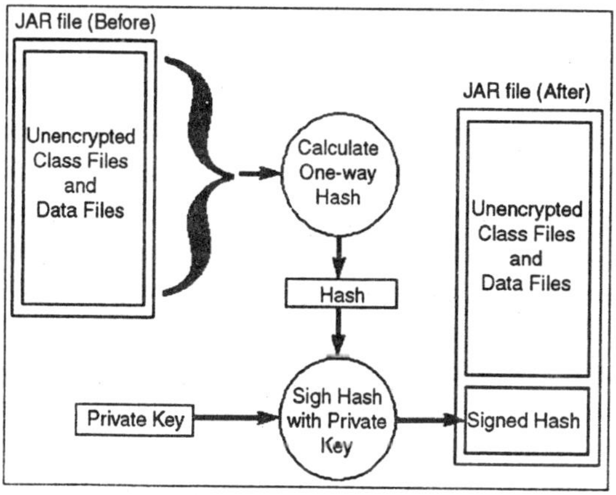

Fig. Digitally Signing a JAR File.

To authenticate a JAR file that you have purportedly signed, the recipient must decrypt the signed hash with your public key. The result should be equal to the original hash that you calculated on the contents of the JAR file. To verify that the JAR file contents were not changed since you signed them, the recipient simply applies the one-way hash algorithm on the contents of the JAR file, just as you did during the signing process. (Remember you never encrypted contents of the JAR file, so anyone can see them.

You only added a digital signature to the JAR file.) If the hash value generated by the algorithm matches the decrypted hash value, the recipient concludes that you did indeed vouch for this JAR file and that the contents of the JAR file did not change since you added your signature. The code contained in the JAR file can be placed inside a relaxed sandbox that represents the trust the recipient places in your signature. The process of verifying a digitally signed JAR file is shown in Figure.

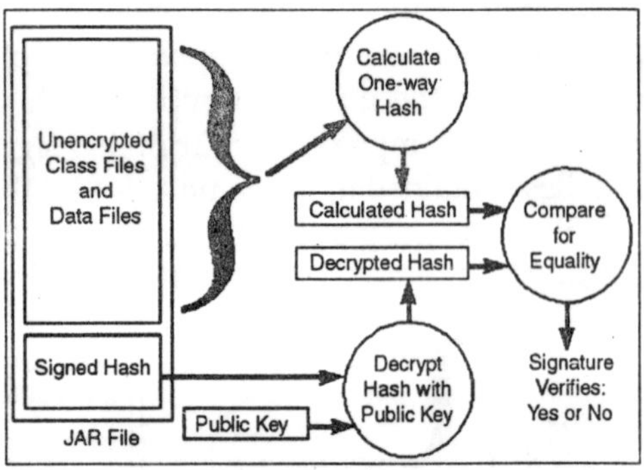

Fig. Authenticating a Digitally Signed JAR File.

Although the authentication technology first introduced in Java version 1.1 is firmly founded in reliable mathematics, the math doesn't solve every problem. In fact, several questions are raised by Java's authentication technology. For example, the authentication technology says nothing about who you should trust, and to what extent you should trust them. To what extent do you trust some small company that you've never heard of? To what extent do you trust a big company whose name is a household word? To what extent do you trust a different department in your own company? What are the chances that any particular company (or department) has a rogue employee who managed to slip a time bomb into a JAR file the company signed? No cryptographic algorithm can answer these questions for you.

Another security issue stems from the assumption inherent in the authentication technology that private keys will be kept under lock and, well, key. If private keys are not kept private, the entire authentication scheme is reduced to strenuous mathematical activity that is not only ineffective, but dangerous, because it can give a false sense of security. You are responsible for keeping your own private keys private. You can only hope that any entity on whose signature authority you grant code access to your system has kept their private keys private. For any party, establishing a key management scheme that prevents private keys from being leaked (remember those rogue employees?) can be a challenging task.

Another question raised by the technology involves the distribution of public keys. Although it may seem surprising at first, the assumption inherent in the authentication technology that public keys will be made public creates some security issues of its own. For example, imagine you want to relax your sandbox for code vouched for by a guy named Evan. To do so, you need Evan's public key. But how exactly do you get his public key? If you know Evan personally, you can invite him over for coffee and ask him to bring his public key so he can give it to you in person.

But what if you don't know Evan personally? You might think you could simply visit Evan's web site and grab his public key off a web page. Or alternatively, perhaps you could phone Evan and ask him to send you his public key in an e-mail. Evan should have no problem sending you, a stranger, his public key, because public keys after all are designed to be public. Evan doesn't need to worry about who gets his public key. He could hire a biplane to write his public key on the sky over Silicon Valley and still feel confident he was operating within the rules delineated by Java's authentication technology. So what's the problem? The problem is that even though Evan doesn't need to worry about your identity when he sends you his public key, you need to worry about his. Evan will be happy to send you his public key, but how do you know that the public key you receive is really the one that Evan sent?

The difficulty of public key distribution is that no matter what the means of communication, the message — the public key — could potentially be tampered with in transit. When you visit Evan's web page, it is possible that the web page is intercepted and changed en route to your browser, perhaps by Dastardly Doug, a cracker of international repute. When you think you are copying Evan's public key off his web page, you could actually be copying Dastardly Doug's.

Doug could also have intercepted Evan's e-mail and replaced Evan's beneficent public key with his own dastardly public key. Doug could even have donned one of his many clever disguises and piloted the biplane high above Silicon Valley, inscribing his public key among the clouds in place of Evan's. If Doug can successfully replace Evan's public key with his own, Doug can pretend to be Evan and take advantage of the trust you place in Evan's signature to break into your system.

But wait a minute, isn't the difficulty of public key distribution just another authentication problem, the kind of problem the authentication technology itself is designed to address? In fact it is, and by turning authentication back on itself, Evan can make it far more difficult for Dastardly Doug to replace Evan's public key with his own.

To address the difficulties of public key distribution, several *certificate authorities* have been established for the purpose of vouching for public keys. Evan, for example, could go to a certificate authority and present his credentials (birth certificate, drivers license, passport, and so on) and his public key. Once convinced that Evan is who he says he is, the certificate authority would sign Evan's public key with the certificate authority's private key. The resulting sequence of numbers is called a *certificate*. Instead of distributing his public key, then, Evan would distribute his certificate. You could grab Evan's certificate off of his web page, out of an e-mail, or via any other unsecured communications medium. When you get the certificate, you decrypt it with the certificate authority's public key and are rewarded with Evan's public key. The certificate scheme makes it much less likely that Doug will be able to swap his public key for Evan's because to do so, Doug would need the certificate authority's private key.

Although certificates improve the public key distribution situation immensely, some issues still remain. First of all, how exactly to you get the certificate authority's public key? You need this public key to authenticate the public keys of anyone else. Well, if you know any employees of the certificate authority personally, you could invite them over for coffee and ask them to bring their public key to give to you in person. But what if you don't know any employees of the certificate authority personally? And then there is the nagging question: why should you trust the certificate authority? A certificate authority can pretend to be anyone. Isn't a certificate authority just as susceptible as the next company to the vagaries of rogue employees?

Despite all these issues, the code signing capabilities introduced in Java 1.1 generally offer you *enough* security to enable you to relax your sandbox when you need to. Although the authentication technology doesn't eliminate all risk associated with relaxing the sandbox, it can help minimize the risks. Security is a tradeoff between cost and risk: the lower the security risk, the higher the cost of security.

You must weigh the costs associated with any computer or network security strategy against the costs of the theft or destruction of the information or computing resources being protected. The nature of your computer or network security strategy should be shaped by the value of the assets you are trying to protect. Java's authentication technology is a useful tool that, in concert with Java's sandbox, can help you manage the costs and risks of running network-mobile code on your systems.

A CODE SIGNING EXAMPLE

For an example of code signing with the jarsigner tool of

the Java 2 SDK 1.2, consider the following types, Doer, Friend, and Stranger. The first type, Doer, defines an interface that the other two types, classes Friend andStranger implement:

```
// On CD-ROM in file
// security/ex2/com/artima/security/doer/Doer.java
package com.artima.security.doer;
public interface Doer {
void doYourThing();
}
```

Doer declares just one method, doYourThing(). Class Friend and classStranger implement this method in the exact same way. In fact, besides their names, the two classes are identical:

```
// On CD-ROM in file
// security/ex2/com/artima/security/friend/
Friend.java
package com.artima.security.friend;
import com.artima.security.doer.Doer;
import java.security.AccessController;
import java.security.PrivilegedAction;

public class Friend implements Doer {

  private Doer next;
  private boolean direct;

  public Friend(Doer next, boolean direct) {
    this.next = next;
    this.direct = direct;
  }

  public void doYourThing() {

    if (direct) {

      next.doYourThing();
    }
    else {
```

```
      AccessController.doPrivileged(
         new PrivilegedAction() {
            public Object run() {
               next.doYourThing();
               return null;
            }
         }
      );
    }
  }
}

// On CD-ROM in file
// security/ex2/com/artima/security/stranger/
Stranger.java
package com.artima.security.stranger;
import com.artima.security.doer.Doer;
import java.security.AccessController;
import java.security.PrivilegedAction;

public class Stranger implements Doer {

   private Doer next;
   private boolean direct;

   public Stranger(Doer next, boolean direct) {
      this.next = next;
      this.direct = direct;
   }

   public void doYourThing() {

      if (direct) {

         next.doYourThing();
      }
      else {
         AccessController.doPrivileged(
```

```
            new PrivilegedAction() {
              public Object run() {
                next.doYourThing();
                return null;
              }
            }
        );
      }
   }
}
```

These types — Doer, Friend, and Stranger — are designed to illustrate the stack inspection mechanism of the access controller. The motivation behind their design will be made clear later in this chapter, when several examples of stack inspection are given.

At this point, however, the class files generated by compiling Friend and Stranger must be signed to prepare them for the upcoming stack inspection examples. The class files generated from Friend.java will be signed by a party referred to fondly as "friend." The class files generated from Stranger.java will be signed by a party referred to somewhat suspiciously as "stranger." The class file generated by Doer will not be signed.

To prepare the class files for signing, they must first be placed into JAR files. Because the class files for Friend andStranger need to be signed by two different parties, they will be collected into two different JAR files. The two class files generated by compiling Friend.java, Friend.class and Friend$1.class, will be placed into a JAR file calledfriend.jar. Similarly, the two class files generated by compiling Stranger.java, Stranger.class andStranger$1.class, will be placed into a JAR file called stranger.jar.

(Note that although all of the files in these examples are in the security/ex2 directory of the CD-ROM, to repeat any of the commands that generate files, you'll have to copy the entire security/ex2 directory hierarchy to a writable media, such as a hard disk. But you probably knew that already.) Friend.java's class files are dropped by the javac compiler in the security/

ex2/com/artima/security/frienddirectory. Because class Friend is declared in the com.artima.security. friend package, Friend.java's class files must be placed in the JAR file in the com/artima/security/friend directory. The following command, executed in thesecurity/ex2 directory, will place Friend.class and Friend$1.class into a newly created JAR file calledfriend.jar, which is placed in the current directory, security/ex2:

```
jar cvf friend.jar com/artima/security/friend/
*.class
```

Once the previous command completes, the class files for Friend.java must be removed so they won't be found by the Java virtual machine when it runs the access control examples:

```
rm com/artima/security/friend/Friend.class
rm com/artima/security/friend/Friend$1.class
```

Filling a JAR file with Stranger.java's class files, which are dropped by javac in thesecurity/ex2/com/artima/security/stranger directory, requires a similar process. From the security/ex2directory, the following command must be executed:

```
jar cvf stranger.jar com/artima/security/stranger/
*.class
rm com/artima/security/stranger/Stranger.class
rm com/artima/security/stranger/Stranger$1.class
```

To sign a JAR file with the jarsigner tool from the Java 2 SDK 1.2, a public/private key pair for the signer must already exist in a *keystore file*, which is a file for storing named, password-protected keys.

The keytool programme of the Java 2 SDK 1.2, can be used to generate a new key pair, associate the key pair with a name or *alias*, and protect it with a password. The alias, which is unique within each keystore file, is used to identify a particular key pair in a particular keystore file. The password for a key pair is required to access or change the information contained in the keystore file for that key pair.

The access control examples expect a keystore file named ivjmkeys in the security/ex2 directory containing key pairs for the aliases "friend" and "stranger." The following command, executed from the security/ex2 directory, will generate the key pair for the alias, friend, with the password, friend4life. In the process, it will create the keystore file named ijvmkeys:

```
keytool -genkey -alias friend -keypass friend4life
-validity 10000 -
keystore ijvmkeys
```

The -validity 10000 command line argument of the previous keytool command indicates that the key pair should be valid for 10000 days, which at over 27 years, is likely enough time to outlive the product lifecycle of this edition of this book. When the command runs, it will prompt for a keystore password, which is a general password required for any kind of access or change of the keystore file. The keystore password given to ijvmkeys is "ijvm2ed".

The key pair for stranger can be generated with a similar command:

```
keytool -genkey -alias stranger -keypass
stranger4life -validity 10000 -
keystore ijvmkeys
```

Now that the keystore file ijvmkeys contains key pairs for friend and stranger, and the JAR files friend.jar andstranger.jar contain the appropriate class files, the JAR files can finally be signed. The following jarsigner command, executed from the examples/ex2 directory, will sign the class files contained in friend.jar using friend's private key:

```
jarsigner -keystore ijvmkeys -storepass ijvm2ed
-keypass friend4life
friend.jar friend
```

A similar command will sign the class files contained in stranger.jar with stranger's private key:

```
jarsigner -keystore ijvmkeys -storepass ijvm2ed
-keypass stranger4life
stranger.jar stranger
```

Whew, that was a lot of work just to sign two JAR files. And keep in mind that in the real world, you'd have to make sure no one with bad intent got a hold of your private keys, and that you kept track of them. That means not losing the keystore file, remembering the passwords, and so on. In addition, you'll have to get your public keys to anyone who is going to use your signature to give your code access to their system.

Policy

As mentioned previously, one of the greatest advantages of Java's sandbox security model is that the sandbox can be customised. The code signing and authentication technology introduced in Java version 1.1 enables your running application to differentiate code to which you attribute different degrees of trust. By customizing the sandbox, trusted code can be given more access to system resources than untrusted code. This prevents untrusted code from accessing the system, but allows trusted code to access the system and do useful work. The real power of Java's security architecture, however, lies in the ability to grant code with varying degrees of trust different levels of *partial*access to the system.

Microsoft offers an authentication technology similar to Java's for ActiveX controls, but ActiveX controls don't run inside a sandbox. Thus with ActiveX, a chunk of mobile code is either completely trusted or completely untrusted. If untrusted, the ActiveX control is denied the opportunity to run. If trusted, the ActiveX control is allowed to run and given full access to the system. While this is a big improvement over no authentication at all, if some malicious or buggy code gets authenticated, the dangerous code has full access to the system. One of the strengths of Java's security architecture is that code can be given access only to the resources it needs. If some malicious or buggy code gets authenticated, it has less opportunity to do damage. For example, instead of being able to delete all files on a local hard disk, the malicious or buggy code might only be able to delete the files in a particular directory set aside just for it.

One major goal of the 1.2 security infrastructure is to make it easier and less error prone to establish fine-grained access control policies based on signed code. To be able to assign different system access privileges to different units of code, Java's access control mechanism must be able to ascertain what privileges should be given to each individual piece of code. To facilitate this process, each piece of code (each class file) loaded into a 1.2 or beyond Java virtual machine is associated with a *code source.*

The code source basically says where the code came from and who, if anyone, has vouched for the code by signing it. In the 1.2 security model, permissions (system access privileges) are assigned to code sources. Thus, if a piece of code requests access to a particular system resource, the Java virtual machine will grant the code access to that resource only if such access is a privilege associated with that code's code source.

In the 1.2 security infrastructure, an access control policy for an entire Java application is represented by a single instance of a subclass of the abstract class java.security.Policy. Each application has just one Policy object in effect at any given time. Code that has permission can replace the current Policy object with a new one by invokingPolicy.setPolicy() and passing a reference to the new Policy object. Class loaders consult the Policy object to help them to decide what privileges to grant code as they import the code into the virtual machine.

A security policy is a mapping from a set of properties that characterize running code to the permissions granted the code. In the 1.2 security infrastructure, the properties that characterize running code are collectively called the code source. A code source is represented by a java.security.Code Source object, which contains a java.net.URL to represent the codebase and an array of zero or more certificate objects to represent the signers. Certificate objects are instances of subclasses of the abstract class java.security.cert.Certificate.

A Certificate is an abstraction that represents a binding of a principal to a public key, and another principal (the certificate authority mentioned previously) that vouches for that binding. The CodeSource object contains an array of Certificate objects, because the same code can be signed (vouched for) by more than one party. The signatures are usually obtained from a JAR file. All of the tools and access control infrastructure that accompanies the concrete SecurityManager in version 1.2 work only with certificates.

None work with bare public keys. If you don't have a certificate authority handy, you can sign your own public key with your private key and generate a self-signed certificate. The keytool programme from the Java 2 SDK version 1.2 always generates a self-signed certificate when it generates keys. In the code signing example given earlier in this chapter, for instance, the keytool created not only public/private key pairs, but also self-signed certificates for the aliasesfriend and stranger.

A permission is represented by an instance of a subclass of the abstract class java.security.Permission. A permission object has three properties: a type, a name, and an optional action. A permission's type is indicated by the name of the permission class. Some examples of permission types are: java.io.FilePermission,java.net.SocketPermission, and java.awt.AWTPermission.

A permission's name is encapsulated inside thePermission object. For example, the name of a FilePermission might be: "/ my/finances.dat"; the name of anSocketPermission might be "applets.artima.com: 2000"; and the name of an AWTPermission might be" show Window Without Banner Warning". The third property of a Permission object is its action. Not all permissions have an action. An example of an action for a FilePermission is: "read,write", and for a SocketPermission is: "accept,connect". A FilePermission with the name/my/finances.dat and action read,write represents permission to read and write to the file/my/finances.dat. Both name and action are represented by Strings.

The Java API has a large hierarchy of permissions that represent potentially dangerous actions code may wish to take. You can also create your own permission classes to represent custom permissions that you use for your own purposes. For example, you could create permission classes that represent permission to access particular records of your proprietary database. Defining custom permission classes is one way you can extend the 1.2 security mechanism to reflect your own needs. If you create your own Permission classes, you can use them like any of the built-in Permission classes from the Java API.

In the Policy object, each CodeSource is associated with one or more Permission objects. The Permission objects with which a CodeSource is associated are encapsulated in an instance of a subclass ofjava.security.PermissionCollection. Class loaders can invoke Policy.getPolicy() to get a reference to the policy object currently in effect. They can then invoke getPermissions() on the Policy object, passing in a CodeSourceto get a PermissionCollection of Permission objects for the passed CodeSource. A class loader can then use thePermissionCollection retrieved from the Policy object to help it decide what permissions the code it is about to import will be granted.

POLICY

java.security.Policy is an abstract class. One of the implementation details of concrete Policy subclasses is how an instance of the subclass learns what the policy should be. Subclasses can take various approaches, such as deserializing a previously serialized policy object, extracting the policy from a database, or reading the policy from a file. The concrete policy subclass supplied by Sun with the version 1.2 Java Platform takes the latter approach: it enables you to express your security policy in a context free grammar in an ASCII *policy file.*

A policy file is consists of a series *grant clauses,* each of which grants a code source a set of permissions. As mentioned previously, a code source consists of a codebase, which is a URL from which code was loaded, and a set of signers. In the policy file, signers are designated with the alias with which the signer's public key is stored in a keystore file. The keystore can be explicitly specified in the policy file in a keystore statement.

As an example of a policy file, consider the policyfile.txt file from the security/ex2 directory of the CD-ROM:

```
keystore "ijvmkeys";
grant signedBy "friend" {
permission java.io.FilePermission "question.txt",
"read";
```

```
permission java.io.FilePermission "answer.txt",
"read";
};
grant signedBy "stranger" {
permission java.io.FilePermission "question.txt",
"read";
};
grant                                     codeBase
"file:${com.artima.ijvm.cdrom.home}/security/ex2/
*" {
 permission java.io.FilePermission "question.txt",
"read";
 permission java.io.FilePermission "answer.txt",
"read";
};
```

The first statement in the policyfile.txt file is a keystore statement:

```
keystore "ijvmkeys";
```

This keystore statement indicates that the key aliases mentioned in the rest of the policy file refer to certificates stored in a file named "ijvmkeys". Because this filename includes no path, the file must be located in the current directory — the directory in which the Java application using this policy file is started.

The second statement in the policy file is a grant statement:

```
grant signedBy "friend" {
permission java.io.FilePermission "question.txt",
"read";
permission java.io.FilePermission "answer.txt",
"read";
};
```

This statement grants two permissions to any code signed by the entity with the alias "friend". The granted permissions are: permission to read a file named question.txt and permission to read a file named answer.txt. Because these filenames appear with no path, both files must be in the current directory, the directory in which the application is started. Because no codebase is mentioned in the grant clause, code signed by friend can come from any codebase. All code signed by friend, regardless of codebase, will be awarded permission to read question.txt and answer.txt.

The third statement in policyfile.txt is another grant statement, similar in form to the first:

```
grant signedBy "stranger" {
permission java.io.FilePermission "question.txt",
"read";
};
```

This statement grants one permission to any code signed by the entity with the alias "stranger": permission to read a file named question.txt. This file must be sitting in the current directory, the directory in which the application is started. Because no codebase is mentioned in the grant clause, code signed by stranger can come from any codebase and will still be awarded permission to read question.txt. Note that although stranger is allowed to read the question contained in question.txt, stranger is not allowed to peek at the answer contained in answer.txt. This contrasts with the privileges awarded to friend, who is allowed to read both the question and the answer.

The fourth and final statement in this policy file is yet another grant statement:

```
grant                                    codeBase
"file:${com.artima.ijvm.cdrom.home}/security/ex2/
*" {
 permission java.io.FilePermission "question.txt",
"read";
 permission java.io.FilePermission "answer.txt",
"read";
};
```

This final grant statement grants two permissions to any code that was loaded from a particular directory, permission to read a file named question.txt and permission to read a file named answer.txt. Both files must be in the current directory, the directory in which the application is started. Note that this grant statement does not mention any signers. The code can be signed by anyone or no one. So long as it is loaded from the indicated directory, the code will be granted the listed permissions. The codebase URL in this grant statement takes the form of a file: URL that includes a property, ${com. artima.ijvm. cdrom.home}. If you run the AccessControl example programs described later in this chapter, you'll have to set the com.artima.ijvm.cdrom.home property to the path of the CD-ROM that comes with this book, or to whatever directory you have moved the security subdirectory from the CD-ROM. The Policy object that is instantiated based on the contents of policyfile.txt will take the com.artima. ijvm.cdrom. home property into account when it constructs the URL for the CodeSource for this grant clause.

PROTECTION DOMAINS

As class loaders load types into the Java virtual machine, they assign each type into a *protection domain*. A protection domain defines all the permissions that are granted to a particular code source. (A protection domain corresponds to one or more grant clauses in a policy file.) Each type loaded into a Java virtual machine belongs to one and only one protection domain.

The class loader knows the codebase and the signers of any class or interface it loads. It uses that information to create a CodeSource object. It passes the CodeSource object to the getPermissions() method of the currently in-force Policy object to get an instance of a subclass of the abstract class java.security.PermissionCollection. ThePermissionCollection holds references to all Permission objects granted to the given code source by the current policy.

With both the CodeSource that it created and the PermissionCollection it got from the Policy object, it can instantiate a new ProtectionDomain object. It places the code into a protection domain by passing the appropriate Protection Domain object to the defineClass() method, an instance method of class ClassLoader that user-defined class loaders call to import type data into the Java virtual machine. This assigning classes into protection domains is a critical job which, as mentioned earlier in this chapter, is one of three ways the class loader architecture supports Java's sandbox security model. Although the Policy object represents a global mapping from code sources to permissions, in the end the class loader is the responsible party that decides what permissions code is going to get when it runs.

A class loader could, for example, completely ignore the current policy and just assign permissions off the cuff. Or, a class loader could add permissions to those returned by the policy object's getPermissions() method. For example, a class loader for loading applet code could add a permission to make a socket connection back to the host from which the applet came to the permissions, if any, granted to the code by the policy. As you can see, the class loader plays a crucial security role as it loads classes.

For a graphical depiction of protection domains, code sources, and permissions, consider Figure 3-5. In Figure 3-5, the method area and heap are shown after the code inside friend.jar is loaded under the policy defined bypolicyfile.txt. friend.jar is a JAR file in the security/ex2/jars directory of the CD-ROM, andpolicyfile.txt is an ASCII policy file in the security/ex2 directory. The friend.jar file contains two class files,Friend.class and Friend$1.class. As described in the code signing example earlier in this chapter, both of these class files have been signed by friend.

When these classes are defined by the class loader, they are placed into a protection domain whose CodeSource object indicates two things. First, the CodeSource indicates that the class files were loaded from a local jar file, whose URL is: file:/ //f l /security/ex2/jars/friend.jar. And second, theCodeSource indicates that the class files were signed by friend, an alias associated with a certificate in the local keystore. The ProtectionDomain object encapsulates a reference to the CodeSource object and to ajava.security.

Permissions object. java.security.Permissions, a concrete subclass of the abstractjava.security. Permission Collection class, represents a heterogeneous collection of permissions. ThePermissions object holds references to two java.io.File Permission objects. These two FilePermissions grant the privilege to read files named question.txt and answer.txt in the current directory.

When a class loader imported Friend and Friend$1 into the method area shown in Figure, the class loader passed a reference to the ProtectionDomain object to defineClass() along with the bytes of the class files. ThedefineClass() method associated the type data in the method area for Friend and Friend$1 with the passedProtectionDomain object. This association is shown graphically in Figure, which includes arrows that represent references to the ProtectionDomain object held as part of the type data in the method area for Friend and Friend$1.

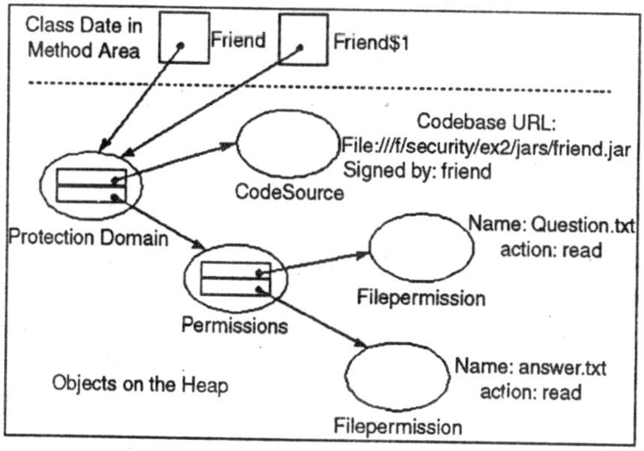

Fig. Protection Domains, Code Sources, and Permissions.

THE ACCESS CONTROLLER

Class java.security.AccessController provides a default security policy enforcement mechanism that uses stack inspection to determine whether potentially unsafe actions should be permitted. The access controller can't be instantiated. It isn't an object. Rather, it is a bundle of static methods collected in a single class. The central method of the AccessController is its static checkPermission() method, which decides whether or not a particular action is allowed. This method returns void and takes a reference to a Permission object as its only parameter. Similar to the check methods of the security manager, if the AccessController decides the operation should be allowed, its checkPermission() method simply returns silently. But if the AccessController decides that an operation should be forbidden, its checkPermission() method completes abruptly by throwing anAccess ControlException, or one of its subclasses.

As mentioned previously, the concrete SecurityManager's implementation of the legacy check methods (such ascheckRead() and checkWrite()) simply instantiate an appropriate Permission object and invoke the concrete SecurityManager's checkPermission() method. The concrete SecurityManager's checkPermission() method simply invokes checkPermission() on the AccessController. Thus, if you install the concrete SecurityManager, theAccessController is the ultimate entity that decides whether or not potentially unsafe actions will be allowed.

The basic algorithm implemented by the Access Controller's checkPermission() method makes certain that every frame on the call stack has permission to perform the potentially unsafe action. Each stack frame represents some method that has been invoked by the current thread. Each method is defined in some class. Each class belongs to some protection domain.

And each protection domain contains a set of permissions. Thus, each stack frame is indirectly associated with a set of permissions. For an action represented by the Permission object passed to the Access Controller' scheck Permission() method to be allowed, the basic algorithm of the AccessController requires that the permissions associated with each frame on the call stack must include or imply the Permission passed to checkPermission().

The AccessController's checkPermission() method inspects the stack from the top down. As soon as it encounters a frame that doesn't have permission, it throws an AccessControlException. By throwing the exception, theAccess Controller, indicates that the action should not be allowed. On the other hand, if the checkPermission()method reaches the bottom of the stack without encountering any frames that don't have permission to perform the potentially unsafe action, checkPermission() returns silently. By returning rather than throwing an exception, theAccessController indicates the action should be allowed The actual algorithm implemented by the Access Controller's checkPermission() method is a bit more complex than the basic algorithm described here. By invoking any of several doPrivileged() methods of class Access Controller, programs can in effect cause the AccessController to stop its frame by frame search before it reaches the bottom of the stack. The doPrivileged() method will be described later in this chapter.

The Implies() Method

To determine whether or not the action represented by the Permission object passed to the Access Controller' scheckPermission() method is included among (or implied by) the permissions associated with the code on the call stack, the AccessController makes use of an important method named implies(). The implies() method is declared in class Permission, as well as in classes PermissionCollection and Protection Domain. implies()takes a Permission object as its only parameter and returns a boolean true or false.

The implies() method of classPermission determines whether the permission represented by one Permission object is naturally implied by the permission represented by a different Permission object. The implies() methods of PermissionCollection andProtection Domain determine whether the passed Permission is included among or implied by the collection ofPermission objects encapsulated in the PermissionCollection or Protection Domain.

For example, a permission to read all files in the/tmp directory would naturally imply a permission to read/tmp/f, a specific file in the/tmp directory, but not vice versa. If you asked a FilePermission object that represents the permission to read any file in the/tmp directory if it implies the permission to read file/tmp/f, the implies() method should returntrue. But if you ask a FilePermission object representing the permission to read/tmp/f if it implies the permission to read any file in the/tmp directory, the implies() method should return false.

The Example1 application from the security/ex1 directory of the CD-ROM demonstrates this meaning of implies():

```
import java.security.Permission;
import java.io.FilePermission;
import java.io.File;

// On CD-ROM in file security/ex1/Example1.java
class Example1 {

 public static void main(String[] args) {

   char sep = File.separatorChar;

 // Read permission for "/tmp/f"
   Permission file = new FilePermission(
     sep + "tmp" + sep + "f", "read");

  // Read permission for "/tmp/*", which
  // means all files in the/tmp directory
 // (but not any files in subdirectories
 // of/tmp)
    Permission star = new FilePermission(
     sep + "tmp" + sep + "*", "read");

  boolean starImpliesFile = star.implies(file);
  boolean fileImpliesStar = file.implies(star);

 // Prints "Star implies file = true"
   System.out.println("Star implies file = "
      + starImpliesFile);

 // Prints "File implies star = false"
    System.out.println("File implies star = "
    + fileImpliesStar);
  }
}
```

The Example1 application creates two FilePermission objects, one that represents read permission for a particular directory and another that represents read permission for a particular file in that same directory. The FilePermissionobject referenced from local variable star represents permission to read any file in/tmp. The FilePermission object referenced from local variable file represents permission to read file/tmp/f. When executed, this application prints:

```
Star implies file = true
File implies star = false
```

The implies() method is used by the AccessController to determine whether a thread has permission to take actions. If the checkPermission() method of the AccessController is invoked to determine whether that thread has permission to read file/tmp/f, for example, the AccessController can invoke the implics() method on the ProtectionDomainobjects associated with each frame of that thread's call stack. To each implies() method, the AccessController can pass the FilePermission object representing permission to read file/tmp/ f that was passed to itscheckPermission() method.

The implies() method of each ProtectionDomain object can invoke implies() on thePermissionCollection it encapsulates, passing along the same FilePermission. Each Permission Collectioncan in turn invoke implies() on the Permission objects it contains, once again passing along a reference to the sameFilePermission object. As soon as a PermissionCollection's implies() method encounters one Permissionobject whose implies() method returns true, the PermissionCollection's implies() method returns true.

Only if none of the implies() methods of the Permission objects contained in a PermissionCollection return true does the PermissionCollection return false. The ProtectionDomain's implies() method simply returns what thePermission Collection's implies() method returns. If the AccessController gets back a true from the implies()method of a Protection Domain associated with a particular stack frame, the code represented by that stack frame has permission to perform the potentially unsafe action.

STACK INSPECTION EXAMPLES

The several examples to illustrate the manner in which

the AccessController performs stack inspection. In the upcoming examples, code signed by both friend and stranger will be trusted to some extent, but friend code will be trusted more than stranger code.

In particular, code signed by both friend and stranger will be given permission to read a file named question.txt, which contains a question. But although code signed by friend will be given permission to read a file named answer.txt, which contains the answer to the question asked inquestion.txt, code signed by stranger will not. These permissions granted to friend and stranger are those outlined in the policyfile.txtfile from the security/ex2 directory of the CD-ROM, which was described earlier in this chapter. Each of the upcoming examples will take their policy from policyfile.txt.

The stack inspection examples all make use of classes that implement the Doer interface:

```
// On CD-ROM in file
// security/ex2/com/artima/security/doer/Doer.java
package com.artima.security.doer;
public interface Doer {
void doYourThing();
}
```

To be a Doer, a class must provide an implementation for one method: doYourThing(). Classes that implement Doercan do whatever they feel like in their doYourThing() method. For example, here's a class that implements Doer namedText FileDisplayer whose "thing" is to display the contents of a text file:

```
// On CD-ROM in file security/ex2/
TextFileDisplayer.java

import com.artima.security.doer.Doer;
import java.io.FileReader;
import java.io.CharArrayWriter;
import java.io.IOException;

public class TextFileDisplayer implements Doer {
 private String fileName;
```

```
  public TextFileDisplayer(String fileName) {
    this.fileName = fileName;
  }

  public void doYourThing() {

    try {
    FileReader fr = new FileReader(fileName);

     try {
   CharArrayWriter caw = new CharArrayWriter();

      int c;
       while ((c = fr.read()) != -1) {
         caw.write(c);
        }

        System.out.println(caw.toString());
      }
      catch (IOException e) {
      }
      finally {
        try {
          fr.close();
        }
        catch (IOException e) {
        }
      }
    }
    catch (IOException e) {
    }
  }
}
```

When you create a TextFileDisplayer object, you must pass a file path name to its constructor. TheTextFileDisplayer constructor stores the passed path name in the filename instance variable. When you invokedoYourThing() on the TextFileDisplayer object, it will attempt to open and read the contents of the file and print them at the standard output.

Another example of a doYourThing() method comes from classes Friend and Stranger, which appeared earlier in this chapter in the code signing example and are shown again here to refresh your memory:

```
// On CD-ROM in file
//  security/ex2/com/artima/security/friend/
Friend.java
package com.artima.security.friend;
import com.artima.security.doer.Doer;
import java.security.AccessController;
import java.security.PrivilegedAction;

public class Friend implements Doer {

  private Doer next;
  private boolean direct;

  public Friend(Doer next, boolean direct) {
    this.next = next;
    this.direct = direct;
  }

  public void doYourThing() {

    if (direct) {

      next.doYourThing();
    }
    else {
      AccessController.doPrivileged(
        new PrivilegedAction() {
          public Object run() {
            next.doYourThing();
            return null;
          }
```

```
            }
        );
      }
    }
}

// On CD-ROM in file
//  security/ex2/com/artima/security/stranger/
Stranger.java
package com.artima.security.stranger;
import com.artima.security.doer.Doer;
import java.security.AccessController;
import java.security.PrivilegedAction;

public class Stranger implements Doer {

    private Doer next;
    private boolean direct;

    public Stranger(Doer next, boolean direct) {
        this.next = next;
        this.direct = direct;
    }

    public void doYourThing() {

        if (direct) {

            next.doYourThing();
        }
        else {
            AccessController.doPrivileged(
                new PrivilegedAction() {
                    public Object run() {
                        next.doYourThing();
                        return null;
                    }
                }
```

```
        );
      }
    }
}
```

Friend and Stranger have much in common. They have identical instance variables, constructors, and doYourThing()methods. They differ only in their package and simple names. When you create a new Friend or Stranger object, you must pass to the constructor a boolean value and a reference to another object whose class implements the Doer interface. The constructor stores the passed Doer reference in the instance variable, next, and the boolean value in the instance variable, direct.

When doYourThing() is invoked on either a Friend or Stranger object, the method invokesdo YourThing(), either directly or indirectly, on the Doer reference contained in next. If direct is true, Friend orStranger's doYourThing() just invokes doYourThing() directly on next. Otherwise, Friend or Stranger'sdoYourThing() invokes doYourThing() on next indirectly, by way of a doPrivileged() call.

3

Java Network

INTRODUCTION

Platform independence deals with the challenge that many different kinds of computers and devices are usually connected to the same network. The security model deals with the challenge that networks represent a convenient way to transmit viruses and other forms of malicious or buggy code. This chapter describes not how Java's architecture deals with a challenge, but how it seizes an opportunity made possible by the network.

One of the fundamental reasons Java is a useful tool for networked software environments is that Java's architecture enables the network mobility of software. In fact, it was primarily this aspect of Java technology that was considered by many in the software industry to represent a paradigm shift. This chapter examines the nature of this new paradigm of network-mobile software, and how Java's architecture makes it possible.

NEED OF NETWORK MOBILITY

Prior to the advent of the personal computer, the dominant computing model was the large mainframe computer serving multiple users. By time-sharing, a mainframe computer divided its attention among several users, who logged onto the mainframe at dumb terminals. Software applications were stored on disks attached to the mainframe computer, allowing multiple users to share the same applications while they shared the same CPU. A drawback of this model was that if one user ran a CPU-intensive job, all other users would experience degraded performance.

The appearance of the microprocessor led to the proliferation of the personal computer. This change in the hardware status quo changed the software paradigm as well. Rather than sharing software applications stored at a mainframe computer, individual users had individual copies of software applications stored at each personal computer. Because each user ran software on a dedicated CPU, this new model of computing addressed the difficulties of dividing CPU-time among many users attempting to share one mainframe CPU.

Initially, personal computers operated as unconnected islands of computing. The dominant software model was of isolated executables running on isolated personal computers. But soon, personal computers began to be connected to networks. Because a personal computer gave its user undivided attention, it addressed the CPU-time sharing difficulties of mainframes. But unless personal computers were connected to a network, they couldn't replicate the mainframe's ability to let multiple users view and manipulate a central repository of data.

As personal computers connected to networks became the norm, another software model began to increase in importance: client/server. The client/server model divided work between two processes running on two different computers: a client process ran on the end-user's personal computer, and a server process ran on some other computer hooked to the same network.

The client and server processes communicated with one another by sending data back and forth across the network. The server process often simply accepted data query commands from clients across the network, retrieved the requested data from a central database, and sent the retrieved data back across the network to the client. Upon receiving the data, the client processed, displayed, and allowed the user to manipulate the data. This model allowed users of personal computers to view and manipulate data stored at a central repository, while not forcing them to share a central CPU for all of the processing of that data. Users did share the CPU running the server process, but to the extent that data processing was performed by the clients, the burden on the central CPU hosting the server process was lessened.

The client/server architecture was soon extended to include more than two processes. The original client/server model began to be called 2-tier client/server, to indicate two processes: one client and one server. More elaborate architectures were called 3-tier, to indicate three processes, 4-tier, to indicate four processes, or N-tier, to indicate people were getting tired of counting processes. Eventually, as more processes became involved, the distinction between client and server blurred, and people just started using the term *distributed processing* to encompass all of these schemes.

The distributed processing model leveraged the network and the proliferation of processors by dividing processing work loads among many processors while allowing those processors to share data. Although this model had many advantages over the mainframe model, there was one notable disadvantage: distributed processing systems were more difficult to administer than mainframe systems. On mainframe systems, software applications were stored on a disk attached to the mainframe.

Even though an application could serve many users, it only needed to be installed and maintained in one place. When an application was upgraded, all users got the new version the next time they logged on and started the application. By contrast, the software executables for different components of a distributed processing system were usually stored on many different disks. In a client/server architecture, for example, each computer that hosted a client process usually had its own copy of the client software stored on its local disk.

As a result, a system administrator had to install and maintain the various components of a distributed software system in many different places. When a software component was upgraded, the system administrator had to physically upgrade each copy of the component on each computer that hosted it. As a result, system administration was more difficult for the distributed processing model than for the mainframe model.

The arrival of Java, with an architecture that enabled the network-mobility of software, heralded yet another model for computing. Building on the prevailing distributed processing model, the new model added the automatic delivery of software across networks to computers that ran the software. This addressed the difficulties involved in system administration of distributed processing systems. For example, in a client/server system, client software could be stored at one central computer attached to the network. Whenever an end-user needed to use the client software, the binary executable would be sent from the central computer across the network to the end-user's computer, where the software would run.

So network-mobility of software represented another step in the evolution of the computing model. In particular, it addressed the difficulty of administering a distributed processing system. It simplified the job of distributing any software that was to be used on more than one CPU. It allowed data to be delivered together with the software that knows how to manipulate or display the data. Because code was sent along with data, end-users would always have the most up-to-date version of the code. Thus, because of network- mobility, software can be administered from a central computer, reminiscent of the mainframe model, but processing can still be distributed among many CPUs.

SOFTWARE PARADIGM

The shift away from the mainframe model towards the distributed processing model was a consequence of the personal computer revolution, which was made possible by the rapidly increasing capabilities and decreasing costs of processors. Similarly, lurking underneath the latest software paradigm shift towards distributed processing with network-mobile code is another hardware trend—the increasing capabilities and decreasing costs of network bandwidth. As bandwidth, the amount of information that can be carried by a network, increases, it becomes practical to send new kinds of information across a network; and with each new kind of information a network carries, the network takes on a new character. Thus, as bandwidth grows, simple text sent across a network can become enhanced with graphics, and the network begins to take on an appearance reminiscent of newspapers or magazines.

Once bandwidth expands enough to support live streams of audio data, the network begins to act like a radio, a CD-player, or a telephone. With still more bandwidth, video becomes possible, resulting in a network that competes with TV and VCRs for the attention of couch potatoes. But there is still one other kind of bandwidth-hungry content that becomes increasingly practical as bandwidth improves: computer software. Because networks by definition interconnect processors, one processor can, given enough bandwidth, send code across a network for another processor to execute. Once networks begin to move software as well as data, the network begins to look like a computer in its own right.

As software begins to travel across networks, not only does the network begin to take on a new character, but so does the software itself. Network-mobile code makes it easier to ensure that an end-user has the necessary software to view or manipulate some data sent across the network, because the software can be sent along with the data. In the old model, software executables from a local disk were invoked to view data that came across the network, thus the software application was usually a distinct entity, easily discernible from the data. In the new model, because software and data are both sent across the network, the distinction between software and data is not as stark—software and data blur together to become "content."

As the nature of software evolves, the end-user's relationship to software evolves as well. Prior to network-mobility, an end-user had to think in terms of software applications and version numbers. Software was generally distributed on media such as tapes, floppy disks, or CD-ROMs.

To use an application, an end- user had to get the installation media, physically insert them into a drive or reader attached to the computer, and run an installation programme that copied files from the installation media to the computer's hard disk. Moreover, the end-user often did this process multiple times for each application, because software applications were routinely replaced by new versions that fixed old bugs and added new features (and usually added new bugs too). When a new version was released, end-users had to decide whether or not to upgrade. If an end-user decided to upgrade, the installation process had to repeated. Thus, end-users had to think in terms of software applications and version numbers, and take deliberate action to keep their software applications up-to-date.

In the new model, end-users think less in terms of software applications with discrete versions, and more in terms of self-evolving "content services." Whereas installing a traditional software application or an upgrade was a deliberate act on the part of the end-user, network-mobility of software enables installation and upgrading that is more automatic. Network-delivered software need not have discrete version numbers that are known to the end-user. The end-user need not decide whether to upgrade, and need not take any special action to upgrade. Network-delivered software can just evolve of its own accord. Instead of buying discrete versions of a software application, end-users can subscribe to a content service—software that is delivered across a network along with relevant data—and watch as both the software and data evolve automatically over time.

Once you move away from delivering software in discrete versions towards delivering software as self- evolving streams of interactive content, your end-user loses some control. In the old model, if a new version appeared that had serious bugs, an end-user could simply opt not to upgrade. But in the new model, an end- user can't necessarily wait until the bugs are worked out of a new version before upgrading to the new version, because the end-user may have no control over the upgrading process.

For certain kinds of products, especially those that are large and full-featured, end-users may prefer to retain control over whether and when to upgrade. Consequently, in some situations software vendors may publish discrete versions of a content service over the network. At the very least, a vendor can publish two branches of a service: a beta branch and a released branch. End-users that want to stay on the bleeding edge can subscribe to the beta service, and the rest can subscribe to the released service that, although it may not have all the newest features, is likely more robust.

Yet for many content services, especially simple ones, most end-users won't want to have to worry about versions, because worrying about versions makes software harder to use. The end-user has to have knowledge about the differences between versions, make decisions about when and if to upgrade, and take deliberate action to cause an upgrade. Content services that are not chopped up into discrete versions are easier to use, because they evolve automatically. Such a content service, because the end-user doesn't have to maintain it but can just simply use it, takes on the feel of a "software appliance."

Many self-evolving content services will share two fundamental characteristics with common household appliances: a focused functionality and a simple user-interface. Consider the toaster. A toaster's functionality is focused exclusively on the job of preparing toast, and it has a simple user-interface. When you walk up to a toaster, you don't expect to have to read a manual. You expect to put the bread in at the top and push down a handle until it clicks. You expect to be able to peer in and see orange wires glowing, and after a moment, to hear that satisfying pop and see your bread transformed into toast.

If the result is too light or too dark, you expect to be able to slide a knob to indicate to the toaster that the next time, you want your toast a bit darker or lighter. That's the extent of the functionality and user-interface of a toaster. Likewise, the functionality of many content services will be as focused and the user-interface will be as simple. If you want to order a movie through the network, for example, you don't want to worry whether you have the correct version of movie-ordering software. You don't want to have to install it. You just want to switch on the movie-ordering content service, and through a simple user-interface, order your movie. Then you can sit back and enjoy your network-delivered movie as you eat your toast.

A good example of a content service is a World Wide Web page. If you look at an HTML file, it looks like a source file for some kind of programme. But if you see the browser as the programme, the HTML file looks more like data. Thus, the distinction between code and data is blurred. Also, people who browse the World Wide Web expect web pages to evolve over time, without any deliberate action on their part. They don't expect to see discrete version numbers for web pages. They don't expect to have to do anything to upgrade to the latest version of a page besides simply revisiting the page in their browser.

In the coming years, many of today's media may to some extent be assimilated by the network and transformed into content services. (As with the Borg from Star Trek, resistance is futile.) Broadcast radio, broadcast and cable TV, telephones, answering machines, faxes, video rental stores, newspapers, magazines, books, computer software—all of these will be affected by the proliferation of networks. But just as TV didn't supplant radio entirely, network-delivered content services will not entirely supplant existing media. Instead, content services will likely take over some aspects of existing media, leaving the existing media to adjust accordingly, and create some new forms that didn't previously exist.

In the computer software domain, the content service model will not completely replace the old models either. Instead, it will likely take over certain aspects of the old models that fit better in the new model, add new forms that didn't exist before, and leave the old models to adjust their focus slightly in light of the newcomer.

This book is an example of how the network can affect existing media. The book was not entirely replaced by a content service counterpart, but instead of including resource pointers (sources where you can find further information on topics presented in the book) as part of the book, they were placed on a web page. Because resource pointers change so often, it made sense to let the network assimilate that part of the book. Thus, the resource pointers portion of the book has become a content service.

The crux of the new software paradigm, therefore, is that software begins to act more like appliances. End-users no longer have to worry about installation, version numbers, or upgrading. As code is sent along with data across the network, software delivery and updating become automatic. In this way, simply by making code mobile, Java unleashes a whole new way to think about software development, delivery, and use.

JAVA'S ARCHITECTURAL SUPPORT FOR NETWORK-MOBILITY

Java's architectural support for network-mobility begins with its support for platform independence and security. Although they are not strictly required for network-mobility, platform independence and security help make network-mobility practical. Platform independence makes it easier to deliver a programme across the network because you don't have to maintain a separate version of the programme for different platforms, and you don't have to figure out how to get the right version to each computer. One version of a programme can serve all computers. Java's security features help promote network-mobility because they give end-users confidence to download class files from untrusted sources. In practice, therefore, Java's architectural support for platform independence and security facilitate the network-mobility of its class files.

Beyond platform independence and security, Java's architectural support for network-mobility is focused on managing the time it takes to move software across a network. If you store a programme on a server and download it across a network when you need it, it will likely take longer for your programme to start than if you had started the same programme from a local disk. Thus, one of the primary issues of network- mobile software is the time it takes to send a programme across a network. Java's architecture addresses this issue by rejecting the traditional monolithic binary executable in favour of small binary pieces: Java class files.

Class files can travel across networks independently, and because Java programs are dynamically linked and dynamically extensible, an end-user needn't wait until all of a program's class files are downloaded before the programme starts. The programme starts when the first class file arrives. Class files themselves are designed to be compact, so that they fly more quickly across networks. Therefore, the main way Java's architecture facilitates network-mobility directly is by breaking up the monolithic binary executable into compact class files, which can be loaded as needed.

The execution of a Java application begins at a main() method of some class, and other classes are loaded and dynamically linked as they are needed by the application. If a class is never actually used during one session, that class won't ever be loaded during that session. For example, if you are using a word processor that has a spelling checker, but during one session you never invoke the spelling checker, the class files for the spelling checker will not be loaded during that session.

In addition to dynamic linking, Java's architecture also enables dynamic extension. Dynamic extension is another way the loading of class files (and the downloading of them across a network) can be delayed in a Java application. Using user-defined class loaders or the forname() method of class Class, a Java programme can load extra classes at run-time, which then become a part of the running programme. Therefore, dynamic linking and dynamic extension give a Java programmer some flexibility in designing when class files for a programme are loaded, and as a result, how much time an end-user must spend waiting for class files to come across the network.

Besides dynamic linking and dynamic extension, another way Java's architecture directly supports network mobility is through the class file format itself. To reduce the time it takes to send them across networks, class files are designed to be compact. In particular, the bytecode streams they contain are designed to be compact. They are called "bytecodes" because each instruction occupies only one byte. With only two exceptions, all opcodes and their ensuing operands are byte aligned to make the bytecode streams smaller. The two exceptions are opcodes that may have one to three bytes of padding after the opcode and before the start of the operands, so that the operands are aligned on word boundaries.

One of the implications of the compactness goal for class files is that Java compilers are not likely to do much local optimization. Because of binary compatibility rules, Java compilers can't perform global optimizations such as inlining the invocation of another class's method. (Inlining means replacing the method invocation with the code performed by the method, which saves the time it takes to invoke and return from the method as the code executes.)

Binary compatibility requires that a method's implementation can be changed without breaking compatibility with pre-existing class files that depend on the method. Inlining could be performed in some circumstances on methods within a single class, but in general that kind of optimization is not done by Java compilers, partly because it goes against the grain of class file compactness. Optimizations are often a tradeoff between execution speed and code size. Therefore, Java compilers generally leave optimization up to the Java virtual machine, which can optimize code as it loads classes for interpreting, just-in-time compiling, or adaptive optimization.

Beyond the architectural features of dynamic linking, dynamic extension and class file compactness, there are some strategies that, although they are really not necessarily part of the architecture, help manage the time it takes to move class files across a network. Because HTTP protocols require that each class file of Java applet be requested individually, it turns out that often a large percentage of applet download time is due not to the actual transmission of class files across the network, but to the network handshaking of each class file request. The overhead for a file request is multiplied by the number of class files being requested. To address this problem, Java 1.1 included support for JAR (Java ARchive) files. JAR files enable many class files to be sent in one network transaction, which greatly reduces the overhead time required to move class files across a network compared with sending one class file at a time. Moreover, the data inside a JAR file can be compressed, which results in an even shorter download time. So sometimes it pays to send software across a network in one big chunk. If a set of class files is definitely needed by a programme before that programme can start, those class files can be more speedily transmitted if they are sent together in a JAR file.

One other strategy to minimize an end-user's wait time is to not download class files on-demand. Through various techniques, such as the subscription model used by Marimba Castanet, class files can be downloaded before they are needed, resulting in a programme that starts up faster. You can obtain more information about such approaches from the resource page for this chapter.

Therefore, other than platform independence and security, which help make network-mobility practical, the main focus of Java's architectural support for network-mobility is managing the time it takes to send class files across a network. Dynamic linking and dynamic extension allow Java programs to be designed in small functional units that are downloaded as needed by the end-user. Class file compactness helps reduce the time it takes to move a Java programme across the network. The JAR file enables compression and the sending of multiple class files across the network in a single network file-transfer transaction.

EXAMPLE OF NETWORK-MOBILE CODE

Java is a network-oriented technology that first appeared at a time when the network was looking increasingly like the next revolution in computing. The reason Java was adopted so rapidly and so widely, however, was not simply because it was a timely technology, but because it had timely marketing.

Java was not the only network-oriented technology being developed in the early to mid 1990s. And although it was a good technology, it wasn't the necessarily the best technology—but it probably had the best marketing. Java was the one technology to hit a slim market window in early 1995, resulting in such a strong response that many companies developing similar technologies canceled their projects. Companies that carried on with their technologies, such as AT&T did with a network-oriented technology named Inferno, saw Java steal much of their potential thunder.

There were several important factors in how Java was initially unleashed on the world that contributed to its successful marketing. First, it had a cool name—one that could be appreciated by programmers and non-programmers alike. Second, it was, for all practical purposes, free—always a strong selling point among prospective buyers. But the most critical factor contributing to the successful marketing of Java, however, was that Sun's engineers hooked Java technology to the World Wide Web at the precise moment Netscape was looking to transform their web browser from a graphical hypertext viewer to a full-fledged computing platform.

As the World Wide Web swept through the software industry (and the global consciousness) like an ever-increasing tidal wave, Java rode with it. Therefore, in a sense Java became a success because Java "surfed the web." It caught the wave at just the right time and kept riding it as one by one, its potential competitors dropped uneventfully into the cold, dark sea. The way the engineers at Sun hooked Java technology to the World Wide Web—and therefore, the key way Java was successfully marketed—was by creating a special flavour of Java programme that ran inside a web browser: the Java applet.

The Java applet showed off all of Java's network-oriented features: platform independence, network- mobility, and security. Platform independence was one of the main tenets of the World Wide Web, and Java applets fit right in. Java applets can run on any platform so long as there is a Java-capable browser for that platform. Java applets also demonstrated Java's security capabilities, because they ran inside a strict sandbox. But most significantly, Java applets demonstrated the promise of network-mobility. As shown in Figure, Java applets can be maintained on one server, from which they can travel across a network to many different kinds of computers. To update an applet, you only need to update the server. Users will automatically get the updated version the next time they use the applet. Thus, maintenance is localized, but processing is distributed.

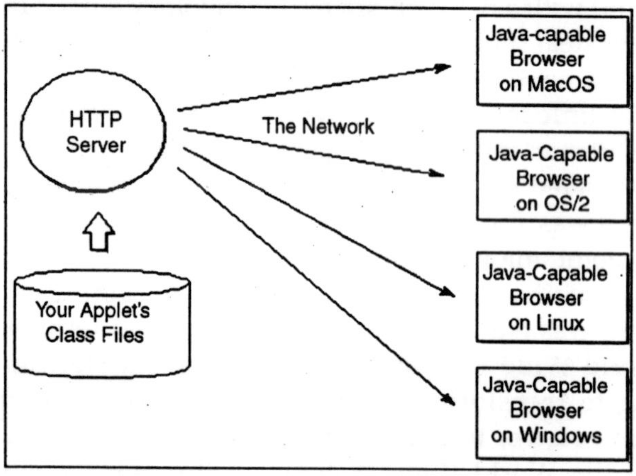

Fig. The Java Applet and the Network.

Java-capable browsers fire off a Java application that hosts the applets the browser displays. To display a web page, a web browser requests an HTML file from an HTTP server. If the HTML file includes an applet, the browser will see an HTML tag such as this:

```
<applet CODE="HeapOfFish.class"
CODEBASE="gcsupport/classes"
WIDTH=525
HEIGHT=360></applet>
```

This "applet" tag provides enough information to enable the browser to display the applet. The CODE attribute indicates the name of the applet's starting class file, in this case: HeapOfFish.class. The CODEBASE attribute gives the location of the applet's class files relative to the base URL of the web page. The WIDTH and HEIGHT attributes indicate the size in pixels of the applet's panel, the visible portion of the applet that is displayed as part of the web page. When a browser encounters a web page that includes an applet tag, it passes information from the tag to the running Java application. The Java application either creates a new user-defined class loader object, or re-uses an existing one, to download the starting class file for the applet. It then initializes the applet, by invoking first the init() and then the start()method of the applet's starting class.

The other class files for the applet are downloaded on an as needed basis, by the normal process of dynamic linking. For example, when a new class is first used by the applet's starting class, the symbolic reference to the new class must be resolved. During resolution, if the class has not already been loaded, the Java virtual machine will ask the same user-defined class loader that loaded the applet's starting class to load the new class. If the user-defined class loader is unable to load the class from the local trusted repository through the bootstrap class loader, the user-defined class loader will attempt to download the class file across the network from the same location it retrieved the applet's starting class. Once initialization of the applet is complete, the applet appears as part of the web page inside the browser.

NETWORK-MOBILE OBJECTS

Although the network-mobility of code made possible by Java's architecture and demonstrated by Java applets represented an important step in the evolution of computing models, Java's architecture held one other promise: the network mobility of objects. An object can move across a network as a combination of code, which defines the object's class, plus data that gives a snapshot of the object's state.

Where network mobility of code can help simplify the work of systems administrators, network mobility of objects can help simplify the work of software developers designing and deploying distributed systems. Through object serialization and Remote Method Invocation (RMI), the Java API supplies a distributed object model that extends Java's local object model beyond the boundaries of the Java virtual machine. The distributed object model enables objects in one virtual machine to hold references to objects in other virtual machines, to invoke methods on those remote objects, and to exchange objects between virtual machines as parameters, return values, and exceptions of those method invocations. These capabilities, which are made practical by Java's underlying network-oriented architecture, can simplify the task of designing a distributed system because they in effect bring object-oriented programming to the network.

One technology that takes full advantage of the network mobility of objects made possible by Java's underlying network-friendly architecture, object serialization, and RMI, is Sun's Jini. Jini is a set of protocols and APIs that support the building and deployment of distributed systems that is targeted at the emerging proliferation of diskless embedded devices connected to networks. One particular piece of the Jini architecture, the service object, provides a good illustration of the way in which network-mobility of objects can be useful.

A Jini system is centered on a lookup service in which services register themselves by sending, among other objects, a service object. The service object represents the service to clients. Clients who want to access the service retrieve a copy of the service object from the lookup service and then interact with the service by invoking methods on the service object. The service object is responsible for implementing the service, either locally or by talking across the network to a software process or piece of hardware that implements the service.

JINI

To the Jini way of thinking, the network is made up of "services" that can be used by clients or other services. A *service* can be anything that sits on the network ready to perform a useful function. Hardware devices, software servers, communications channels — even human users themselves — can be services. A Jini-enabled disk drive, for example, could offer a "storage" service. A Jini-enabled printer could offer a "printing" service.

To perform a task, a client enlists the help of services. For example, a client programme might upload pictures from the image storage service in a digital camera, download the pictures to a persistent storage service offered by a disk drive, and send a page of thumbnail-sized versions of the images to the printing service of a colour printer. In this example, the client programme builds a distributed system consisting of itself, the image storage service, the persistent storage service, and the colour-printing service. The client and services of this distributed system work together to perform the task: to offload and store images from a digital camera and print out a page of thumbnails.

Working

Jini provides a *runtime infrastructure* that enables service providers to offer their services to clients, and enables clients to locate and access services. The runtime infrastructure resides on the network in three places: in lookup services that sit on the network; in the service providers (such as Jini- enabled devices); and in clients. *Lookup services* are the central organizing mechanism for Jini- based systems. When new services become available on the network, they register themselves with a lookup service. When clients wish to locate a service to assist with some task, they consult a lookup service.

The runtime infrastructure uses one network-level protocol, called *discovery,* and two object-level protocols, called *join* and*lookup*. Discovery enables clients and services to locate lookup services. Join enables a service to register itself in a lookup service. Lookup enables a client to query a lookup service for services that can help the client accomplish its goals.

The Discovery Process

The discovery process begins automatically when a service provider, such as a Jini-enabled disk drive that offers a storage service, is plugged into the network. When a service provider is connected to the network, it broadcasts a *presence announcement* by dropping a multicast packet onto a well-known port. Included in the presence announcement is an IP address and port number where the service provider can be contacted by a lookup service. Lookup services monitor the well-known port for presence announcement packets. When a lookup service receives a presence announcement, it opens and inspects the packet. The packet contains information that enables the lookup service to determine whether or not it should contact the sender of the packet. If so, it contacts the sender directly by making a TCP connection to the IP address and port number extracted from the packet.

Using RMI, the lookup service sends an object, called a *service registrar*, across the network to the originator of the packet. The purpose of the service registrar object is to facilitate further communication with the lookup service. By invoking methods on the service registrar object, the sender of the announcement packet can perform join and lookup on the lookup service. In the case of a disk drive, the lookup service would make a TCP connection to the disk drive and would send it a service registrar object, through which the disk drive would then register its storage service via the join process.

The Join Process

Once a service provider has a service registrar object, the end product of discovery, it is ready to do a join — to become registered in the lookup service. To do a join, the service provider invokes the register() method on the service registrar object, passing as a parameter an object called a *service item*, a bundle of objects that describe the service. Theregister() method sends a copy of the service item up to the lookup service, where the service item is stored. Once this has completed, the service provider has finished the join process: its service has become registered in the lookup service.

The service item is a container for several objects, including the object called the *service object*, which clients can use to interact with the service. The service item can also include any number of *attributes*, which can be any kind of object. Some potential attributes are icons, classes that provide GUIs for the service, and objects that give more information about the service.

Service objects usually implement one or more interfaces through which clients interact with the service. For example, a lookup service is a Jini service, and its service object is the service registrar. The register() method invoked by service providers during join is declared in the ServiceRegistrar interface, which all service registrar objects implement. Clients and service providers talk to the lookup service through the service registrar object by invoking methods declared in theServiceRegistrar interface. Likewise, a disk drive would provide a service object that implemented some well-known storage service interface. Clients would look up and interact with the disk drive by this storage service interface.

The Lookup Process

Once a service has registered with a lookup service via the join process, that service is available for use by clients that query that lookup service. To build a distributed system of services that will work together to perform some task, a client must locate and enlist the help of the individual services. To find a service, clients query lookup services via a process called *lookup*.

To perform a lookup, a client invokes the lookup() method on a service registrar object. (A client, like a service provider, gets a service registrar through the process of discovery, described previously.) The client passes as an argument tolookup() a *service template,* an object that serves as search criteria for the query. The service template can include a reference to an array of Class objects. These Class objects indicate to the lookup service the Java type (or types) of the service object desired by the client.

The service template can also include a *service ID,* which uniquely identifies a service, and attributes, which must exactly match the attributes uploaded by the service provider in the service item. The service template can also contain wildcards for any of these fields. A wildcard in the service ID field, for example, will match any service ID. The lookup() method sends the service template to the lookup service, which performs the query and sends back zero to many matching service objects. The client gets a reference to the matching service objects as the return value of the lookup() method.

In the general case, a client looks up a service by Java type, usually an interface. For example, if a client needed to use a printer, it would compose a service template that included a Class object for a well-known interface to printer services. All printer services would implement this well-known interface. The lookup service would return a service object (or objects) that implemented this interface. Attributes can be included in the service template to narrow the number of matches for such a type-based search. The client would use the printer service by invoking on the service object methods declared in the well-known printer service interface.

BENEFITS OF THE SERVICE OBJECT

In Jini systems, network-mobile objects fly all over the place. When a client or service performs discovery, for example, it receives a service registrar object from a lookup service. When a service registers itself with a lookup service through the join process, it sends to the lookup service a service item object, which itself is a container of many objects, including attributes and the service object. When a client performs lookup, it sends a service template object, a bundle of objects that serves as a search criteria for the lookup query. If the lookup is successful, the client receives either the service object or the entire service item for the service or services that matched the query.

How do all the objects flying across the network between clients, services, and the lookup service actually make distributed programming easier? In short, Jini's use of network-mobile objects (in particular, the network-mobile service object) raises the level of abstraction for distributed systems programming, effectively turning network programming into object-oriented programming.

Jini's architecture brings object-oriented programming to the network by enabling network services to take advantage of one of the fundamentals of object-oriented programming: the separation of interface and implementation. For example, a service object can grant clients access to the service in many ways. The object can actually represent the entire service, which is downloaded to the client during lookup and then executed locally. Alternatively, the service object can serve merely as a proxy to a remote server. When the client invokes methods on the service object, it sends the requests across the network to the server, which does the real work. The local service object and a remote server could also share the work.

One important consequence of Jini's architecture is that the network protocol used to communicate between a proxy service object and a remote server does not need to be known to the client. As illustrated in Figure 4-2, the network protocol is part of the service's implementation. This protocol is a private matter decided upon by the developer of the service. The client can communicate with the service via this private protocol because the service injects its own service object into the client's address space — the service object moves across the network from service to client.

The injected service object could communicate with a back-end server via RMI, CORBA, DCOM, some home-brewed protocol built on top of sockets and streams, or anything else. The client simply doesn't need to care about network protocols, because it can talk to the well-known interface that the service object implements. The service object takes care of any necessary communication on the network.

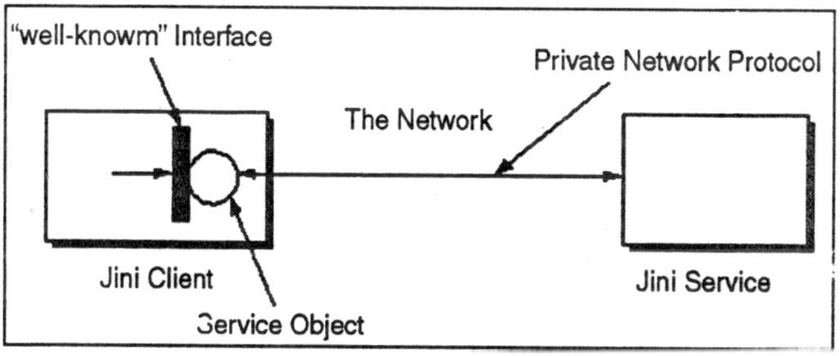

Fig. The Client Talks to the Service Through a Well-known Interface.

Different implementations of the same service interface can use completely different implementation approaches and completely different network protocols. A service can use specialized hardware to fulfill client requests, or it can do all its work in software. Different implementations of a service can be tuned for different environments. In addition, the implementation approach taken by a single service provider can evolve over time. The client can be sure it has a service object that understands the current implementation of the service, because the client receives the service object (by way of the lookup service) from the service provider itself. To the client, a service looks like the well-known interface, regardless of how the service is implemented.

Thus, Jini attempts to raise the level of abstraction for distributed systems programming, from the network protocol level to the object interface level. In the emerging proliferation of embedded devices connected to networks, many pieces of a distributed system may come from different vendors. Jini makes it unnecessary for vendors of devices to agree on low-level network protocols that allow their devices to interact. Instead, vendors will need to agree on high-level Java interfaces through which their devices can interact. Raising the level of discourse, from the network protocol level to the object interface level, will allow vendors to focus more on high-level concepts and less on low-level details. The higher level of discourse made possible by Jini should facilitate the process by which vendors of similar products come to an agreement on how their services will interact with clients.

In addition, Jini's architecture enables software developers to enjoy the benefits of separation of interface and implementation when they develop distributed systems. One such benefit is that well-defined object interfaces can help software developers work together effectively on large distributed systems projects. Similar to the way in which object interfaces define the contract between the parts of any object-oriented programme, object interfaces can also serve to clarify the contract between the various members and teams of a large project who are responsible for individual pieces of the programme. Another benefit of the separation of interface and implementation is that programmers can use it to reduce the impact of change by minimize coupling. The only point of coupling of a well-designed object is its interface; The implementation of an object can change without affecting code in any other object.

Jini brings the object-oriented benefits resulting from raising the level of abstraction and clearly separating interface from implementation to distributed systems programming by taking advantage of Java's support for network-mobile objects. The network-mobility of objects made possible by the combination of Java's underlying architecture, object serialization, and RMI, and demonstrated by the Jini service object, enables Jini to bring the benefits of object-oriented programming to the network.

DESIGN CENTER OF JAVA

Network-mobile Java software can come in many forms besides just the two forms, Java applets and Jini service objects, described in the previous sections. Yet although network-mobile Java is not limited to applets and service objects, the framework that supports any other form of network-mobile Java will likely look similar to the framework that supports applets and service objects. Like applets and service objects, for example, other forms of network-mobile Java will execute in the context of a host Java application, and the class files for the network-mobile Java code will be loaded by user-defined class loaders.

User-defined class loaders can download class files across a network in custom ways that bootstrap class loaders usually can't. And because network-mobile class files are not always known to be trustworthy, the separate name-spaces provided by user-defined class loaders are needed to protect malicious or buggy code from interfering with code loaded from other sources. Lastly, because network-mobile class files can't always be trusted, there will generally be a security manager or access controller establishing a security policy for the network-mobile code.

The key to understanding Java's architecture, then, is to see enabling the network mobility of code and objects as the design center of Java. Although Java can offer valuable benefits, such as increased programmer productivity and increased programme robustness, in situations that don't even remotely involve a network, the main focus of Java's architecture is the network. The Java virtual machine, Java class file, Java API, and Java programming language work in concert to make network mobile software both possible and practical. Through its support for network mobile code and objects, Java helps software developers meet challenges and seize opportunities presented by the ever-progressing network age.

4

Loading and Linking

INTRODUCTION

The Java virtual machine makes types available to the running programme through a process of *loading, linking,* and *initialization.* Loading is the process of bringing a binary form for a type into the Java virtual machine. Linking is the process of incorporating the binary type data into the runtime state of the virtual machine. Linking is divided into three sub-steps: *verification, preparation,* and*resolution.* Verification ensures the type is properly formed and fit for use by the Java virtual machine. Preparation involves allocating memory needed by the type, such as memory for any class variables. Resolution is the process of transforming symbolic references in the constant pool into direct references. Implementations may delay the resolution step until each symbolic reference is actually used by the running programme. After verification, preparation, and (optionally) resolution are completed, the type is ready for initialization. During initialization, the class variables are given their proper initial values. See Figure for a graphical depiction of this process.

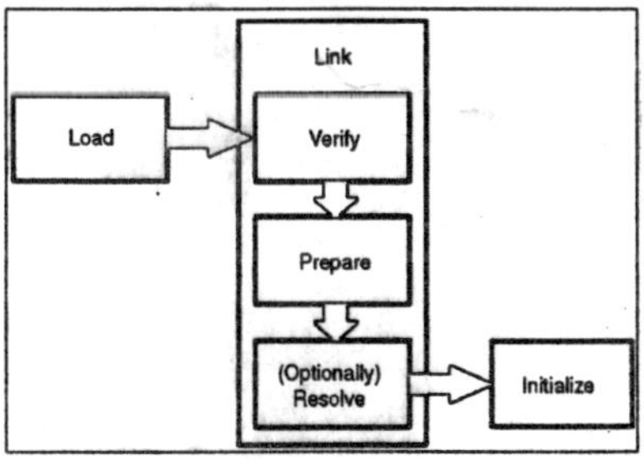

Fig. The Beginning of a Type's Lifetime.

As you can see from Figure, the processes of:

- Loading,
- Linking, and
- Initialization must take place in that order.

The only exception to this required ordering is the third phase of linking, resolution, which may optionally take place after initialization.

The Java virtual machine specification gives implementations flexibility in the timing of class and interface loading and linking, but strictly defines the timing of initialization. All implementations must initialize each class or interface on its first*active use.*

The following six situations qualify as active uses:

1. A new instance of a class is created (in bytecodes, the execution of a new instruction. Alternatively, via implicit creation, reflection, cloning, or deserialization.)
2. The invocation of a static method declared by a class (in bytecodes, the execution of an invokestatic instruction)
3. The use or assignment of a static field declared by a class or interface, except for static fields that are final and initialized by a compile-time constant expression (in bytecodes, the execution of a getstatic or putstaticinstruction)
4. The invocation of certain reflective methods in the Java API, such as methods in class Class or in classes in thejava.lang.reflect package
5. The initialization of a subclass of a class (Initialization of a class requires prior initialization of its superclass.)
6. The designation of a class as the initial class (with the main()< method) when a Java virtual machine starts up

All other uses of a type besides the six listed here are *passive uses,* which don't trigger an initialization of the type. Several examples illustrating the difference between active and passive uses are given later in this chapter. As mentioned in the previous list, initialization of a class requires prior initialization of its superclass. Applied recursively, this rule means that all of a class's superclasses must be initialized prior to the initialization of the class. The same is not true, however, of interfaces. An interface is initialized only because a non-constant field declared by the interface is used, never because a subinterface or class that implements the interface needs to be initialized. Thus, initialization of a class requires prior initialization of all its superclasses, but not its superinterfaces. Initialization of an interface does not require initialization of its superinterfaces.

The "initialize on first active use" rule drives the mechanism that loads, links, and initializes classes. On its first active use, a type must be initialized. Before it can be initialized, however, it must be linked. And before it can be linked, it must be loaded. At their option, implementations may load and link types early. They need not wait until the type's first active use to load and link the type. If a type hasn't been loaded and linked before its first active use, however, it must be loaded and linked at that time, so that it can be initialized.

LOADING

The loading process consists of three basic activities.

To load a type, the Java virtual machine must:

- Given the type's fully qualified name, produce a stream of binary data that represents the type
- Parse the stream of binary data into internal data structures in the method area
- Create an instance of class java.lang.Class that represents the type

The stream of binary data may adhere to the Java class file format, but could alternatively follow some other format. As mentioned in previous chapters, all Java virtual machine implementations must recognize the Java class file format, but individual implementations may also recognize other binary formats.

The Java virtual machine specification does not say how the binary data for a type must be produced.

Some potential ways to produce binary data for a type are:

- Load a Java class file from the local file system
- Download a Java class file across a network
- Extract a Java class file from a ZIP, JAR, CAB, or other archive file
- Extract a Java class file from a proprietary database
- Compile a Java source file on the fly into the class file format
- Compute the class file data for a type on the fly
- Any of the above, but using a binary file format other than the Java class file

Given the binary data for a type, the Java virtual machine must process that data to a great enough extent that it can create an instance of class java.lang.Class. The virtual machine must parse the binary data into implementation-dependent internal data structures. ("The Java Virtual Machine," for a discussion of potential internal data structures for storing class data.) The Class instance, the end product of the loading step, serves as an interface between the programme and the internal data structures. To access information about a type that is stored in the internal data structures, the programme invokes methods on the Class instance for that type. Together, the processes of parsing the binary data for a type into internal data structures in the method area and instantiating a Class object on heap are called *creating* the type.

As described in previous chapters, types are loaded either through the bootstrap class loader or through user-defined class loaders. The bootstrap class loader, a part of the virtual machine implementation, loads types (including the classes and interfaces of the Java API) in an implementation-dependent way. User- defined class loaders, instances of subclasses ofjava.lang.ClassLoader, load classes in custom ways. The inner workings of user-defined class loaders are described in more detail later in Chapter, "The Linking Model."

Class loaders (bootstrap or user-defined) need not wait until a type's first active use before they load the type. Class loaders are allowed to cache binary representations of types, load types early in anticipation of eventual use, or load types together in related groups. If a class loader encounters a problem during early loading, however, it must report that problem (by throwing a subclass of LinkageError) only upon the type's first active use. In other words, if a class loader encounters a missing or malformed class file during early loading, it must wait to report that error until the class's first active use by the programme. If the class is never actively used by the programme, the class loader will never report the error.

VERIFICATION

After a type is loaded, it is ready to be linked. The first step of the linking process is verification— ensuring that the type obeys the semantics of the Java language and that it won't violate the integrity of the virtual machine.

Verification is another area in which implementations of the Java virtual machine have some flexibility. Implementation designers can decide how and when to verify types. The Java virtual machine specification lists all the exceptions that a virtual machine can throw and under what circumstances it must throw them. No matter what kind of trouble a Java virtual machine might encounter, there is an exception or error it is supposed to throw. The specification says what exception or error should be thrown in each situation. In some cases, the specification says exactly when the exception or error should be thrown, but usually doesn't dictate precisely how or when the error condition should be detected.

Nevertheless, certain kinds of checks are very likely to take place at certain times in most Java virtual machine implementations. For example, during the loading process, the virtual machine must parse the stream of binary data that represents the type and build internal data structures. At this point, certain checks will have to be done just to ensure the initial act of parsing the binary data won't crash the virtual machine. During this parsing, implementations will likely check the binary data to make sure it has the expected overall format. Parsers of the Java class file format might check the magic number, make sure each component is in the right place and of the proper length, verify that the file isn't too short or too long, and so on. Although these checks take place during loading, before the official verification phase of linking, they are still logically part of the verification phase. The entire process of detecting any kind of problem with loaded types is placed under the category of verification.

Another check that likely occurs during loading is making sure that every class except Object has a superclass. This may be done during loading because when the virtual machine loads a class, it must also make sure all of the class's superclasses are loaded also. The only way a virtual machine can know the name of a given class's superclass is by peering into the binary data for the class. Since the virtual machine is looking at every class's superclass data during loading anyway, it may as well make this check during the loading phase.

Another check—one that likely occurs after the official verification phase in most implementations—is the verification of symbolic references. As described in earlier chapters, the process of dynamic linking involves locating classes, interfaces, fields, and methods referred to by symbolic references stored in the constant pool, and replacing the symbolic references with direct references. When the virtual machine searches for a symbolically referenced entity (type, field, or method), it must first make sure the entity exists. If the virtual machine finds that the entity exists, it must further check that the referencing type has permission to access the entity, given the entity's access permissions. These checks for existence and access permission are logically a part of verification, the first phase of linking, but most likely happen during resolution, the third phase of linking. Resolution itself can be delayed until each symbolic reference is first used by the programme, so these checks may even take place after initialization.

So what gets checked during the official verification phase? Anything that hasn't already been checked before the official verification phase and that won't get checked after it. Here are two lists of some of the things that are good candidates for checking during the official verification phase.

This first list is composed of checks that ensure classes are binary compatible with each other:

- Checking that final classes are not subclassed
- Checking that final methods are not overridden
- Making sure no incompatible method declarations (such as two methods that have the same name, the same number, order, and types of parameters, but different return types) appear between the type and its supertypes

Note that while these checks require looking at other types, they only require looking at supertypes. Superclasses need to be initialized before subclasses, so these classes are likely already loaded. Superinterfaces do not need to be initialized when a class that implements them is initialized. However, superinterfaces must be loaded when the class that implements them (or the interface that extends them) is loaded. (They won't be initialized, just loaded and possibly linked at the option of the virtual machine implementation.) All a class's supertypes will be loaded when the class is loaded. At verification time, the class and all its supertypes will be to make sure they are all still binary compatible with one another.

- Checking that all constant pool entries are consistent with each other. (For example, the string_index item of aCONSTANT_String_info entry must be the index of a CONSTANT_Utf8_info entry.)
- Checking that all special strings contained in the constant pool (class names, field and method names, field and method descriptors) are well-formed
- Verifying the integrity of the bytecodes

The most complicated task in the above list is the last one: bytecode verification. All Java virtual machines must in some way verify the integrity of the bytecodes for every method they execute. For example, implementations are not allowed to crash because a jump instruction sends the virtual machine beyond the end of a method. They must detect that the jump instruction is invalid through some process of bytecode verification, and throw an error. Java virtual machine implementations are not required to verify bytecodes during the official verification phase of linking. Implementations are free, for example, to verify individual instructions as each instruction is executed. One of the design goals of the Java virtual machine instruction set, however, was that it yield bytecodes streams that can be verified all at once by a data flow analyser. The ability to verify bytecode streams all at once during linking, rather than on the fly as the programme runs, gives a big boost to the potential execution speed of Java programs.

When verifying bytecodes via a data flow analyser, the virtual machine may have to load other classes to ensure that the semantics of the Java language are being followed. For example, imagine a class contained a method that assigned a reference to an instance of java.lang.Float to a field of type java.lang.Number. In this case, the virtual machine would have to load class Float during bytecode verification to make sure it was a subclass of class Number. It would have to load Number to make sure it wasn't declared final. The virtual machine must not initialize class Float at this time, just load it. Float will be initialized only upon its first active use.

PREPARATION

After a Java virtual machine has loaded a class and performed whatever verification it chooses to do up front, the class is ready for preparation. During the preparation phase, the Java virtual machine allocates memory for the class variables and sets them to default initial values. The class variables are not initialized to their proper initial values until the initialization phase. (No Java code is executed during the preparation step.) During preparation, the Java virtual machine sets the newly allocated memory for the class variables to a default value determined by the type of the variable. The default values for the various types are shown in Table.

Table. Default Initial Values for the Primitive and Reference Types

Type	Initial Value
Int	0
Long	0L

Short	(short) 0
Char	'\u0000'
Byte	(byte) 0
Boolean	false
Reference	null
Float	0.0f
Double	0.0d

Although the boolean type appears in Table 7-1, the Java virtual machine itself has very little support for booleans. Internally, boolean is usually implemented as an int, which gets set to zero (boolean false) by default. Therefore,boolean class variables, even if they are implemented internally as ints, are initialized to false.

During the preparation phase, Java virtual machine implementations may also allocate memory for data structures that are intended to improve the performance of the running programme. An example of such a data structure is a method table, which contains a pointer to the data for every method in a class, including those inherited from its superclasses. A method table enables an inherited method to be invoked on an object without a search of superclasses at the point of invocation. Method tables are described in more detail in Chapter, "The Linking Model."

RESOLUTION

After a type has been through the first two phases of linking: verification and preparation, it is ready for the third and final phase of linking: resolution. Resolution is the process of locating classes, interfaces, fields, and methods referenced symbolically from a type's constant pool, and replacing those symbolic references with direct references. As mentioned above, this phase of linking is optional until (and unless) each symbolic reference is first used by the programme.

INITIALIZATION

The final step required to ready a class or interface for its first active use is initialization, the process of setting class variables to their proper initial values. As used here, a "proper" initial value is the programmer's desired starting value for a class variable. A proper initial value contrasts with the default initial value given to class variables during preparation. As described above, the virtual machine assigns default values based only on each variable's type. Proper initial values, by contrast, are based on some master plan known only to the programmer.

In Java code, a proper initial value is specified via a class variable initializer or static initializer. A class variable initializer is an equals sign and expression next to a class variable declaration, as in:

```
// On CD-ROM in file classlife/ex1/Example1a.java
class Example1a {
  // "= 3 * (int) (Math.random() * 5.0)" is the
class variable
 // initializer
static int size = 3 * (int) (Math.random() *
5.0);
}
```

A static initializer is a block of code introduced by the static keyword, as in:

```
// On CD-ROM in file classlife/ex1/Example1b.java
class Example1b {
static int size;
  // This is the static initializer
static {
size = 3 * (int) (Math.random() * 5.0);
  }
}
```

All the class variable initializers and static initializers of a type are collected by the Java compiler and placed into one special method. For classes, this method is called the *class initialization method*; for interfaces, the *interface initialization method*. In Java class files for both classes and interfaces, this method is named "". Regular methods of a Java application cannot invoke a method. This kind of method can only be invoked by the Java virtual machine, which invokes it to set a type's static variables to their proper initial values.

Initialization of a class consists of two steps:

1. Initializing the class's direct superclass (if any), if the direct superclass hasn't already been initialized
2. Executing the class's class initialization method, if it has one

When initializing a class's direct superclass, the same two steps listed above must be followed. As a result, the first class that will be initialized will always be Object, then all the classes on down the inheritance hierarchy to the class being actively used. Superclasses will be initialized before subclasses.

Initialization of an interface does not require initialization of its superinterfaces. Initialization of an interface consists of only one step:

- Executing the interface's interface initialization method, if it has one

The code of a () method does not explicitly invoke a superclass's () method. Before a Java virtual machine invokes the ()method of a class, therefore, it must make certain the () methods of superclasses have been executed.

Java virtual machines must also make sure the initialization process is properly synchronized. If multiple threads need to initialize a class, only one thread should be allowed to perform the initialization while the other threads wait. After the active thread completes the initialization process, it must notify any waiting threads."Thread Synchronization," for information about synchronization, wait and notify.

THE () METHOD

As mentioned above, Java compilers place the code for class variable initializers and static initializers into the () method of the class file in the order in which they appear in the class or interface declaration. For example, given this class:

```
// On CD-ROM in file classlife/ex1/Example1c.java
class Example1c {

  static int width;
 static int height = (int) (Math.random() * 2.0);
```

```
// This is the static initializer
  static {

    width = 3 * (int) (Math.random() * 5.0);
  }
}
```

The Java compiler generates the following () method:

```
// The code for height's class variable initializer
begins here
                              //              Invoke
Math.random(), which will push
                              // a double return value
 0 invokestatic #6 <Method double random()>
 3 ldc2_w #8 <Double 2.0>// Push double constant
2.0
 6 dmul                      // Pop two doubles,
multiply, push result
 7 d2i                       // Pop double, convert to
                                int, push int
                             // Pop int, store into
                                class variable
         // height
 8 putstatic #5 <Field int height>

// The code for the static initializer begins
here
11 iconst_3     // Push int constant 3
                             // Invoke Math.random(),
                                which will push
         // a double return value
12 invokestatic #6 <Method double random()>
15 ldc2_w #10 <Double 5.0>// Push double constant
5.0
18 dmul                      // Pop two doubles,
multiply, push result
19 d2i                       // Pop double, convert to
```

```
int, push int
20 imul                    // Pop two ints, multiply,
push int result               // Pop int, store into
class variable
          // width
21 putstatic #7 <Field int width>
24 return           // Return void from <clinit>
method
```

This () method first executes the code for Example1c's only class variable initializer, which initializes height, then executes the code for the static initializer, which initializes width. The initialization is done in this order because the class variable initializer appears textually before the static initializer in the source code of the Example1c class.

Not all classes will necessarily have a () method in their class file. If a class declares no class variables or static initializers, it won't have a () method.

If a class declares class variables, but doesn't explicitly initialize them with class variable initializers or static initializers, it won't have a () method. If a class contains only class variable initializers for static final variables, and those class variable initializers use compile-time constant expressions, that class won't have a () method. Only those classes that actually require Java code to be executed to initialize class variables to proper initial values will have a class initialization method.

Here's an example of a class that won't be awarded a () method by the Java compiler:

```
// On CD-ROM in file classlife/ex1/Example1d.java
class Example1d {

  static final int angle = 35;
  static final int length = angle * 2;
}
```

Class Example1d declares two constants, angle and length, and initializes them with expressions that are compile-time constants. The compiler knows that angle represents the value 35 and length represents the value 70. When theExample1d class is loaded by a Java virtual machine, angle and length are not stored as class variables in the method area. As a result, no () method is needed to initialize them. The angle and length fields are not class variables, they are constants, which are treated specially by the Java compiler.

Instead of treating Example1d's angle and length fields as class variables, the Java compiler places the constant intvalues they represent into the constant pool or bytecode streams of any class that uses them. For example, if a class usesExample1d's angle field, that class will not have in its constant pool a symbolic reference to the angle field of classExample1d. Instead, the class will have operands embedded in its bytecode streams that have the value 35. If the constant value of angle were outside the range of a short (-32,768 to 32,767), say 35,000, the class would have aCONSTANT_Integer_info entry in its constant pool with the value of 35,000.

Here's a class that uses both a constant and a class variable from other classes:

```
// On CD-ROM in file classlife/ex1/Example1e.java
class Example1e {

 // The class variable initializer for symbolicRef
uses a symbolic
// reference to the size class variable of class
Example1a
  static int symbolicRef = Example1a.size;

// The class variable initializer for localConst
doesn't use a
// symbolic reference to the length field of class
Example1d.
    // Instead, it just uses a copy of the constant
value 70.
  static int localConst = Example1d.length * (int)
(Math.random()
    * 3.0);
}
```

The Java compiler generates the following () method for class Example1e:

```
// The code for symbolicRef's class variable
initializer begins here:
          // Push int value from Example1a.size.
                              // This getstatic
                                instruction refers to
                                    a
                                // symbolic reference
                                  to Example1a.size.
 0 getstatic #9 <Field int size>
          // Pop int, store into class variable
          // symbolicRef
 3 putstatic #10 <Field int symbolicRef>

// The code for localConst's class variable
intializer begins here:
          // Expand byte operand to int, push
int
          // result. This is the local copy of
 6 bipush 70                // Example1d's length
constant, 70.
                              // Invoke Math.random(),
                                 which will push
                              // a double return value
 8 invokestatic #8 <Method double random()>
11 ldc2_w #11 <Double 3.0>// Push double constant
3.0
14 dmul // Pop two doubles, multiply, push result
15 d2i        // Pop double, convert to int, push
int
16 imul  // Pop two ints, multiply, push int
result
          // Pop int, store into class variable
          // localConst
17 putstatic #7 <Field int localConst>
20 return          // Return void from <clinit>
method
```

The getstatic instruction at offset zero uses a symbolic reference (in constant pool entry nine) to the size field of classExample1a. The bipush instruction at offset six is followed by a byte that contains the constant value represented byExample1d.length. Example1e's constant pool contains no symbolic reference to anything in class Example1d.

Interfaces may also be awarded a () method in the class file. All fields declared in an interface are implicitly public, static, and final and must be initialized with a field initializer. If an interface has any field initializers that don't resolve at compile-time to a constant, that interface will have a () method. Here's an example:

```
// On CD-ROM in file classlife/ex1/Example1f.java
interface Example1f {

  int ketchup = 5;
  int mustard = (int) (Math.random() * 5.0);
}
```

The Java compiler generates the following () method for interface Example1f:

```
// The code for mustard's class variable
initializer begins here
        // Invoke Math.random(), which will push
          // a double return value
 0 invokestatic #6 <Method double random()>
 3 ldc2_w #7 <Double 5.0>// Push double constant
2.0
 6 dmul                  // Pop two doubles,
multiply, push result
 7 d2i        // Pop double, convert to int, push
int
                         // Pop int, store into
class variable
         // mustard
 8 putstatic #5 <Field int mustard>
11 return     // Return void from <clinit> method
```

Note that only the mustard field is initialized by this () method. Because the ketchup field is initialized to a compile-time constant, it is treated specially by the compiler. Although types that use Example1f.mustard will contain a symbolic reference to the field, types that use Example1f.ketchup will contain a local copy of ketchup's constant value, 5.

ACTIVE VERSUS PASSIVE USE

As mentioned previously, the Java virtual machine initializes types on their first active use. Only six activities constitute an active use: creating a new instance of a class, invoking a static method declared in a class, accessing a non-constant static field declared in a class or interface, the invocation of certain reflective methods in the Java API, the initialization of a subclass of a class, and the designation of a class as the initial class when a Java virtual machine starts up.

A use of a non-constant static field is an active use of only the class or interface that actually declares the field. For example, a field declared in a class may be referred to via a subclass. A field declared in an interface may be referred to via a subinterface or class that implements the interface. These are passive uses of the subclass, subinterface, or class that implements the interface—uses that won't trigger their initialization. They are an active use only of the class or interface in which the field is actually declared. Here's an example that illustrates this principle:

```
// On CD-ROM in file classlife/ex2/NewParent.java
class NewParent {
  static int hoursOfSleep = (int) (Math.random()
* 3.0);

  static {
    System.out.println("NewParent was
            initialized.");
  }
}

// On CD-ROM in file classlife/ex2/
     NewbornBaby.java
class NewbornBaby extends NewParent {
```

```
   static int hoursOfCrying = 6 + (int)
       (Math.random() * 2.0);

   static {
     System.out.println("NewbornBaby was
           initialized.");
   }
}

// On CD-ROM in file classlife/ex2/Example2.java
class Example2 {

// Invoking main() is an active use of
       Example2
   public static void main(String[] args) {

   // Using hoursOfSleep is an active use
             of NewParent,
   // but a passive use of NewbornBaby
     int hours = NewbornBaby.hoursOfSleep;
     System.out.println(hours);
   }

   static {
     System.out.println("Example2 was
           initialized.");
   }
}
```

In the above example, executing main() of Example2 causes only Example2 and NewParent to be initialized. NewbornBaby is not initialized and need not be loaded. The following text is printed to the standard output:

```
Example2 was initialized.
NewParent was initialized.
2
```

A use of a field that is both static and final, and initialized by a compile-time constant expression, is not an active use of the type that declares the field. As mentioned above, the Java compiler resolves references to such fields to a local copy of the constant value that resides either in the referring class's constant pool, in its bytecode streams, or both. Here's an example that illustrates this special treatment of static final fields:

```
// On CD-ROM in file classlife/ex3/Angry.java
interface Angry {

  String greeting = "Grrrr!";

  int angerLevel = Dog.getAngerLevel();
}

// On CD-ROM in file classlife/ex3/Dog.java
class Dog {

  static final String greeting = "Woof, woof,
  world!";

  static {
    System.out.println("Dog was
         initialized.");
  }

  static int getAngerLevel() {

    System.out.println("Angry was
          initialized");
    return 1;
  }
}

// On CD-ROM in file classlife/ex3/Example3.java
class Example3 {

// Invoking main() is an active use of Example3
  public static void main(String[] args) {
```

```
    // Using Angry.greeting is a passive use
              of Angry
       System.out.println(Angry.greeting);


    // Using Dog.greeting is a passive use
               of Dog
       System.out.println(Dog.greeting);
    }

    static {
       System.out.println("Example3 was
                  initialized.");
    }
}
```

Running the Example3 application yields the following output:

```
Example3 was initialized.
Grrrr!
Woof, woof, world!
```

Had Angry been initialized, the string "Angry was initialized." would have been written to the standard output. Likewise, had Dog been initialized, the string "Dog was initialized." would have been written to the standard output. As you can see from the above output, neither interface Angry or class Dog were ever initialized during the execution of the Example application.

CLASS INSTANTIATION

In Java programs, classes can be instantiated explicitly or implicitly. The four ways a class can be instantiated explicitly are with the new operator, by invoking newInstance()on a Class orjava.lang.reflect.Constructor object, by invoking clone() on any existing object, or by deserializing an object via the getObject() method of classjava.io.ObjectInputStream. Here is an example showing three ways to create a new class instance:

```
// On CD-ROM in file classlife/ex4/Example4.java
```

```
class Example4 implements Cloneable {

  Example4() {
      System.out.println("Created by invoking
newInstance()");
  }

  Example4(String msg) {
    System.out.println(msg);
  }

  public static void main(String[] args)
          throws ClassNotFoundException,
InstantiationException,
                       IllegalAccessException,
CloneNotSupportedException {

  // Create a new Example4 object with the new
operator
     Example4 obj1 = new Example4("Created with
new.");

  // Get a reference to the Class instance for
Example4, then
  // invoke newInstance() on it to create a new
Example4 object
     Class myClass = Class.forName("Example4");
          Example4 obj2 = (Example4)
myClass.newInstance();

  // Make an identical copy of the the second
Example4 object
     Example4 obj3 = (Example4) obj2.clone();
  }
}
```

When executed, the Example4 application prints this output:

```
Created with new.
Created by invoking newInstance()
```

Besides the four ways listed previously to explicitly instantiate objects in Java source code, there are several situations in which objects will be instantiated implicitly—without an explicit new, newInstance(), clone(), orObject Input Stream.readObject() appearing in the source.

Possibly the first implicitly instantiated objects of any Java application are the String objects that hold the command line arguments. References to these objects, one for each command-line argument, are delivered in the String array passed as the sole parameter to the main() method of every application.

Two other ways a class can be instantiated implicitly involve the process of class loading. First, for every type a Java virtual machine loads, it implicitly instantiates a new Class object to represent that type. Second, when the Java virtual machine loads a class that contains CONSTANT_String_info entries in its constant pool, it may instantiate new String objects to represent those constant string literals. The process of transforming a CONSTANT_String_info entry in the method area to a String instance on the heap is part of the process of constant pool resolution. This process is described in detail in Chapter, "The Linking Model."

Another way objects can be created implicitly is through the process of evaluating an expression that involves the string concatenation operator. If such an expression is not a compile-time constant, intermediate String and StringBufferobjects will be created in the process of evaluating the expression. Here's an example:

```
// On CD-ROM in file classlife/ex5/Example5.java
class Example5 {

  public static void main(String[] args) {

     if (args.length < 2) {
          System.out.println("Must enter any two
args.");
        return;
     }
     System.out.println(args[0] + args[1]);
```

```
   }
}
```

javac generates these bytecodes for Example5's main() method:

```
// On CD-ROM in file classlife/ex5/Example5.java
class Example5 {

  public static void main(String[] args) {

     if (args.length < 2) {
         System.out.println("Must enter any two
args.");
        return;
     }

     System.out.println(args[0] + args[1]);
  }
}
```

javac generates these bytecodes for Example5's main() method:

```
0 aload_0       // Push the objref from loc var 0
                   (args)
1 arraylength  // Pop arrayref, calc array length,
                  push int length
2 iconst_2      // Push int constant 2
               // Pop 2 ints, compare, branch if
                  (length >= 2) to
3 if_icmpge 15 // offset 15.
                // Push objref from System.out
6 getstatic #11 <Field java.io.PrintStream out>
               // Push objref of string literal
9 ldc #1 <String "Must enter any two args.">
              // Pop objref to String param,
                 objref to System.out,
              // invoke println()
11 invokevirtual #12 <Method void
                  println(java.lang.String)>
14 return       // Return void from main()
               // Push objref from System.out
```

```
15 getstatic #11 <Field java.io.PrintStream out>

// The string concatenation operation begins here
              // Allocate mem for new StringBuffer
                 object, and
              // initialize mem to default initial
                values, push
              // objref to new object
18 new #6 <Class java.lang.StringBuffer>
21 dup        // Duplicate objref to StringBuffer
                object
22 aload_0    // Push ref from loc var 0 (args)
23 iconst_0   // Push int constant 0
              // Pop int, arrayref, push String at
                  arrayref[int],
24 aaload     // which is args[0]
              // Pop objref, invoke String's class
                  method
              // valueOf(), passing it the objref
                 to the args[0]
              // String object. valueOf() calls
                 toString() on the
               // ref, and returns (and pushes)
                 the result, which
              // happens to be the original args[0]
                 String. In this
              // case, the stack will look precisely
                  the same
              // before and after this instruction
                  is executed.
              // Thus here, the 1.1 javac compiler
                     has
              // over-enthusiastically generated an
                    unnecessary
             // instruction.
25 invokestatic #14 <Method java.lang.String
valueOf(
        java.lang.Object)>
```

```
                    // Pop objref to args[0] String,
                      objref of the
                   // StringBuffer object, invoke
                      <init>() method on the
                   // StringBuffer object passing the
                        args[0] objref as
                   // the only parameter.
28 invokespecial #9 <Method
 java.lang.StringBuffer(java.lang.String)>
31 aload_0         // Push objref from loc var 0 (args)
32 iconst_1        // Push int constant 1
                   // Pop int, arrayref, push String
                       at arrayref[int],
33 aaload            // which is args[1]
                     // Pop objref to args[1] String,
objref of the
                      // StringBuffer object (there's
                         still another objref
                    // to this same object on the stack
                             because of the
                    // dup instruction above), invoke
                         append() method on
                      // StringBuffer object, passing
                           args[1] as the only
                    // parameter. append() will return
                          an objref to this
                    // StringBuffer object, which will
                         be pushed back
                     // onto the stack.
34 invokevirtual #10 <Method
java.lang.StringBuffer
append(java.lang.String)>
                    // Pop objref to StringBuffer
                      (pushed by append()),
                   // invoke toString() on it, which
                     returns the value
                   // of the StringBuffer as a String
                      object. Push
```

```
                    // objref of String object.
37 invokevirtual #13 <Method java.lang.String
toString()>
                  // The string concatenation
                     operation is now complete

                   // Pop objref of concatenated
                      String, objref of
                   // System.out that was pushed
                      by the getstatic
                 // instruction at offset 15. Invoke
                        println() on
                 // System.out, passing the
                       concatenated String as
                 // the only parameter.
40 invokevirtual #12 <Method void
println(java.lang.String)>
43 return        // Return void from main()
```

The bytecodes for Example5's main() method contain three implicitly generated String objects and one implicitly generated StringBuffer object. References to two of the String objects appear as arguments passed to main() in theargs array, which are pushed onto the stack by the aaload instructions at offset 24 and 33. The StringBuffer is created with the new instruction at offset 18 and initialized with the invokespecial instruction at offset 28. The final String, which represents the concatenation of args[0] and args[1], is created by calling toString() on the StringBuffer object via the invokevirtual instruction at offset 37.

When the Java virtual machine creates a new instance of a class, either implicitly or explicitly, it first allocates memory on the heap to hold the object's instance variables. Memory is allocated for all variables declared in the object's class and in all its superclasses, including instance variables that are hidden. As described in Chapter, "The Java Virtual Machine," memory for other implementation-dependent components of an object's image on the heap, such as a pointer to class data in the method area, are also likely allocated at this point. As soon as the virtual machine has set aside the heap memory for a new object, it immediately initializes the instance variables to default initial values. These are the same values shown above in Table 7-1 as default initial values for class variables.

Once the virtual machine has allocated memory for the new object and initialized the instance variables to default values, it is ready to give the instance variables their proper initial values. The Java virtual machine uses one of three techniques to do this, depending upon how the object is being created. If the object is being created because of a clone() invocation, the virtual machine copies the values of the instance variables of the object being cloned into the new object. If the object is being deserialized via a readObject() invocation on an ObjectInputStream, the virtual machine initializes non-transient instance variables of the object from values read from the input stream. Otherwise, the virtual machine invokes an*instance initialization method* on the object. The instance initialization method initializes the object's instance variables to their proper initial values.

The Java compiler generates at least one instance initialization method for every class it compiles. In the Java class file, the instance initialization method is named "<init>." For each constructor in the source code of a class, the Java compiler generates one <init>() method. If the class declares no constructors explicitly, the compiler generates a default no-arg constructor that just invokes the superclass's no-arg constructor. As with any other constructor, the compiler creates an<init>() method in the class file that corresponds to this default constructor. An <init>() method can contain three kinds of code: an invocation of another <init>() method, code that implements any instance variable initializers, and code for the body of the constructor. If a constructor begins with an explicit invocation of another constructor in the same class (a this() invocation) its corresponding <init>() method will be composed of two parts:

1. An invocation of the same-class <init>() method
2. The bytecodes that implement the body of the corresponding constructor

If a constructor does not begin with a this() invocation and the class is not Object, the <init>() method will have three components:

- An invocation of a superclass <init>() method
- The bytecodes for any instance variable initializers
- The bytecodes that implement the body of the corresponding constructor

If a constructor does not begin with a this() invocation and the class *is* Object, the first component in the above list is missing. Because Object has no superclass, its <init>() method's can't begin with a superclass <init>() method invocation.

If a constructor begins with an explicit invocation of a superclass constructor (a super() invocation), its <init>() method will invoke the corresponding superclass <init>() method. For example, if a constructor begins with an explicit invocation of the "super(int, String) constructor," the corresponding <init>() method will begin by invoking the superclass's "<init>(int, String)" method. If a constructor does not begin with an explicit this() or super() invocation, the corresponding <init>() method will invoke the superclass's no-arg <init>() method by default.

Here's an example with three constructors, numbered one through three:

```
// On CD-ROM in file classlife/ex6/Example6.java
class Example6 {

  private int width = 3;

// Constructor one:
// This constructor begins with a this()
     constructor invocation,
// which gets compiled to a same-class <init>()
     method
// invocation.
  Example6() {
     this(1);
     System.out.println("Example6(), width = " +
width);
```

```
    }

 // Constructor two:
 // This constructor begins with no explicit
        invocation of another
 // constructor, so it will get compiled to an
        <init>() method
 // that begins with an invocation of the
         superclass's no-arg
 // <init>() method.
   Example6(int width) {
     this.width = width;
    System.out.println("Example6(int), width = "
+ width);
   }

 // Constructor three:
 // This constructor begins with super(), an
        explicit invocation
 // of the superclass's no-arg constructor. Its
        <init>() method
 // will begin with an invocation of the
        superclass's no-arg
 // <init>() method.
   Example6(String msg) {
     super();
     System.out.println("Example6(String), width
= " + width);
     System.out.println(msg);
   }

   public static void main(String[] args) {
     String msg
       = "The Agapanthus is also known as Lily of
the Nile.";
     Example6 one = new Example6();
     Example6 two = new Example6(2);
     Example6 three = new Example6(msg);
```

```
  }
}
```

When executed, the Example6 application prints this output:

```
Example6(int), width = 1
Example6(), width = 1
Example6(int), width = 2
Example6(String), width = 3
The Agapanthus is also known as Lily of the Nile.
```

The bytecodes for Example6's no-arg <init>() method (the <init>() method that corresponds to constructor one) are:

```
// The first component, the same-class <init>()
invocation, begins
// here:
 0 aload_0  // Push the objref from loc var 0
              (this)
 1 iconst_1 // Push int constant 1
            // Pop int and objref, invoke <init>()
              method on
            // objref (this), passing the int (a
               1) as the
            // only parameter.
 2 invokespecial #12 <Method Example6(int)>

            // The second component, the body of
              the constructor, begins
           // here:
           // Push objref from System.out
 5 getstatic #16 <Field java.io.PrintStream out>
           // Allocate mem for new StringBuffer
               object, and
           // initialize mem to default initial
               values, push
           // objref to new object
 8 new #8 <Class java.lang.StringBuffer>
11 dup     // Duplicate objref to StringBuffer
object
          // Push objref to String literal from
             constant pool
```

```
12 ldc #1 <String "Example6(), width = ">
         // Pop objref to literal String, pop
              objref of the
         // StringBuffer object, invoke <init>()
            method on the
        // StringBuffer object passing the
             args[0] objref as
        // the only parameter.
14      invokespecial     #14     <Method
java.lang.StringBuffer(
    java.lang.String)>
17 aload_0 // Push objref from loc var 0 (this)
        // Pop this reference, Push int value of
            width field
18 getfield #19 <Field int width>
        // Pop int (width), pop objref
          (StringBuffer object),
        // invoke append() on StringBuffer object
             passing the
        // width int as the only parameter.
             append() will add
        // the string representation of the int
             to the end of
        // the buffer, and return an objref to
            the same
        // StringBuffer object.
          21  invokevirtual  #15  <Method
java.lang.StringBuffer append(int)>
        // Pop objref to StringBuffer (pushed by
             append()),
        // invoke toString() on it, which returns
            the value
        // of the StringBuffer as a String object.
              Push
        // objref of String object.
24 invokevirtual #18 <Method java.lang.String
toString()>
        // Pop objref of String, pop objref of
```

```
System.out
          // that was pushed by the getstatic
instruction at
        // offset 5. Invoke println() on
            System.out,
        // passing the String as the only
               parameter:
        // System.out.println("Example6(), width
            = "
       //    + width);
27   invokevirtual   #17   <Method   void
println(java.lang.String)>
30 return   // Return void from <init>()
```

Note that the <init>() method for constructor one begins with an invocation of a same-class <init>() method, then executes the body of the corresponding constructor. Because the constructor begins with a this() invocation, its corresponding <init>() method doesn't contain bytecodes for the instance variable initializer.

The bytecodes for Example6's <init>() method that takes an int parameter (the <init>() method that corresponds to constructor two) is:

```
// The first component, the superclass <init>()
invocation, begins
// here:
 0 aload_0  // Push the objref from loc var 0
                (this)
            // Pop objref (this), invoke the
                 superclass's
            // no-arg<init>() method on objref.
 1 invokespecial #11 <Method java.lang.Object()>

            // The second component, the instance
               variable initializers, begins
            // here:
 4 aload_0 // Push the objref from loc var 0
(this)
 5 iconst_3 // Push int constant 3
```

```
            // Pop int (3), pop objref (this),
               store 3 into
            // width instance variable of this
                 object
 6 putfield #19 <Field int width>

            // The third component, the body of
               the constructor, begins
            // here:
 9 aload_0  // Push the objref from loc var 0
(this)
10 iload_1  // Push int from loc var 1 (int param
width)
            // Pop int (param width), pop objref
                 (this), store
            // int param value into width field
                 of this object:
            // this.width = width
              11 putfield #19 <Field int width>
            // Push objref from System.out
14 getstatic #16 <Field java.io.PrintStream out>
            // Allocate mem for new StringBuffer
               object, and
            // initialize mem to default initial
               values, push
            // objref to new object
17 new #8 <Class java.lang.StringBuffer>
20 dup      // Duplicate objref to StringBuffer
object
            // Push objref to String literal from
               constant pool
21 ldc #3 <String "Example6(int), width = ">
            // Pop objref to literal String, pop
               objref of the
            // StringBuffer object, invoke
               <init>() method on the
            // StringBuffer object passing the
                 args[0] objref as
```

```
          // the only parameter.
23    invokespecial    #14    <Method
java.lang.StringBuffer(
    java.lang.String)>
26 iload_1 // Push int from loc var 1 (int param
width)
          // Pop int (width), pop objref
             (StringBuffer object),
         // invoke append() on StringBuffer
            object passing the
         // width int as the only parameter.
append() will add
         // the string representation of the int
            to the end of
         // the buffer, and return an objref to
            the same
         // StringBuffer object.
27 invokevirtual #15 <Method
java.lang.StringBuffer append(int)>
        // Pop objref to StringBuffer (pushed by
              append()),
        // invoke toString() on it, which returns
           the value
        // of the StringBuffer as a String object.
             Push
         // objref of String object.
30 invokevirtual #18 <Method java.lang.String
toString()>
          // Pop objref of String, pop objref of
             System.out
          // that was pushed by the getstatic
              instruction at
         // offset 14. Invoke println() on
             System.out,
         // passing the String as the only
             parameter:
         // System.out.println("Example6(int),
            width = "
```

```
        //    + width);
33 invokevirtual #17 <Method void
println(java.lang.String)>
36 return   // Return void from <init>()
```

The <init>() method for constructor two has three components. First it has an invocation of the superclass's (Object's) no-arg <init>() method. The compiler generated this invocation by default, because no explicit super() invocation appears as the first statement in the body of constructor two. Following the superclass <init>() invocation is the second component: the bytecodes for width's instance variable initializer. Third, the <init>() method contains the bytecodes for the body of constructor two.

The bytecodes for Example6's <init>() method that takes a String parameter (the <init>() method that corresponds to constructor three) are:

```
// The first component, the superclass <init>()
invocation, begins
// here:
 0 aload_0 // Push the objref from loc var 0
(this)
            // Pop objref (this), invoke the
               superclass's
           // no-arg<init>() method on objref.
 1 invokespecial #11 <Method java.lang.Object()>

          // The second component, the instance
             variable initializers, begins
           // here:
 4 aload_0 // Push the objref from loc var 0
(this)
 5 iconst_3 // Push int constant 3
            // Pop int (3), pop objref (this),
            store 3 into
            // width instance variable of this
               object
 6 putfield #19 <Field int width>
```

```
            // The third component, the body of
                the constructor, begins
// here:
           // Push objref from System.out
 9 getstatic #16 <Field java.io.PrintStream out>
          // Allocate mem for new StringBuffer
            object, and
          // initialize mem to default initial
              values, push
       // objref to new object
12 new #8 <Class java.lang.StringBuffer>
15 dup    // Duplicate objref to StringBuffer
object
           // Push objref to String literal from
               constant pool
16 ldc #2 <String "Example6(String), width = ">
           // Pop objref to literal String, pop
                objref of the
           // StringBuffer object, invoke <init>()
               method on the
           // StringBuffer object passing the
                args[0] objref as
           // the only parameter.
18      invokespecial     #14     <Method
java.lang.StringBuffer(
     java.lang.String)>
21 aload_0 // Push objref from loc var 0 (this)
             // Pop this reference, Push int value
                  of width field
22 getfield #19 <Field int width>
              // Pop int (width), pop objref
                   (StringBuffer object),
              // invoke append() on StringBuffer
                    object passing the
               // width int as the only parameter.
                    append() will add
               // the string representation of the
                   int to the end of
```

```
        // the buffer, and return an objref to
             the same
        // StringBuffer object.
25      invokevirtual      #15      <Method
java.lang.StringBuffer append(int)>
        // Pop objref to StringBuffer (pushed
           by append()),
        // invoke toString() on it, which returns
           the value
        // of the StringBuffer as a String
              object. Push
        // objref of String object.
28 invokevirtual #18 <Method java.lang.String
toString()>
        // Pop objref of String, pop objref of
             System.out
        // that was pushed by the getstatic
             instruction at
        // offset 9. Invoke println() on
               System.out,
        // passing the String as the only
             parameter:
        // System.out.println("Example6(String),
              width = "
        //   + width);
31   invokevirtual   #17   <Method   void
println(java.lang.String)>
        // Push objref from System.out
34 getstatic #16 <Field java.io.PrintStream out>
37 aload_1 // Push objref from loc var 1 (param
msg)
         // Pop objref of String, pop objref of
              System.out
         // that was pushed by the getstatic
               instruction at
          // offset 37. Invoke println() on
                System.out,
          // passing the String as the only
```

```
parameter:
            // System.out.println(msg);
38   invokevirtual   #17   <Method   void
println(java.lang.String)>
41 return  // Return void from <init>()
```

The <init>() method for constructor three has the same three components as the <init>() method for constructor two: a superclass <init>() invocation, the bytecodes for width's initializer, and the bytecodes for the constructor body. One difference between constructor two and three is that constructor two does not begin with an explicit this() or super()invocation. As a result, the compiler places an invocation of the superclass's no-arg <init>() method in constructor two's<init>() method. By contrast, constructor three begins with an explicit super() invocation, which the compiler converts into the corresponding superclass <init>() invocation in constructor three's <init>() method.

For every class except Object, an <init>() method must begin with an invocation of another <init>() method belonging either to the same class or to the direct superclass. <init>() methods are not allowed to catch exceptions thrown by the <init>() method they invoke. If a subclass <init>() method invokes a superclass <init>() method that completes abruptly, for example, the subclass <init>() method must also complete abruptly.

GARBAGE COLLECTION AND FINALIZATION OF OBJECTS

As mentioned in earlier chapters, implementations of the Java virtual machine must have some kind of automatic storage management strategy for the heap, most likely a garbage collector. Applications can allocate memory for objects via the explicit and implicit ways described earlier in this chapter, but cannot explicitly free that memory. When an object becomes unreferenced by the application, the virtual machine may reclaim (garbage collect) that memory. Implementations can decide when to garbage collect unreferenced objects—even whether to garbage collect them at all. Java virtual machine implementations are not required to free memory occupied by unreferenced objects. If a class declares a method named finalize() that returns void, the garbage collector will execute that method (called a "finalizer") once on an instance of that class, before it frees the memory space occupied by that instance. Here's an example of a class that declares a finalizer:

```
// On CD-ROM in file classlife/ex7/Finale.java
class Finale {
  protected void finalize() {
      System.out.println("A Finale object was
finalized.");
  //...
  }
//...
}
```

Because a finalizer is a regular Java method, it may be invoked directly by the application. Such a direct invocation will not affect the automatic invocation of the finalizer by the garbage collector. The garbage collector may invoke an object's finalizer at most once, sometime after the object becomes unreferenced and before the memory it occupies is reused. If the object becomes referenced again (resurrected) as a result of executing the finalizer code, and then becomes unreferenced again later, the garbage collector must not automatically invoke the finalizer a second time.

5

Security on JBoss

INTRODUCTION

Security is a fundamental part of any enterprise application. You need to be able to restrict who is allowed to access your applications and control what operations application users may perform. The J2EE specifications define a simple role-based security model for EJBs and web components. The JBoss component framework that handles security is the JBossSX extension framework.

The JBossSX security extension provides support for both the role-based declarative J2EE security model as well as integration of custom security via a security proxy layer. The default implementation of the declarative security model is based on Java Authentication and Authorization Service (JAAS) login modules and subjects. The security proxy layer allows custom security that cannot be described using the declarative model to be added to an EJB in a way that is independent of the EJB business object. Before getting into the JBoss security implementation details, we will review EJB and Servlet specification security models as well as JAAS to establish the foundation for these details.

DECLARATIVE SECURITY

The security model advocated by the J2EE specification is a declarative model. It is declarative in that you describe the security roles and permissions using a standard XML descriptor rather than embedding security into your business component. This isolates security from business-level code because security tends to be a more a function of where the component is deployed, rather than an inherent aspect of the component's business logic. For example, consider an ATM component that is to be used to access a bank account. The security requirements, roles and permissions will vary independent of how one accesses the bank account based on what bank is managing the account, where the ATM machine is deployed, and so on. Securing a J2EE application is based on the specification of the application security requirements via the standard J2EE deployment descriptors. You secure access to EJBs and web components in an enterprise application by using the ejb-jar.xml and web.xml deployment descriptors. We'll look at the purpose and usage of the various security elements in the following subsections.

SECURITY REFERENCES

Both EJBs and servlets may declare one or more security-role-ref elements. This element is used to declare that a component is using the role-name value as an argument to the isCallerInRole(String) method. Using the isCallerInRole method, a component can verify if the caller is in a role that has been declared with a security-role-ref/role-name element. The role-name element value must link to a security-role element through the role-link element. The typical use of isCallerInRole is to perform a security check that cannot be defined using the role basedmethod-permissions elements.

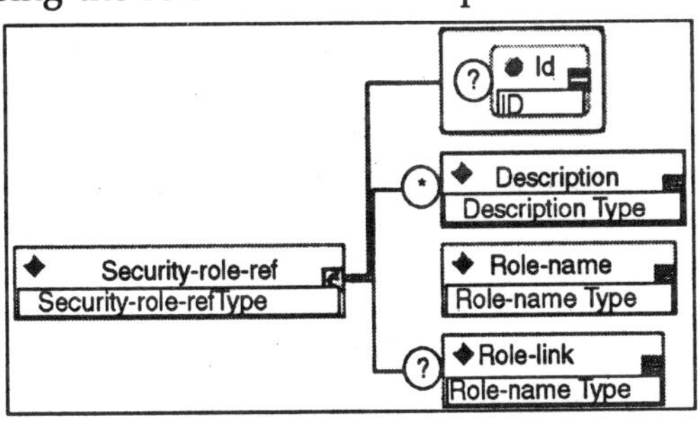

Fig. The Security-role-ref Element

```
<!-- A sample ejb-jar.xml fragment -->
<ejb-jar>
 <enterprise-beans>
```

```
   <session>
    <ejb-name>ASessionBean</ejb-name>
   ...
    <security-role-ref>
      <role-name>TheRoleICheck</role-name>
      <role-link>TheApplicationRole</role-link>
    </security-role-ref>
   </session>
  </enterprise-beans>
...
</ejb-jar>
```

An example web.xml descriptor fragment that illustrates the security-role-ref element usage.

```
<web-app>
  <servlet>
    <servlet-name>AServlet</servlet-name>
    ...
    <security-role-ref>
      <role-name>TheServletRole</role-name>
      <role-link>TheApplicationRole</role-link>
    </security-role-ref>
  </servlet>
...
</web-app>
```

SECURITY IDENTITY

An EJB has the capability to specify what identity an EJB should use when it invokes methods on other components using the security-identityelement.

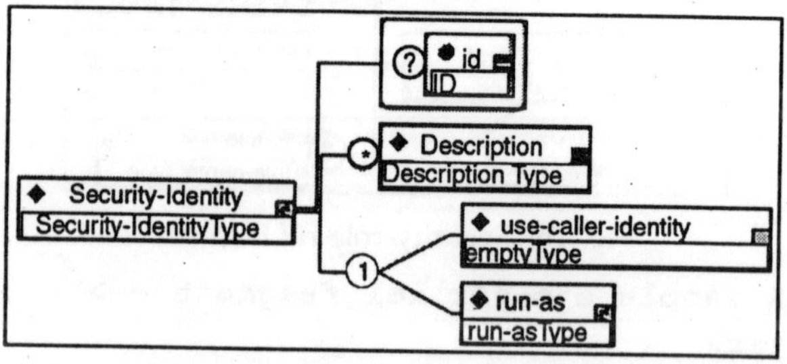

Fig. The Security-identity Element

The invocation identity can be that of the current caller, or a specific role. The application assembler uses the security-identity element with ause-caller-identity child element to indicate the current caller's identity should be propagated as the security identity for method invocations made by the EJB. Propagation of the caller's identity is the default used in the absence of an explicit security-identity element declaration.

Alternatively, the application assembler can use the run-as/role-name child element to specify that a specific security role given by the role-name value should be used as the security identity for method invocations made by the EJB. Note that this does not change the caller's identity as seen by EJBContext.getCallerPrincipal(). Rather, the caller's security roles are set to the single role specified by the run-as/role-nameelement value. One use case for the run-as element is to prevent external clients from accessing internal EJBs. This is accomplished by assigning the internal EJB method-permission elements that restrict access to a role never assigned to an external client. EJBs that need to use internal EJB are then configured with a run-as/role-name equal to the restricted role. An example descriptor fragment that illustratessecurity-identity element usage is presented.

An example ejb-jar.xml descriptor fragment that illustrates the security-identity element usage.

```
<!-- A sample ejb-jar.xml fragment -->
<ejb-jar>
  <enterprise-beans>
    <session>
      <ejb-name>ASessionBean</ejb-name>
      <!--... -->
      <security-identity>
        <use-caller-identity/>
      </security-identity>
    </session>
    <session>
      <ejb-name>RunAsBean</ejb-name>
      <!--... -->
      <security-identity>
```

```
        <run-as>
         <description>A private internal role</
description>
           <role-name>InternalRole</role-name>
        </run-as>
      </security-identity>
    </session>
  </enterprise-beans>
  <!--... -->
</ejb-jar>
```

SECURITY ROLES

The security role name referenced by either the security-role-ref or security-identity element needs to map to one of the application's declared roles. An application assembler defines logical security roles by declaring security-role elements. The role-name value is a logical application role name like Administrator, Architect, SalesManager, etc.

What is a role? The J2EE specifications note that it is important to keep in mind that the security roles in the deployment descriptor are used to define the logical security view of an application. Roles defined in the J2EE deployment descriptors should not be confused with the user groups, users, principals, and other concepts that exist in the target enterprise's operational environment.

The deployment descriptor roles are application constructs with application domain specific names. For example, a banking application might use role names like BankManager, Teller, and Customer.

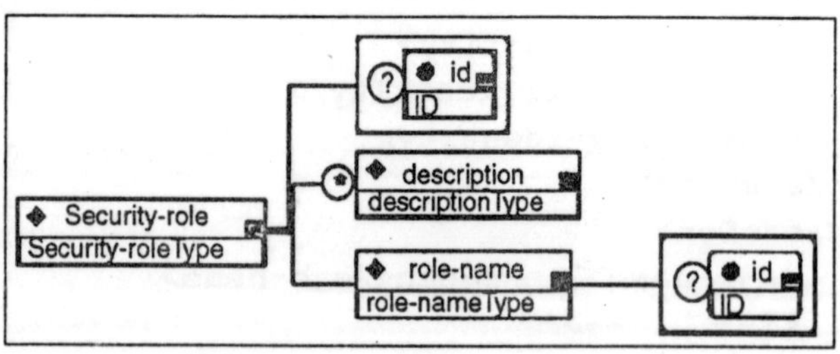

Fig. The Security-role Element

In JBoss, a security-role is only used to map security-role-ref/role-name values to the logical role that the component role referenced. The user's assigned roles are a dynamic function of the application's security manager, as you will see when we discuss the JBossSX implementation details. JBoss does not require the definition of security-roles in order to declare method permissions. However, the specification of security-role elements is still a recommended practice to ensure portability across application servers and for deployment descriptor maintenance. An example ejb-jar.xml descriptor fragment that illustrates the security-role element usage.

```
<!-- A sample ejb-jar.xml fragment -->
<ejb-jar>
  <!--... -->
  <assembly-descriptor>
    <security-role>
     <description>The single application role</
description>
      <role-name>TheApplicationRole</role-name>
    </security-role>
  </assembly-descriptor>
</ejb-jar>
```

An example web.xml descriptor fragment that illustrates the security-role element usage.

```
<!-- A sample web.xml fragment -->
<web-app>
  <!--... -->
  <security-role>
    <description>The single application role</
description>
    <role-name>TheApplicationRole</role-name>
  </security-role>
</web-app>
```

EJB METHOD PERMISSIONS

An application assembler can set the roles that are allowed to invoke an EJB's home and remote interface methods through method-permission element declarations.

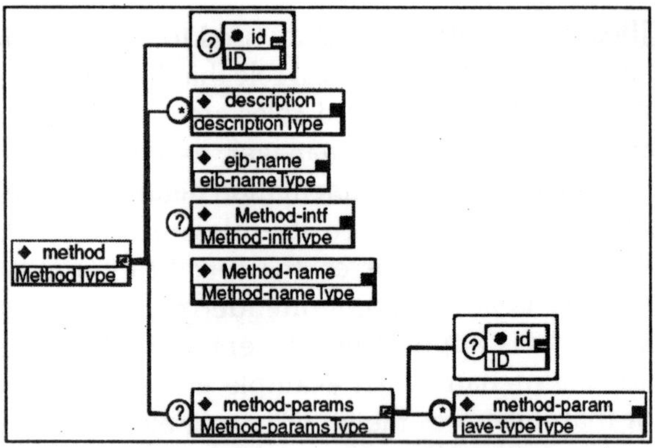

Fig. The Method-permissions Element

Each method-permission element contains one or more role-name child elements that define the logical roles allowed access the EJB methods as identified by method child elements. You can also specify an unchecked element instead of the role-name element to declare that any authenticated user can access the methods identified by method child elements. In addition, you can declare that no one should have access to a method with the exclude-list element. If an EJB has methods that have not been declared as accessible by a role using a method-permission element, the EJB methods default to being excluded from use. This is equivalent to defaulting the methods into the exclude-list.

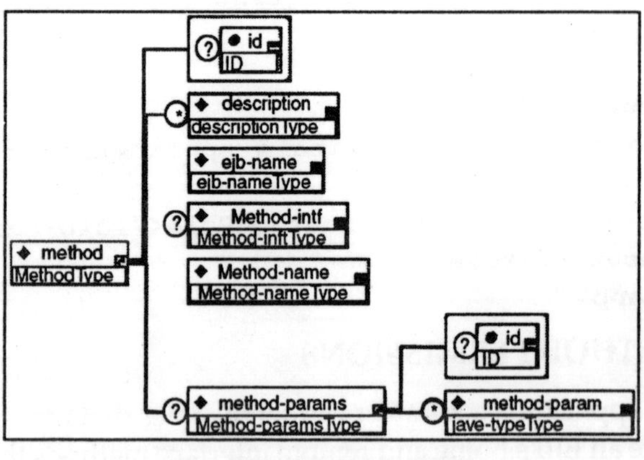

Fig. The Method Element

There are three supported styles of method element declarations.

- Style 1 is used for referring to all of the home and component interface methods of the named enterprise bean.

```
<method>
  <ejb-name>EJBNAME</ejb-name>
  <method-name>*</method-name>
</method>
```

- Style 2 is used for referring to a specified method of the home or component interface of the named enterprise bean. If there are multiple methods with the same overloaded name, this style refers to all of the overloaded methods.

```
<method>
      <ejb-name>EJBNAME</ejb-name>
      <method-name>METHOD</method-name>
</method>
```

- Style 3 is used to refer to a specified method within a set of methods with an overloaded name. The method must be defined in the specified enterprise bean's home or remote interface. The method-param element values are the fully qualified name of the corresponding method parameter type. If there are multiple methods with the same overloaded signature, the permission applies to all of the matching overloaded methods.

```
<method>
  <ejb-name>EJBNAME</ejb-name>
  <method-name>METHOD</method-name>
  <method-params>
    <method-param>PARAMETER_1</method-param>
    <!--... -->
    <method-param>PARAMETER_N</method-param>
  </method-params>
</method>
```

The optional method-intf element can be used to differentiate methods with the same name and signature that are defined in both the home and remote interfaces of an enterprise bean. An example ejb-jar.xml descriptor fragment that illustrates the method-permission element usage.

```
<ejb-jar>
  <assembly-descriptor>
    <method-permission>
     <description>The employee and temp-employee
roles may access any
          method of the EmployeeService bean </
description>
      <role-name>employee</role-name>
      <role-name>temp-employee</role-name>
      <method>
        <ejb-name>EmployeeService</ejb-
                  name>
        <method-name>*</method-name>
      </method>
    </method-permission>
    <method-permission>
      <description>The employee role may
             access the findByPrimaryKey,
              getEmployeeInfo, and the
updateEmployeeInfo(String) method of
        the AardvarkPayroll bean </description>
      <role-name>employee</role-name>
      <method>
        <ejb-name>AardvarkPayroll</ejb-name>
         <method-name>findByPrimaryKey</method-
name>
      </method>
      <method>
        <ejb-name>AardvarkPayroll</ejb-name>
          <method-name>getEmployeeInfo</method-
name>
      </method>
      <method>
        <ejb-name>AardvarkPayroll</ejb-name>
      <method-name>updateEmployeeInfo</
```

```
            method-name>
        <method-params>
    <method-param>java.lang.String</
              method-param>
        </method-params>
      </method>
    </method-permission>
    <method-permission>
     <description>The admin role may access
           any method of the
    EmployeeServiceAdmin bean </description>
      <role-name>admin</role-name>
      <method>
        <ejb-name>EmployeeServiceAdmin</ejb-
             name>
              <method-name>*</method-name>
      </method>
    </method-permission>
    <method-permission>
            <description>Any authenticated user
             may access any method of the
        EmployeeServiceHelp bean</description>
      <unchecked/>
      <method>
                 <ejb-name>EmployeeServiceHelp</
                    ejb-name>
        <method-name>*</method-name>
      </method>
    </method-permission>
    <exclude-list>
      <description>No fireTheCTO methods
of the EmployeeFiring bean may be
     used in this deployment</description>
      <method>
       <ejb-name>EmployeeFiring</ejb-name>
      <method-name>fireTheCTO</method-name>
      </method>
    </exclude-list>
```

```
  </assembly-descriptor>
</ejb-jar>
```

WEB CONTENT SECURITY CONSTRAINTS

In a web application, security is defined by the roles allowed access to content by a URL pattern that identifies the protected content. This set of information is declared using the web.xml security-constraint element.

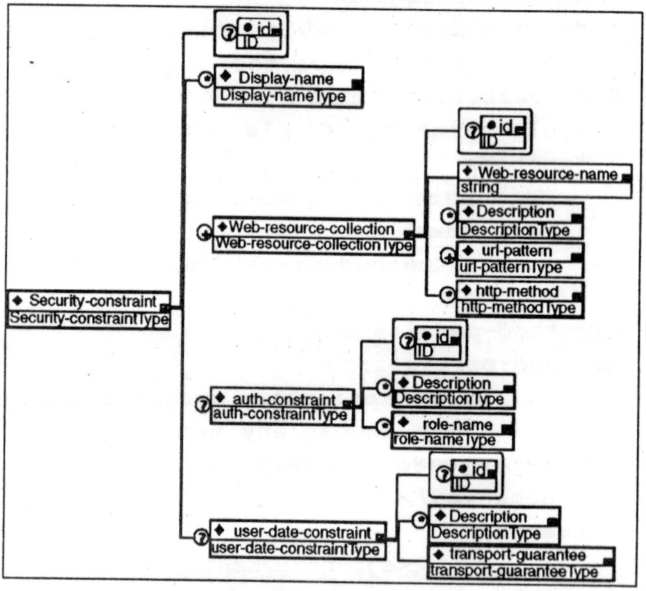

Fig. The security-constraint Element

The content to be secured is declared using one or more web-resource-collection elements. Each web-resource-collection element contains an optional series of url-pattern elements followed by an optional series of http-method elements. The url-pattern element value specifies a URL pattern against which a request URL must match for the request to correspond to an attempt to access secured content. The http-methodelement value specifies a type of HTTP request to allow.

The optional user-data-constraint element specifies the requirements for the transport layer of the client to server connection. The requirement may be for content integrity (preventing data tampering in the communication process) or for confidentiality (preventing reading while in transit). The transport-guarantee element value specifies the degree to which communication between client and server should be protected. Its values are NONE, INTEGRAL, or CONFIDENTIAL. A value of NONE means that the application does not require any transport guarantees. A value of INTEGRAL means that the application requires the data sent between the client and server be sent in such a way that it can't be changed in transit. A value of CONFIDENTIAL means that the application requires the data to be transmitted in a fashion that prevents other entities from observing the contents of the transmission. In most cases, the presence of the INTEGRAL or CONFIDENTIAL flag indicates that the use of SSL is required.

The optional login-config is used to configure the authentication method that should be used, the realm name that should be used for this application, and the attributes that are needed by the form login mechanism.

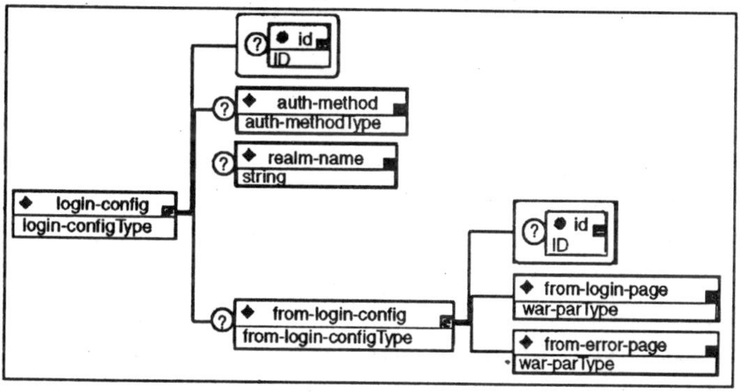

Fig. The Login-config Rlement

The auth-method child element specifies the authentication mechanism for the web application. As a prerequisite to gaining access to any web resources that are protected by an authorization constraint, a user must have authenticated using the configured mechanism. Legal values for auth-method are BASIC, DIGEST, FORM, or CLIENT-CERT. The realm-name child element specifies the realm name to use in

HTTP basic and digest authorization. The form-login-config child element specifies the log in as well as error pages that should be used in form-based login. If the auth-method value is not FORM, form-login-config and its child elements are ignored.

A web.xml descriptor fragment which illustrates the use of the security-constraint and related elements.

```
<web-app>
  <!--... -->
  <security-constraint>
    <web-resource-collection>
        <web-resource-name>Secure Content</web-
resource-name>
       <url-pattern>/restricted/*</url-pattern>
    </web-resource-collection>
    <auth-constraint>
       <role-name>AuthorizedUser</role-name>
    </auth-constraint>
    <user-data-constraint>
         <transport-guarantee>NONE</transport-
guarantee>
    </user-data-constraint>
  </security-constraint>
  <!--... -->
  <login-config>
    <auth-method>BASIC</auth-method>
   <realm-name>The Restricted Zone</realm-name>
  </login-config>
  <!--... -->
  <security-role>
      <description>The role required to access
restricted content </description>
    <role-name>AuthorizedUser</role-name>
  </security-role>
</web-app>
```

ENABLING DECLARATIVE SECURITY IN JBOSS

The J2EE security elements that have been covered

describe only the security requirements from the application's perspective. Since J2EE security elements declare logical roles, the application deployer maps the roles from the application domain onto the deployment environment. The J2EE specifications omit these application-server-specific details. In JBoss, mapping the application roles onto the deployment environment entails specifying a security manager that implements the J2EE security model using JBoss server specific deployment descriptors. We will avoid discussion the details of this step for now..

JAAS

The JBossSX framework is based on the JAAS API. It is important that you understand the basic elements of the JAAS API to understand the implementation details of JBossSX. This section provides an introduction to JAAS to prepare you for the JBossSX architecture discussion.

DEFINITION

The JAAS 1.0 API consists of a set of Java packages designed for user authentication and authorization. It implements a Java version of the standard Pluggable Authentication Module (PAM) framework and compatibly extends the Java 2 Platform's access control architecture to support user-based authorization. JAAS was first released as an extension package for JDK 1.3 and is bundled with JDK 1.4+. Because the JBossSX framework uses only the authentication capabilities of JAAS to implement the declarative role-based J2EE security model, this introduction focuses on only that topic.

JAAS authentication is performed in a pluggable fashion. This permits Java applications to remain independent from underlying authentication technologies and allows the JBossSX security manager to work in different security infrastructures. Integration with a security infrastructure can be achieved without changing the JBossSX security manager implementation. All that needs to change is the configuration of the authentication stack that JAAS uses.

The JAAS Core Classes

The JAAS core classes can be broken down into three categories: common, authentication, and authorization. The following list presents only the common and authentication classes because these are the specific classes used to implement the functionality of JBossSX covered in this chapter.

Common classes:

- Subject (javax.security.auth.Subject)
- Principal (java.security.Principal)

Authentication classes:

- Callback (javax.security.auth.callback.Callback)
- CallbackHandler (javax.security.auth.callback.CallbackHandler)
- Configuration (javax.security.auth.login.Configuration)
- LoginContext (javax.security.auth.login.LoginContext)
- LoginModule (javax.security.auth.spi.LoginModule)

Subject and Principal

To authorize access to resources, applications first need to authenticate the request's source. The JAAS framework defines the term subject to represent a request's source. The Subject class is the central class in JAAS. A Subject represents information for a single entity, such as a person or service. It encompasses the entity's principals, public credentials, and private credentials. The JAAS APIs use the existing Java 2java.security.Principal interface to represent a principal, which is essentially just a typed name.

During the authentication process, a subject is populated with associated identities, or principals. A subject may have many principals. For example, a person may have a name principal (John Doe), a social security number principal (123-45-6789), and a username principal (johnd), all of which help distinguish the subject from other subjects. To retrieve the principals associated with a subject, two methods are available:

```
public Set getPrincipals() {...}
public Set getPrincipals(Class c) {...}
```

The first method returns all principals contained in the subject. The second method only returns those principals that are instances of class cor one of its subclasses. An empty set will be returned if the subject has no matching principals. Note that the java.security.acl.Group interface is a subinterface of java.security.Principal, and so an instance in the principals set may represent a logical grouping of other principals or groups of principals.

8.2.1.1.2. Authentication of a Subject

Authentication of a subject requires a JAAS login.

The login procedure consists of the following steps:

- An application instantiates a LoginContext passing in the name of the login configuration and a CallbackHandler to populate the Callbackobjects as required by the configuration LoginModules.
- The LoginContext consults a Configuration to load all of the LoginModules included in the named login configuration. If no such named configuration exists the other configuration is used as a default.
- The application invokes the LoginContext.login method.
- The login method invokes all the loaded Login Modules. As each LoginModule attempts to authenticate the subject, it invokes the handle method on the associated CallbackHandler to obtain the information required for the authentication process. The required information is passed to the handle method in the form of an array of Callback objects. Upon success, the LoginModules associate relevant principals and credentials with the subject.
- The LoginContext returns the authentication status to the application. Success is represented by a return from the login method. Failure is represented through a LoginException being thrown by the login method.
- If authentication succeeds, the application retrieves the authenticated subject using the LoginContext. getSubject method.

- After the scope of the subject authentication is complete, all principals and related information associated with the subject by the login method may be removed by invoking the LoginContext.logout method.

The LoginContext class provides the basic methods for authenticating subjects and offers a way to develop an application independent of the underlying authentication technology. The LoginContext consults a Configuration to determine the authentication services configured for a particular application. LoginModule classes represent the authentication services. Therefore, you can plug in different login modules into an application without changing the application itself. The following code shows the steps required by an application to authenticate a subject.

```
CallbackHandler handler = new MyHandler();
LoginContext lc = new LoginContext("some-config",
handler);

try {
  lc.login();
  Subject subject = lc.getSubject();
} catch(LoginException e) {
  System.out.println("authentication failed");
  e.printStackTrace();
}

// Perform work as authenticated Subject
//...

// Scope of work complete, logout to remove
authentication info
try {
  lc.logout();
} catch(LoginException e) {
  System.out.println("logout failed");
  e.printStackTrace();
}
```

```
// A sample MyHandler class
class MyHandler
  implements CallbackHandler
{
 public void handle(Callback[] callbacks) throws
    IOException, UnsupportedCallbackException
  {
    for (int i = 0; i < callbacks.length; i++) {
      if (callbacks[i] instanceof NameCallback)
{
                          NameCallback   nc   =
(NameCallback)callbacks[i];
          nc.setName(username);
          } else if (callbacks[i] instanceof
PasswordCallback) {
                      PasswordCallback   pc   =
(PasswordCallback)callbacks[i];
          pc.setPassword(password);
        } else {
                                    throw    new
UnsupportedCallbackException(callbacks[i],
                                    "Unrecognized
Callback");
        }
      }
  }
}
```

Developers integrate with an authentication technology by creating an implementation of the LoginModule interface. This allows different authentication technologies to be plugged into an application by administrator.

Multiple LoginModules can be chained together to allow for more than one authentication technology to participate in the authentication process. For example, one LoginModule may perform username/password-based authentication, while another may interface to hardware devices such as smart card readers or biometric authenticators.

The life cycle of a LoginModule is driven by the LoginContext object against which the client creates and issues the login method. The process consists of a two phases.

The steps of the process are as follows:

- The LoginContext creates each configured Login Module using its public no-arg constructor.
- Each LoginModule is initialized with a call to its initialize method. The Subject argument is guaranteed to be non-null. The signature of the initialize method is: public void initialize(Subject subject, CallbackHandler callbackHandler, Map sharedState, Map options).
- The login method is then called to start the authentication process. An example method implementation might prompt the user for a username and password, and then verify the information against data stored in a naming service such as NIS or LDAP. Alternative implementations might interface to smart cards and biometric devices, or simply extract user information from the underlying operating system. The validation of user identity by each LoginModule is considered phase 1 of JAAS authentication. The signature of the loginmethod is: boolean login() throws Login Exception. Failure is indicated by throwing a LoginException. A return of true indicates that the method succeeded, while a return of false indicates that the login module should be ignored.
- If the LoginContext's overall authentication succeeds, commit is invoked on each LoginModule. If phase 1 succeeded for a LoginModule, then the commit method continues with phase 2: associating relevant principals, public credentials, and/or private credentials with the subject. If phase 1 fails for a LoginModule, then commit removes any previously stored authentication state, such as usernames or passwords. The signature of the commit method is: boolean commit() throws LoginException. Failure to

complete the commit phase is indicated by throwing a LoginException. A return of true indicates that the method succeeded, while a return of false indicates that the login module should be ignored.

- If the LoginContext's overall authentication failed, then the abort method is invoked on each LoginModule. The abort method removes/destroys any authentication state created by the login or initialize methods. The signature of the abort method is: boolean abort() throws LoginException. Failure to complete the abort phase is indicated by throwing a LoginException. A return of true indicates that the method succeeded, while a return of false indicates that the login module should be ignored.
- Removal of the authentication state after a successful login is accomplished when the application invokes logout on the LoginContext. This in turn results in a logout method invocation on each LoginModule. The logout method removes the principals and credentials originally associated with the subject during the commit operation. Credentials should be destroyed upon removal. The signature of thelogout method is: boolean logout() throws LoginException. Failure to complete the logout process is indicated by throwing aLoginException. A return of true indicates that the method succeeded, while a return of false indicates that the login module should be ignored.

When a LoginModule must communicate with the user to obtain authentication information, it uses a CallbackHandler object. Applications implement the CallbackHandler interface and pass it to the LoginContext, which forwards it directly to the underlying login modules. Login modules use the CallbackHandler both to gather input from users, such as a password or smart card PIN number, and to supply information to users, such as status information. By allowing the application to specify the CallbackHandler, underlying LoginModules remain independent from the different ways applications interact with users. For example, a Callback

Handler's implementation for a GUI application might display a window to solicit user input. On the other hand, a callbackhandler's implementation for a non-GUI environment, such as an application server, might simply obtain credential information using an application server API. The callbackhandler interface has one method to implement:

```
void handle(Callback[] callbacks)
 throws java.io.IOException,
  UnsupportedCallbackException;
```

The last authentication class to cover is the Callback interface. This is a tagging interface for which several default implementations are provided, including the NameCallback and PasswordCallback used in the earlier example. A LoginModule uses a Callback to request information required by the authentication mechanism. LoginModules pass an array of Callbacks directly to the CallbackHandler.handle method during the authentication's login phase. If a callbackhandler does not understand how to use a Callback object passed into the handle method, it throws an Unsupported Callback Exception to abort the login call.

JBOSS SECURITY MODEL

Similar to the rest of the JBoss architecture, security at the lowest level is defined as a set of interfaces for which alternate implementations may be provided. There are three basic interfaces that define the JBoss server security layer: **org.jboss.security.AuthenticationManager,org.jboss.security.RealmMapping,andorg.jboss.security.SecurityProxy.**

The classes represent the security interfaces while the yellow classes represent the EJB container layer. The two interfaces required for the implementation of the J2EE security model are the org.jboss.security.AuthenticationManager andorg.jboss.security.RealmMapping.

- AuthenticationManager is an interface responsible for validating credentials associated with principals. Principals are identities and examples include usernames, employee numbers, social security numbers, and so on. Credentials are proof of the identity and examples include passwords, session keys, digital signatures, and so on. The isValid method is invoked to see if a user identity and associated credentials as known in the operational environment are valid proof of the user identity.

- RealmMapping is an interface responsible for principal mapping and role mapping. The getPrincipal method takes a user identity as known in the operational environment and returns the application domain identity. The doesUserHaveRole method validates that the user identity in the operation environment has been assigned the indicated role from the application domain.
- SecurityProxy is an interface describing the requirements for a custom SecurityProxyInterceptor plugin. A SecurityProxy allows for the externalization of custom security checks on a per-method basis for both the EJB home and remote interface methods.
- SubjectSecurityManager is a subinterface of AuthenticationManager that simply adds accessor methods for obtaining the security domain name of the security manager and the current thread's authenticated Subject.
- SecurityDomain is an extension of the Authentication Manager, RealmMapping, and SubjectSecurity Manager interfaces. It is a move to a comprehensive security interface based on the JAAS Subject, a java.security. KeyStore, and the JSSEcom. sun.net.ssl. KeyManagerFactory and com.sun.net.ssl. Trust ManagerFactory interfaces. This interface is still a work in progress that will be the basis of a multi-domain security architecture that will better support ASP style deployments of applications and resources.

Note that the AuthenticationManager, RealmMapping and SecurityProxy interfaces have no association to JAAS related classes. Although the JBossSX framework is heavily dependent on JAAS, the basic security interfaces required for implementation of the J2EE security model are not. The JBossSX framework is simply an implementation of the basic security plug-in interfaces that are based on JAAS. The implication of this plug-in architecture is that you are free to replace the JAAS-based JBossSX implementation classes with your own custom security manager implementation that does not make use of JAAS, if you so desire. You'll see how to do this when you look at the JBossSX MBeans available for the configuration of JBossSX in Figure,

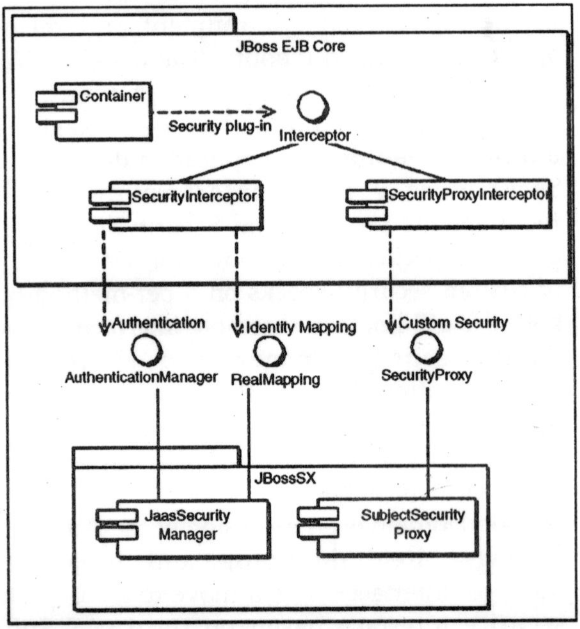

ENABLING DECLARATIVE SECURITY IN JBOSS REVISITED

Recall that our discussion of the J2EE standard security model ended with a requirement for the use of JBoss server specific deployment descriptor to enable security. The details of this configuration is presented here, as this is part of the generic JBoss security model. Figure shows the JBoss-specific EJB and web application deployment descriptor's security-related elements.

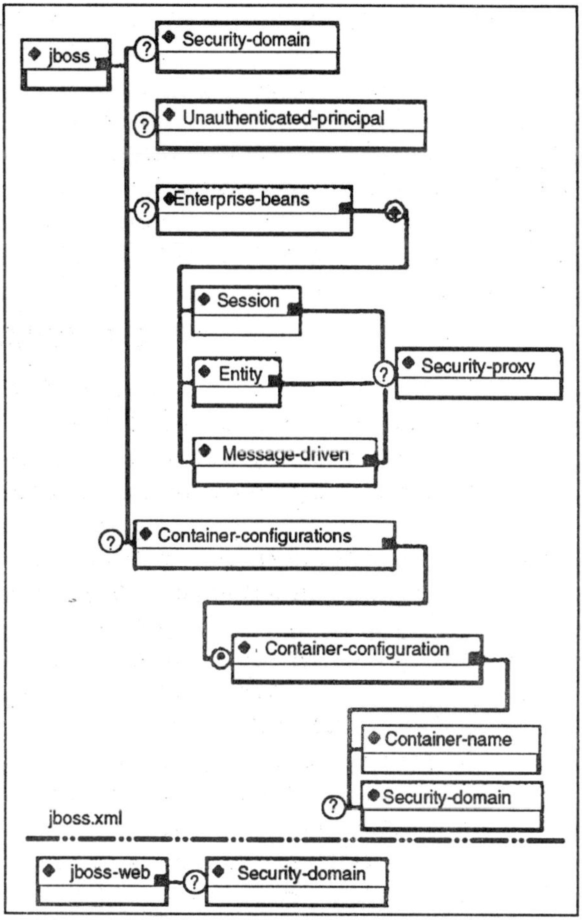

Fig. The Security Element Subsets of the JBoss server jboss.xml and jboss-web.xml Deployment Descriptors.

The value of a security-domain element specifies the JNDI name of the security manager interface implementation that JBoss uses for the EJB and web containers. This is an object that implements both of the AuthenticationManager and Realm Mapping interfaces. When specified as a top-level element it defines what security domain in effect for all EJBs in the deployment unit. This is the typical usage because mixing security managers within a deployment unit complicates inter-component operation and administration. To specify the security domain for an individual EJB, you specify the security-domain at the container configuration level. This will override any top-level security-domain element.

The unauthenticated-principal element specifies the name to use for the Principal object returned by the EJBContext. getUserPrincipal method when an unauthenticated user invokes an EJB. Note that this conveys no special permissions to an unauthenticated caller. Its primary purpose is to allow unsecured servlets and JSP pages to invoke unsecured EJBs and allow the target EJB to obtain a non-null Principal for the caller using the getUserPrincipal method. This is a J2EE specification requirement.

The security-proxy element identifies a custom security proxy implementation that allows per-request security checks outside the scope of the EJB declarative security model without embedding security logic into the EJB implementation. This may be an implementation of theorg.jboss.security. SecurityProxy interface, or just an object that implements methods in the home, remote, local home or local interfaces of the EJB to secure without implementing any common interface. If the given class does not implement the SecurityProxy interface, the instance must be wrapped in a SecurityProxy implementation that delegates the method invocations to the object. Theorg.jboss. security.Subject SecurityProxy is an example SecurityProxy implementation used by the default JBossSX installation.

Take a look at a simple example of a custom SecurityProxy in the context of a trivial stateless session bean. The custom SecurityProxyvalidates that no one invokes the bean's echo method with a four-letter word as its argument. This is a check that is not possible with role-based security; you cannot define a FourLetterEchoInvoker role because the security context is the method argument, not a property of the caller. The code for the custom SecurityProxy is given in Example.

```
package org.jboss.chap8.ex1;

import java.lang.reflect.Method;
```

```
import javax.ejb.EJBContext;

import org.apache.log4j.Category;

import org.jboss.security.SecurityProxy;

/** A simple example of a custom SecurityProxy
implementation
  * that demonstrates method argument based
security checks.
 * @author Scott.Stark@jboss.org
 * @version $Revision: 1.5 $
 */
public class EchoSecurityProxy implements
SecurityProxy
{
  Category log =
Category.getInstance(EchoSecurityProxy.class);
  Method echo;

   public void init(Class beanHome, Class
beanRemote,
            Object securityMgr)
     throws InstantiationException
  {
     log.debug("init, beanHome="+beanHome
          + ", beanRemote="+beanRemote
          + ", securityMgr="+securityMgr);
  // Get the echo method for equality testing in
invoke
     try {
       Class[] params = {String.class};
      echo = beanRemote.getDeclaredMethod("echo",
params);
     } catch(Exception e) {
          String msg = "Failed to finde an
echo(String) method";
       log.error(msg, e);
```

```
        throw new InstantiationException(msg);
      }
   }
   public void setEJBContext(EJBContext ctx)
   {
      log.debug("setEJBContext, ctx="+ctx);
   }
  public void invokeHome(Method m, Object[] args)
      throws SecurityException
   {
   // We don't validate access to home methods
   }
   public void invoke(Method m, Object[] args,
Object bean)
      throws SecurityException
   {
      log.debug("invoke, m="+m);
   // Check for the echo method
      if (m.equals(echo)) {
     // Validate that the msg arg is not 4 letter
word
        String arg = (String) args[0];
        if (arg == null || arg.length() == 4)
         throw new SecurityException("No 4 letter
words");
      }
  // We are not responsible for doing the invoke
   }
}
```

The EchoSecurityProxy checks that the method to be invoked on the bean instance corresponds to the echo(String) method loaded the init method. If there is a match, the method argument is obtained and its length compared against 4 or null. Either case results in aSecurityException being thrown. Certainly this is a contrived example, but only in its application. It is a common requirement that applications must perform security checks based on the value of method arguments. The point of the example is to demonstrate how custom security beyond the scope of the standard declarative security model can be introduced independent of the bean implementation. This allows the specification and coding of the security requirements to be delegated to security experts. Since the security proxy layer can be done independent of the bean implementation, security can be changed to match the deployment environment requirements.

```
<jboss>
   <security-domain>java:/jaas/other</security-
domain>

  <enterprise-beans>
    <session>
      <ejb-name>EchoBean</ejb-name>
                                                    <security-
proxy>org.jboss.chap8.ex1.EchoSecurityProxy</
security-proxy>
    </session>
  </enterprise-beans>
</jboss>
```

Now test the custom proxy by running a client that attempts to invoke the EchoBean.echo method with the arguments Hello and Four as illustrated in this fragment:

```
public class ExClient
{
  public static void main(String args[])
    throws Exception
  {
    Logger log = Logger.getLogger("ExClient");
    log.info("Looking up EchoBean");

   InitialContext iniCtx = new InitialContext();
    Object ref = iniCtx.lookup("EchoBean");
    EchoHome home = (EchoHome) ref;
    Echo echo = home.create();

    log.info("Created Echo");
         log.info("Echo.echo('Hello') =
"+echo.echo("Hello"));
```

```
            log.info("Echo.echo('Four')  =
"+echo.echo("Four"));
  }
}
```

The first call should succeed, while the second should fail due to the fact that Four is a four-letter word. Run the client as follows using Ant from the examples directory:

```
[examples]$ ant -Dchap=chap8 -Dex=1 run-example
run-example1:
     [copy] Copying 1 file to/tmp/jboss-4.0.1/
server/default/deploy
    [echo] Waiting for 5 seconds for deploy...
    [java] [INFO,ExClient] Looking up EchoBean
    [java] [INFO,ExClient] Created Echo
     [java] [INFO,ExClient] Echo.echo('Hello') =
Hello
      [java] Exception in thread "main"
java.rmi.ServerException: RemoteException occurred
in server thread; nested exception is:
      [java]    java.rmi.AccessException:
SecurityException; nested exception is:
     [java]    java.lang.SecurityException: No 4
letter words
...
   [java]   at
org.jboss.chap8.ex1.ExClient.main(ExClient.java:25)
     [java] Caused by: java.rmi.AccessException:
SecurityException; nested exception is:
     [java]    java.lang.SecurityException: No 4
letter words
...
```

The result is that the echo('Hello') method call succeeds as expected and the echo('Four') method call results in a rather messy looking exception, which is also expected. The above output has been truncated to fit in the book. The key part to the exception is that theSecurityException("No 4 letter words") generated by the EchoSecurityProxy was thrown to abort the attempted method invocation as desired.

SECURITY EXTENSION ARCHITECTURE

The preceding discussion of the general JBoss security layer has stated that the JBossSX security extension framework is an implementation of the security layer interfaces. This is the primary purpose of the JBossSX framework.

The details of the implementation are interesting in that it offers a great deal of customization for integration into existing security infrastructures. A security infrastructure can be anything from a database or LDAP server to a sophisticated security software suite. The integration flexibility is achieved using the pluggable authentication model available in the JAAS framework.

The heart of the JBossSX framework is org.jboss. security.plugins.JaasSecurityManager. This is the default implementation of theAuthenticationManager and Realm Mapping interfaces. Figure shows the relationship between the security-domain component deployment descriptor value, the component container and the JaasSecurityManager. shows how the JaasSecurityManager integrates into the EJB and web container layers based on the security-domain element of the corresponding component deployment descriptor.

The EJB and web containers have a request interceptor architecture that includes a security interceptor, which enforces the container security model. At deployment time, the security-domain element value in the jboss.xml and jboss-web.xml descriptors is used to obtain the security manager instance associated with the container. The security interceptor then uses the security manager to perform its role. When a secured component is requested, the security interceptor delegates security checks to the security manager instance associated with the container.

The JBossSX JaasSecurityManager implementation performs security checks based on the information associated with the Subject instance that results from executing the JAAS login modules configured under the name matching the security-domain element value. We will drill into the JaasSecurityManager implementation and its use of JAAS in the following section.

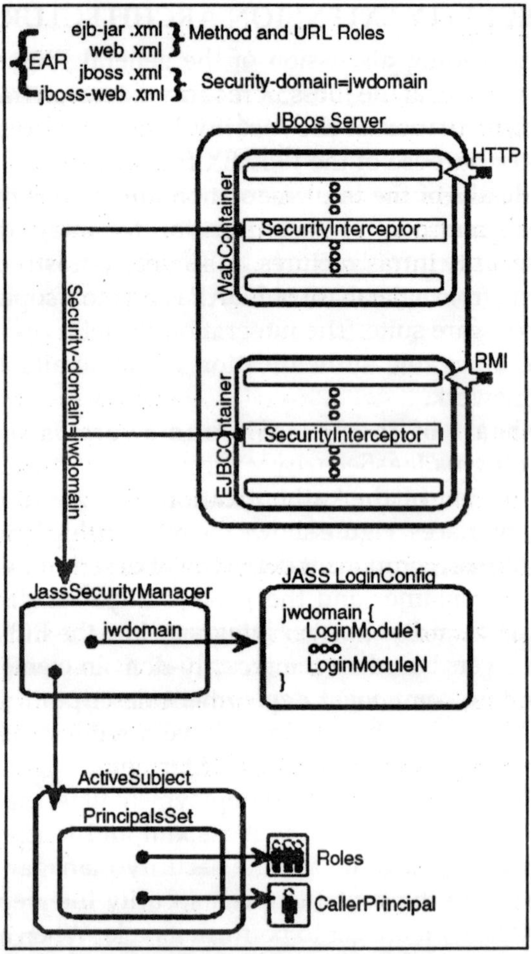

Fig: The Relationship between the Security-domain Component Deployment Descriptor Value, the Component Container and the JaasSecurityManager.

JAASSECURITYMANAGER USAGES

The JaasSecurityManager uses the JAAS packages to implement the AuthenticationManager and RealmMapping interface behaviour. In particular, its behaviour derives from the execution of the login module instances that are configured under the name that matches the security domain to which the JaasSecurityManager has been assigned. The login modules implement the security domain's principal authentication and role-mapping behaviour. Thus, you can use the JaasSecurity Manager across different security domains simply by plugging in different login module configurations for the domains.

To illustrate the details of the JaasSecurityManager's usage of the JAAS authentication process, you will walk through a client invocation of an EJB home method invocation. The prerequisite setting is that the EJB has been deployed in the JBoss server and its home interface methods have been secured using method-permission elements in the ejb-jar.xml descriptor, and it has been assigned a security domain named jwdomain using the jboss.xml descriptor security-domain element.

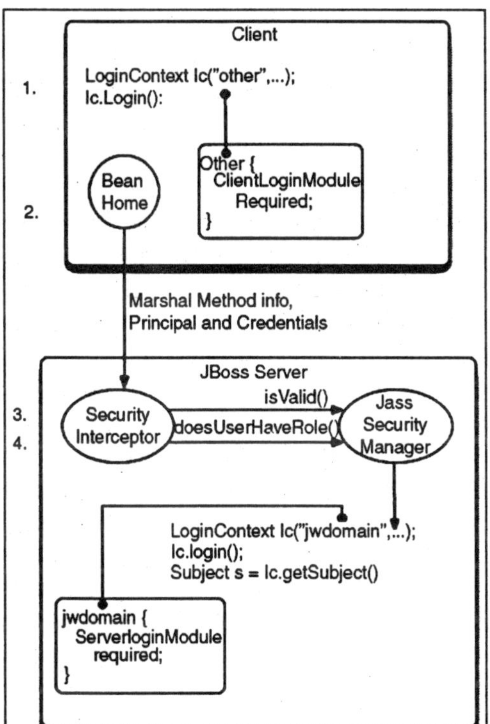

Fig. An Illustration of the steps Involved in the Authentication and Authorization of a Secured EJB home Method Invocation.

The numbered steps shown are:

- The client first has to perform a JAAS login to establish the principal and credentials for authentication, and this is labeled *Client Side Login* in the figure. This is how clients establish their login identities in JBoss. Support for presenting the login information via JNDIInitialContext properties is provided via an alternate configuration. A JAAS login entails creating a LoginContext instance and passing the name of the configuration to use. The configuration name is other. This one-time login associates the login principal and credentials with all subsequent EJB method invocations. Note that the process might not authenticate the user. The nature of the client-side login depends on the login module configuration that the client uses. In this example, the other client-side login configuration entry is set up to use the ClientLoginModule module (an org.jboss.security.ClientLoginModule). This is the default client side module that simply binds the username and password to the JBoss EJB invocation layer for later authentication on the server. The identity of the client is not authenticated on the client.
- Later, the client obtains the EJB home interface and attempts to create a bean. This event is labeled as *Home Method Invocation*. This results in a home interface method invocation being sent to the JBoss server. The invocation includes the method arguments passed by the client along with the user identity and credentials from the client-side JAAS login performed in step 1.
- On the server side, the security interceptor first requires authentication of the user invoking the call, which, as on the client side, involves a JAAS login.
- The security domain under which the EJB is secured determines the choice of login modules. The security domain name is used as the login configuration entry name passed to the LoginContext constructor. The

EJB security domain is jwdomain. If the JAAS login authenticates the user, a JAAS Subject is created that contains the following in its PrincipalsSet:

- A java.security.Principal that corresponds to the client identity as known in the deployment security environment.
- A java.security.acl.Group named Roles that contains the role names from the application domain to which the user has been assigned. org.jboss.security.SimplePrincipal objects are used to represent the role names; SimplePrincipal is a simple string-based implementation of Principal. These roles are used to validate the roles assigned to methods in ejb-jar.xml and theEJBContext.isCallerInRole(String) method implementation.
- An optional java.security.acl.Group named CallerPrincipal, which contains a single org.jboss. security.SimplePrincipal that corresponds to the identity of the application domain's caller. The CallerPrincipal sole group member will be the value returned by theEJBContext. getCaller Principal() method. The purpose of this mapping is to allow a Principal as known in the operational security environment to map to a Principal with a name known to the application. In the absence of a CallerPrincipal mapping the deployment security environment principal is used as the getCallerPrincipal method value. That is, the operational principal is the same as the application domain principal.

- The final step of the security interceptor check is to verify that the authenticated user has permission to invoke the requested method This is labeled as *Server Side*
  - Obtain the names of the roles allowed to access the EJB method from the EJB container. The role names are determined by ejb-jar.xml descriptor

role-name elements of all method-permission elements containing the invoked method.

- If no roles have been assigned, or the method is specified in an exclude-list element, then access to the method is denied. Otherwise, the doesUserHaveRole method is invoked on the security manager by the security interceptor to see if the caller has one of the assigned role names. This method iterates through the role names and checks if the authenticated user's SubjectRoles group contains a SimplePrincipal with the assigned role name. Access is allowed if any role name is a member of the Rolesgroup. Access is denied if none of the role names are members.
- If the EJB was configured with a custom security proxy, the method invocation is delegated to it. If the security proxy wants to deny access to the caller, it will throw a java.lang.SecurityException. If no SecurityException is thrown, access to the EJB method is allowed and the method invocation passes to the next container interceptor. Note that the SecurityProxy Interceptor handles this check and this interceptor is not shown.

Every secured EJB method invocation, or secured web content access, requires the authentication and authorization of the caller because security information is handled as a stateless attribute of the request that must be presented and validated on each request. This can be an expensive operation if the JAAS login involves client-to-server communication. Because of this, the JaasSecurityManager supports the notion of an authentication cache that is used to store principal and credential information from previous successful logins. You can specify the authentication cache instance to use as part of the JaasSecurity Manager configuration as you will see when the associated MBean service is discussed in following section. In the absence of any user-defined cache, a default cache that maintains credential information for a configurable period of time is used.

JAASSECURITYMANAGERSERVICE MBEAN

The JaasSecurityManagerService MBean service manages security managers. Although its name begins with *Jaas,* the security managers it handles need not use JAAS in their implementation. The name arose from the fact that the default security manager implementation is theJaasSecurityManager. The primary role of the JaasSecurityManagerService is to externalize the security manager implementation. You can change the security manager implementation by providing an alternate implementation of the AuthenticationManager and RealmMappinginterfaces. The second fundamental role of the JaasSecurity ManagerService is to provide a JNDI javax. naming. spi.ObjectFactory implementation to allow for simple code-free management of the JNDI name to security manager implementation mapping. It has been mentioned that security is enabled by specifying the JNDI name of the security manager implementation via the security-domain deployment descriptor element.

When you specify a JNDI name, there has to be an object-binding there to use. To simplify the setup of the JNDI name to security manager bindings, the JaasSecurityManagerService manages the association of security manager instances to names by binding a next naming system reference with itself as the JNDI ObjectFactory under the name java:/jaas. This allows one to use a naming convention of the formjava:/jaas/XYZ as the value for the security-domain element, and the security manager instance for the XYZ security domain will be created as needed for you. The security manager for the domain XYZ is created on the first lookup against the java:/jaas/XYZ binding by creating an instance of the class specified by the SecurityManager ClassName attribute using a constructor that takes the name of the security domain. For example, consider the following container security configuration snippet:

```
<jboss>
   <!-- Configure all containers to be secured
under the "hades" security domain -->
   <security-domain>java:/jaas/hades</security-
```

```
domain>
  <!--... -->
</jboss>
```

Any lookup of the name java:/jaas/hades will return a security manager instance that has been associated with the security domain namedhades. This security manager will implement the AuthenticationManager and RealmMapping security interfaces and will be of the type specified by the JaasSecurityManagerService SecurityManagerClassName attribute.

The JaasSecurityManagerService MBean is configured by default for use in the standard JBoss distribution, and you can often use the default configuration as is.

The configurable attributes of the JaasSecurityManagerService include:

- *SecurityManagerClassName*: The name of the class that provides the security manager implementation. The implementation must support both the org.jboss. security.AuthenticationManager and org.jboss. security.RealmMapping interfaces. If not specified this defaults to the JAAS-based org.jboss. security. plugins.JaasSecurityManager.
- *CallbackHandlerClassName*: The name of the class that provides the javax.security. auth.callback. Callback Handler implementation used by the JaasSecurity Manager. You can override the handler used by the JaasSecurityManager if the default implementation (org.jboss.security.auth.callback. Security Association Handler) does not meet your needs. This is a rather deep configuration that generally should not be set unless you know what you are doing.
- *SecurityProxyFactoryClassName*: The name of the class that provides the org.jboss.security. SecurityProxy Factory implementation. If not specified this defaults to org.jboss. security.Subject Security ProxyFactory.
- *AuthenticationCacheJndiName*: Specifies the location of the security credential cache policy. This is first treated as anObjectFactory location capable of

returning CachePolicy instances on a per-security-domain basis. This is done by appending the name of the security domain to this name when looking up the CachePolicy for a domain. If this fails, the location is treated as a singleCachePolicy for all security domains. As a default, a timed cache policy is used.

- *DefaultCacheTimeout*: Specifies the default timed cache policy timeout in seconds. The default value is 1800 seconds (30 minutes). The value you use for the timeout is a tradeoff between frequent authentication operations and how long credential information may be out of synch with respect to the security information store. If you want to disable caching of security credentials, set this to 0 to force authentication to occur every time. This has no affect if the AuthenticationCacheJndiName has been changed from the default value.
- *DefaultCacheResolution*: Specifies the default timed cache policy resolution in seconds. This controls the interval at which the cache current timestamp is updated and should be less than the Default CacheTimeout in order for the timeout to be meaningful. The default resolution is 60 seconds(1 minute). This has no affect if the Authentication CacheJndiName has been changed from the default value.
- *DefaultUnauthenticatedPrincipal*: Specifies the principal to use for unauthenticated users. This setting makes it possible to set default permissions for users who have not been authenticated.

The JaasSecurityManagerService also supports a number of useful operations. These include flushing any security domain authentication cache at runtime, getting the list of active users in a security domain authentication cache, and any of the security manager interface methods.

Flushing a security domain authentication cache can be used to drop all cached credentials when the underlying store has been updated and you want the store state to be used immediately. The MBean operation signature is: public void flushAuthenticationCache(String securityDomain).

This can be invoked programmatically using the following code snippet:

```
MBeanServer server =...;
String jaasMgrName = "jboss.security: service=Jaas
SecurityManager";
ObjectName jaasMgr = new ObjectName(jaasMgrName);
Object[] params = {domainName};
String[] signature = {"java.lang.String"};
server.invoke(jaasMgr, "flushAuthenticationCache",
params, signature);
```

Getting the list of active users provides a snapshot of the Principals keys in a security domain authentication cache that are not expired. The MBean operation signature is: public List getAuthenticationCachePrincipals(String securityDomain).

This can be invoked programmatically using the following code snippet:

```
MBeanServer server =...;
String                    jaasMgrName                   =
"jboss.security:service=JaasSecurityManager";
ObjectName jaasMgr = new ObjectName(jaasMgrName);
Object[] params = {domainName};
String[] signature = {"java.lang.String"};
List users = (List) server.invoke(jaasMgr,
"getAuthenticationCachePrincipals",params,
signature);
```

The security manager has a few additional access methods.

```
public boolean isValid(String securityDomain,
Principal principal, Object credential);
public Principal getPrincipal(String
securityDomain, Principal principal);
public boolean doesUserHaveRole(String
securityDomain, Principal principal,
Object credential, Set roles);
public Set getUserRoles(String securityDomain,
```

```
Principal principal, Object credential);
```

They provide access to the corresponding Authentication Manager and RealmMapping interface method of the associated security domain named by the securityDomain argument.

The JaasSecurityDomain MBean

The org.jboss.security.plugins.JaasSecurityDomain is an extension of JaasSecurityManager that adds the notion of a KeyStore, a JSSEKeyManagerFactory and a TrustManager Factory for supporting SSL and other cryptographic use cases.

The additional configurable attributes of the JaasSecurity Domain include:

- *KeyStoreType*: The type of the KeyStore implementation. This is the type argument passed to thejava. security.KeyStore.getInstance(String type) factory method. The default is JKS.
- *KeyStoreURL*: A URL to the location of the KeyStore database. This is used to obtain an InputStream to initialize the KeyStore. If the string is not a value URL, it is treated as a file.
- *KeyStorePass*: The password associated with the KeyStore database contents. The KeyStorePass is also used in combination with theSalt and IterationCount attributes to create a PBE secret key used with the encode/decode operations. The KeyStore Pass attribute value format is one of the following:
  - The plaintext password for the KeyStore The toCharArray() value of the string is used without any manipulation.
  - A command to execute to obtain the plaintext password. The format is {EXT}... where the... is the exact command line that will be passed to the Runtime.exec(String) method to execute a platform-specific command. The first line of the command output is used as the password.
  - A class to create to obtain the plaintext password. The format is {CLASS}classname[:ctorarg] where

the [:ctorarg] is an optional string that will be passed to the constructor when instantiating the classname. The password is obtained from classname by invoking a toCharArray() method if found, otherwise, the toString() method is used.

- *Salt*: The PBEParameterSpec salt value.
- *IterationCount*: The PBEParameterSpec iteration count value.
- *TrustStoreType*: The type of the TrustStore implementation. This is the type argument passed to thejava.security.KeyStore.getInstance(String type) factory method. The default is JKS.
- *TrustStoreURL*: A URL to the location of the TrustStore database. This is used to obtain an InputStream to initialize the KeyStore. If the string is not a value URL, it is treated as a file.
- *TrustStorePass*: The password associated with the trust store database contents. The TrustStorePass is a simple password and doesn't have the same configuration options as the KeyStorePass.
- *ManagerServiceName*: Sets the JMX object name string of the security manager service MBean. This is used to register the defaults to register the JaasSecurityDomain as a the security manager under java:/jaas/<domain> where <domain> is the name passed to the MBean constructor. The name defaults to jboss.security:service=JaasSecurityManager.

8.4.4. An XML JAAS Login Configuration MBean

The XMLLoginConfig is a service that loads standard JAAS application configurations from a local configuration file. The MBean supports the following attributes:

- *ConfigURL*: specifies the URL of the XML login configuration file that should be loaded by this MBean on startup. This must be a valid URL string representation.
- *ConfigResource*: specifies the resource name of the XML login configuration file that should be loaded

by this MBean on startup. The name is treated as a classpath resource for which a URL is located using the thread context class loader.

- *ValidateDTD*: a flag indicating if the XML configuration should be validated against its DTD. This defaults to true.

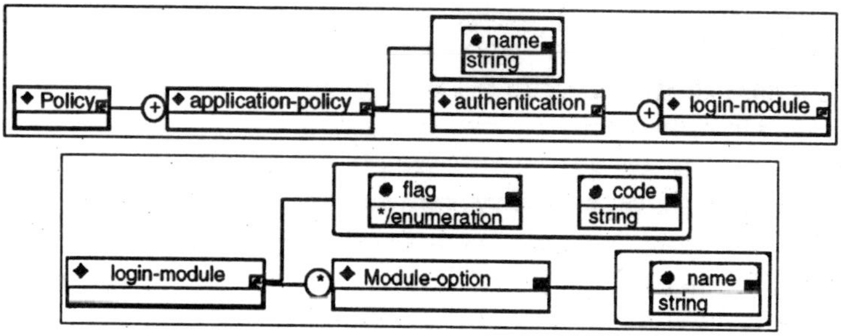

Fig. The XMLLoginConfig DTD

The name attribute of the application-policy is the login configuration name. This corresponds to the portion of the jboss.xml and jboss-web.xmlsecurity-domain element value after the java:/jaas/ prefix. The code attribute of the login-module element specifies the class name of the login module implementation. The flag attribute controls the overall behaviour of the authentication stack.

The allowed values and meanings are:

- *Required*: The LoginModule is required to succeed. If it succeeds or fails, authentication still continues to proceed down the LoginModulelist.
- *Requisite*: the LoginModule is required to succeed. If it succeeds, authentication continues down the LoginModule list. If it fails, control immediately returns to the application (authentication does not proceed down the LoginModule list).
- *Sufficient*: The LoginModule is not required to succeed. If it does succeed, control immediately returns to the application (authentication does not proceed down the LoginModule list). If it fails, authentication continues down the LoginModule list.
- *Optional*: The LoginModule is not required to

succeed. If it succeeds or fails, authentication still continues to proceed down theLoginModule list.

Zero or more module-option elements may be specified as child elements of a login-module. These define name/value string pairs that are made available to the login module during initialization.

```
<policy>
  <application-policy name="srp-test">
    <authentication>
 <login-module

code="org.jboss.security.srp.jaas.SRPCacheLoginModule"
              flag="required">
        <module-option name="cacheJndiName">srp-
test/AuthenticationCache</module-option>
       </login-module>

<login-modulecode="org.jboss.security.auth.spi.
UsersRolesLoginModule"
                flag="required">
             <module-option name="password-
stacking">useFirstPass</module-option>
       </login-module>
     </authentication>
  </application-policy>
</policy>
```

The MBean also supports the following operations that allow one to dynamically extend the login configurations at runtime. Note that any operation that attempts to alter login configuration requires a javax.security.auth.Auth Permission("refreshLoginConfiguration") when running with a security manager. The org.jboss.chap8. service.Security Config service demonstrates how this can be used to add/ remove a deployment specific security config-uration dynamically.

- *Void add AppConfig (String appName, App Configuration Entry[] entries)*: this adds the given login module configuration stack to the current configuration under the given appName. This replaces any existing entry under that name.

- *Void removeAppConfig(String appName)*: this removes the login module configuration registered under the given appName.
- *String[] loadConfig(URL configURL) throws Exception*: this loads one or more login configurations from a URL representing either an XML or legacy Sun login configuration file. Note that all login configurations must be added or none will be added. It returns the names of the login configurations that were added.
- *Void removeConfigs(String[] appNames)*: this removes the login configurations specified appNames array.
- *String displayAppConfig(String appName)*: this operation displays a simple string format of the named configuration if it exists.

JAAS LOGIN CONFIGURATION MANAGEMENT MBEAN

The installation of the custom javax. security. auth. login. Configuration is managed by the org.jboss.The MBean also supports the following operations security.plugins. SecurityConfig MBean.

There is one configurable attribute:

- *LoginConfig*: Specifies the JMX ObjectName string of the that provides the default JAAS login configuration. When the Security Configis started, this mean is queried for its javax.security.auth. login.Configuration by calling its getConfiguration (Configuration currentConfig) operation. If the LoginConfig attribute is not specified then the default Sun Configuration implementation described in the Configurationclass JavaDocs is used.

In addition to allowing for a custom JAAS login configuration implementation, this service allows configurations to be chained together in a stack at runtime. This allows one to push a login configuration onto the stack and latter pop it. This is a feature used by the security unit tests to install custom login configurations into a default JBoss installation. Pushing a new configuration is done using:

```
public void pushLoginConfig(String objectName) throws
JMException, MalformedObjectNameException;
```

The objectName parameters specifies an MBean similar to the LoginConfig attribute. The current login configuration may be removed using:

```
public void popLoginConfig() throws JMException;
```

SING AND WRITING JBOSSSX LOGIN MODULES

The JaasSecurityManager implementation allows complete customization of the authentication mechanism using JAAS login module configurations. By defining the login module configuration entry that corresponds to the security domain name you have used to secure access to your J2EE components, you define the authentication mechanism and integration implementation.

The JBossSX framework includes a number of bundled login modules suitable for integration with standard security infrastructure store protocols such as LDAP and JDBC. These implementations allow for easy integration of your own authentication protocol, if none of the bundled login modules prove suitable.

In this section we will first describe the useful bundled login modules and their configuration, and then end with a discussion of how to create your own custom Log in Module implementations for use with JBoss.

org.jboss.security.auth.spi.IdentityLoginModule

The IdentityLoginModule is a simple login module that associates the principal specified in the module options with any subject authenticated against the module. It creates a SimplePrincipal instance using the name specified by the principal option.

Although this is certainly not an appropriate login module for production strength authentication, it can be of use in development environments when you want to test the security associated with a given principal and associated roles.

The supported login module configuration options include:

- *Principal:* The name to use for the SimplePrincipal all users are authenticated as. The principal name defaults to guest if no principal option is specified.
- *Roles:* The names of the roles that will be assigned to the user principal. The value is a comma-delimited list of role names.
- *Password-stacking:* When password-stacking option is set to useFirstPass, this module first looks for a shared username under the property name javax.security.auth.login.name in the login module shared state map. If found this is used as the principal name. If not found the principal name set by this login module is stored under the property name javax.security.auth.login.name.

A sample XMLLoginConfig configuration entry that would authenticate all users as the principal named jduke and assign role names ofTheDuke, and AnimatedCharacter is:

The corresponding format is:

```
<policy>
 <application-policy name="testIdentity">
  <authentication>
   <login-module code="org.jboss.security.auth.
   spi.IdentityLogin Module"
     flag="required">
  <module-option name="principal">jduke</module-
  option>
  <module-option name="roles">TheDuke,Animated
 Charater</module-option>
    </login-module>
  </authentication>
 </application-policy>
</policy>
```

org.jboss.security.auth.spi.UsersRolesLoginModule

The UsersRolesLoginModule is a simple login module that supports multiple users and user roles loaded from Java properties files. The username-to-password mapping file is called users.properties and the username-to-roles mapping file is called roles.properties. The properties files are loaded during initialization using the initialize method thread context class loader. This means that these files can be placed into the J2EE deployment JAR, the JBoss configuration directory, or any directory on the JBoss server or system classpath. The primary purpose of this login module is to easily test the security settings of multiple users and roles using properties files deployed with the application.

The users.properties file uses a username=password format with each user entry on a separate line as show here:

```
username1=password1
username2=password2
...
```

The roles.properties file uses as username=role1,role2... format with an optional group name value.

For example:

```
username1=role1,role2...
username1.RoleGroup1=role3,role4...
username2=role1,role3...
```

The username.XXX form of property name is used to assign the username roles to a particular named group of roles where the XXX portion of the property name is the group name. The username=... form is an abbreviation for username.Roles=..., where the Roles group name is the standard name the JaasSecurityManager expects to contain the roles which define the users permissions.

The following would be equivalent definitions for the jduke username:

```
jduke=TheDuke,AnimatedCharacter
jduke.Roles=TheDuke,AnimatedCharacter
```

The supported login module configuration options include the following:

- *UnauthenticatedIdentity*: Defines the principal name that should be assigned to requests that contain no authentication information. This can be used to allow unprotected servlets to invoke methods on EJBs that do not require a specific role. Such a principal has no associated roles and so can only access either unsecured EJBs or EJB methods that are associated with the unchecked permission constraint.

- *Password-stacking*: When password-stacking option is set to useFirstPass, this module first looks for a shared username and password under the property names javax.security.auth.login.name and javax.security.auth.login.password respectively in the login module shared state map. If found these are used as the principal name and password. If not found the principal name and password are set by this login module and stored under the property names javax.security.auth.login.name and javax.security.auth.login.passwordrespectively.
- *HashAlgorithm*: The name of the java.security.MessageDigest algorithm to use to hash the password. There is no default so this option must be specified to enable hashing. When hashAlgorithm is specified, the clear text password obtained from the callbackhandler is hashed before it is passed to Username PasswordLoginModule.validatePassword as the input Password argument. The expected Passwordas stored in the users.properties file must be comparably hashed.
- *HashEncoding*: The string format for the hashed pass and must be either base64 or hex. Base64 is the default.
- *HashCharset*: The encoding used to convert the clear text password to a byte array. The platform default encoding is the default.
- *UsersProperties*: The name of the properties resource containing the username to password mappings. This defaults tousers.properties.
- *RolesProperties*: The name of the properties resource containing the username to roles mappings. This defaults to roles.properties.

A sample legacy XMLLoginConfig configuration entry that assigns unauthenticated users the principal name nobody and contains based64 encoded, MD5 hashes of the passwords in a usersb64.properties file is:

```
<policy>
  <application-policy name="testUsersRoles">
    <authentication>
  <login-module
        code="org.jboss.security.auth.spi.Users
            RolesLoginModule"
              flag="required">
                                    <module-option
name="usersProperties">usersb64.properties</
module-option>
      <module-option name="hashAlgorithm">MD5</
module-option>
                                    <module-option
name="hashEncoding">base64</module-option>
                                    <module-option
name="unauthenticatedIdentity">nobody</module-
option>
      </login-module>
    </authentication>
  </application-policy>
</policy>
```

org.jboss.security.auth.spi.LdapLoginModule

The LdapLoginModule is a LoginModule implementation that authenticates against an LDAP server using JNDI login using the login module configuration options. You would use the LdapLoginModule if your username and credential information are store in an LDAP server that is accessible using a JNDI LDAP provider. The LDAP connectivity information is provided as configuration options that are passed through to the environment object used to create JNDI initial context.

The standard LDAP JNDI properties used include the following:

- *Java.naming.factory.initial*: The classname of the InitialContextFactory implementation. This defaults to the Sun LDAP provider implementation com.sun.jndi.ldap.LdapCtxFactory.
- *Java.naming.provider.url*: The LDAP URL for the LDAP server

- *Java.naming.security.authentication*: The security level to use. This defaults to simple.
- Java.naming.security.protocol: The transport protocol to use for secure access, such as, ssl.
- *Java.naming.security.principal*: The principal for authenticating the caller to the service. This is built from other properties as described below.
- *Java.naming.security.credentials*: The value of the property depends on the authentication scheme. For example, it could be a hashed password, clear-text password, key, certificate, and so on.

The supported login module configuration options include the following:

- *PrincipalDNPrefix*: A prefix to add to the username to form the user distinguished name. See principal DNSuffix for more info.
- *PrincipalDNSuffix*: A suffix to add to the username when forming the user distinguished name. This is useful if you prompt a user for a username and you don't want the user to have to enter the fully distinguished name. Using this property and principalDNSuffix the userDNwill be formed as principalDNPrefix + username + principalDNSuffix
- *UseObjectCredential*: A true/false value that indicates that the credential should be obtained as an opaque Object using theorg.jboss.security.auth.callback. ObjectCallback type of Callback rather than as a char[] password using a JAAS PasswordCallback. This allows for passing non-char[] credential information to the LDAP server.
- *RolesCtxDN*: The fixed distinguished name to the context to search for user roles.
- *UserRolesCtxDNAttributeName*: The name of an attribute in the user object that contains the distinguished name to the context to search for user roles. This differs from rolesCtxDN in that the context to search for a user's roles can be unique for each user.

- *RoleAttributeID*: The name of the attribute that contains the user roles. If not specified this defaults to roles.
- *RoleAttributeIsDN*: A flag indicating whether the roleAttributeID contains the fully distinguished name of a role object, or the role name. If false, the role name is taken from the value of roleAttributeID. If true, the role attribute represents the distinguished name of a role object. The role name is taken from the value of the roleNameAttributeId attribute of the context name by the distinguished name. In certain directory schemas (*e.g.*, MS ActiveDirectory), role attributes in the user object are stored as DNs to role objects instead of as simple names, in which case, this property should be set to true. The default is false.
- *RoleNameAttributeID*: The name of the attribute of the in the context pointed to by the roleCtxDN distinguished name value which contains the role name. If the roleAttributeIsDN property is set to true, this property is used to find the role object's name attribute. The default is group.
- *UidAttributeID*: The name of the attribute in the object containing the user roles that corresponds to the userid. This is used to locate the user roles. If not specified this defaults to uid.
- *MatchOnUserDN*: A true/false flag indicating if the search for user roles should match on the user's fully distinguished name. If false, just the username is used as the match value against the uidAttributeName attribute. If true, the full userDN is used as the match value.
- *UnauthenticatedIdentity*: The principal name that should be assigned to requests that contain no authentication information. This behaviour is inherited from the Username Password Login Module superclass.
- *Password-stacking*: When the password-stacking option is set to useFirstPass, this module first looks

for a shared username and password under the property names javax.security.auth.login.name and javax.security.auth.login.password respectively in the login module shared state map. If found these are used as the principal name and password. If not found the principal name and password are set by this login module and stored under the property names javax.security.auth.login.name and javax. security.auth.login.passwordrespectively.

- *AllowEmptyPasswords*: A flag indicating if empty (length 0) passwords should be passed to the LDAP server. An empty password is treated as an anonymous login by some LDAP servers and this may not be a desirable feature. Set this to false to reject empty passwords or true to have the LDAP server validate the empty password. The default is true.

The authentication of a user is performed by connecting to the LDAP server based on the login module configuration options. Connecting to the LDAP server is done by creating an InitialLdapContext with an environment composed of the LDAP JNDI properties described previously in this section. The Context.SECURITY_PRINCIPAL is set to the distinguished name of the user as obtained by the callback handler in combination with the principalDNPrefix and principalDNSuffix option values, and the Context. SECURITY_CREDENTIALS property is either set to theString password or the Object credential depending on the useObjectCredential option.

Once authentication has succeeded by virtue of being able to create an InitialLdapContext instance, the user's roles are queried by performing a search on the rolesCtxDN location with search attributes set to the roleAttributeName and uidAttributeName option values. The roles names are obtaining by invoking the toString method on the role attributes in the search result set.

The following is a sample login-config.xml entry.

```
<policy>
  <application-policy name="testLDAP">
```

```
    <authentication>
                                    <login-module
code="org.jboss.security.auth.spi.LdapLoginModule"
              flag="required">
                                    <module-option
name="java.naming.factory.initial">
           com.sun.jndi.ldap.LdapCtxFactory
           </module-option>
                                    <module-option
name="java.naming.provider.url">
       ldap://ldaphost.jboss.org:1389/
         </module-option>
                                    <module-option
name="java.naming.security.authentication">
           simple
         </module-option>
                                    <module-option
name="principalDNPrefix">uid=</module-option>
       <module-option name="principalDNSuffix">
          ,ou=People,dc=jboss,dc=org
         </module-option>

      <module-option name="rolesCtxDN">
          ou=Roles,dc=jboss,dc=org
         </module-option>
   <module-option name="uidAttributeID">member</
module-option>
     <module-option name="matchOnUserDN">true</
module-option>

   <module-option name="roleAttributeID">cn</
module-option>
   <module-option name="roleAttributeIsDN">false
</module-option>
      </login-module>
    </authentication>
  </application-policy>
</policy>
```

An LDIF file representing the structure of the directory this data operates against is shown below:

```
dn: dc=jboss,dc=org
objectclass: top
objectclass: dcObject
objectclass: organization
dc: jboss
o: JBoss

dn: ou=People,dc=jboss,dc=org
objectclass: top
objectclass: organizationalUnit
ou: People

dn: uid=jduke,ou=People,dc=jboss,dc=org
objectclass: top
objectclass: uidObject
objectclass: person
uid: jduke
cn: Java Duke
sn: Duke
userPassword: theduke

dn: ou=Roles,dc=jboss,dc=org
objectclass: top
objectclass: organizationalUnit
ou: Roles

dn: cn=JBossAdmin,ou=Roles,dc=jboss,dc=org
objectclass: top
objectclass: groupOfNames
cn: JBossAdmin
member: uid=jduke,ou=People,dc=jboss,dc=org
description: the JBossAdmin group
```

Looking back at the testLDAP login module configuration, the java.naming.factory.initial, java.naming.factory.url and java.naming.security options indicate the Sun LDAP JNDI provider implementation will be used, the LDAP server is located on host ldaphost.jboss.org on port 1389, and that the LDAP simple authentication method will be use to connect to the LDAP server.

The login module attempts to connect to the LDAP server using a DN representing the user it is trying to authenticate. This DN is constructed from the principalDNPrefix, passed in, the username of the user and the principalDNSuffix as described above. In this example, the username jduke would map to uid=jduke,ou=People,dc=jboss,dc=org. We've assumed the LDAP server authenticates users using theuserPassword attribute of the user's entry (theduke in this example). This is the way most LDAP servers work, however, if your LDAP server handles authentication differently you will need to set the authentication credentials in a way that makes sense for your server.

Once authentication succeeds, the roles on which authorization will be based are retrieved by performing a subtree search of the rolesCtxDNfor entries whose uidAttributeID match the user. If matchOnUserDN is true the search will be based on the full DN of the user. Otherwise the search will be based on the actual user name entered. In this example, the search is under ou=Roles,dc=jboss,dc=org for any entries that have a member attribute equal to uid=jduke, ou=People,dc=jboss,dc=org. The search would locate cn=JBossAdmin under the roles entry.

The search returns the attribute specified in the roleAttributeID option. In this example, the attribute is cn. The value returned would beJBossAdmin, so the jduke user is assigned to the JBossAdmin role.

It's often the case that a local LDAP server provides identity and authentication services but is unable to use the authorization services. This is because application roles don't always map well onto LDAP groups, and LDAP administrators are often hesitant to allow external application-specific data in central LDAP servers. For this reason, the LDAP authentication module is often paired with another login module, such as the database login module, that can provide roles more suitable to the application being developed.

org.jboss.security.auth.spi.DatabaseServerLoginModule

The DatabaseServerLoginModule is a JDBC based login module that supports authentication and role mapping. You would use this login module if you have your username, password and role information relational database. The DatabaseServerLoginModule is based on two logical tables:

```
Table Principals(PrincipalID text, Password text)
Table Roles(PrincipalID text, Role text, RoleGroup
text)
```

The Principals table associates the user PrincipalID with the valid password and the Roles table associates the user PrincipalID with its role sets. The roles used for user permissions must be contained in rows with a RoleGroup column value of Roles. The tables are logical in that you can specify the SQL query that the login module uses. All that is required is that the java.sql.ResultSet has the same logical structure as the Principals and Roles tables described previously. The actual names of the tables and columns are not relevant as the results are accessed based on the column index. To clarify this notion, consider a database with two tables, Principals and Roles, as already declared. The following statements build the tables to contain a PrincipalID java with a Password of echoman in the Principals table, a PrincipalID java with a role named Echo in the Roles RoleGroup in the Roles table, and a PrincipalID java with a role named caller_java in the CallerPrincipal RoleGroup in the Roles table:

```
INSERT INTO Principals VALUES('java', 'echoman')
INSERT INTO Roles VALUES('java', 'Echo', 'Roles')
INSERT INTO Roles VALUES('java', 'caller_java',
'CallerPrincipal')
```

The supported login module configuration options include the following:

- *DsJndiName*: The JNDI name for the DataSource of the database containing the logical Principals and Roles tables. If not specified this defaults to java:/DefaultDS.
- *PrincipalsQuery*: The prepared statement query equivalent to: select Password from Principals where

PrincipalID=?. If not specified this is the exact prepared statement that will be used.

- *RolesQuery*: The prepared statement query equivalent to: select Role, RoleGroup from Roles where PrincipalID=?. If not specified this is the exact prepared statement that will be used.
- *UnauthenticatedIdentity*: The principal name that should be assigned to requests that contain no authentication information.
- *Password-stacking*: When password-stacking option is set to useFirstPass, this module first looks for a shared username and password under the property names javax.security.auth.login.name and javax. security.auth.login.password respectively in the login module shared state map. If found these are used as the principal name and password. If not found the principal name and password are set by this login module and stored under the property names javax.security.auth.login.name and javax.security. auth.login.passwordrespectively.
- *HashAlgorithm*: The name of the java.security. MessageDigest algorithm to use to hash the password. There is no default so this option must be specified to enable hashing. When hashAlgorithm is specified, the clear text password obtained from the callbackhandler is hashed before it is passed to UsernamePasswordLoginModule.validatePassword as the inputPassword argument. The expected Passwordas obtained from the database must be comparably hashed.
- *HashEncoding*: The string format for the hashed pass and must be either base64 or hex. Base64 is the default.
- *HashCharset*: The encoding used to convert the clear text password to a byte array. The platform default encoding is the default
- IgnorePasswordCase: A boolean flag indicating if the password comparison should ignore case. This can

be useful for hashed password encoding where the case of the hashed password is not significant.

- PrincipalClass: An option that specifies a Principal implementation class. This must support a constructor taking a string argument for the principal name.

As an example DatabaseServerLoginModule configuration, consider a custom table schema like the following:

```
CREATE TABLE Users(username VARCHAR(64) PRIMARY
KEY, passwd VARCHAR(64))
CREATE TABLE UserRoles(username VARCHAR(64),
userRoles VARCHAR(32))
```

A corresponding login-config.xml entry would be:

```
<policy>
  <application-policy name="testDB">
    <authentication>
<login-module
code="org.jboss.security.auth.spi.DatabaseServerLoginModule"
  flag="required">
   <module-option name="dsJndiName">java:/
MyDatabaseDS</module-option>
  <module-option name="principalsQuery">
       select passwd from Users username where
username=?</module-option>
   <module-option name="rolesQuery">
       select userRoles, 'Roles' from UserRoles
where username=?</module-option>
      </login-module>
    </authentication>
  </application-policy>
</policy>
```

BaseCertLoginModule

This is a login module which authenticates users based on X509 certificates. A typical use case for this login module is CLIENT-CERTauthentication in the web tier. This login module only performs authentication. You need to combine it with another login module capable of acquiring the authorization roles to completely define access to a secured web or EJB component. Two subclasses of this login module,CertRolesLoginModule and Database CertLogin Module extend the behaviour to obtain the authorization roles from either a properties file or database.

The BaseCertLoginModule needs a KeyStore to perform user validation. This is obtained through a org.jboss.security. SecurityDomainimplementation. Typically, the Security Domain implementation is configured using the org.jboss. security.plugins.JaasSecurityDomain MBean as shown in this jboss-service.xml configuration fragment:

```
<mbean code="org.jboss. security.
plugins.JaasSecurityDomain"
     name="jboss.web:service=SecurityDomain">
   <constructor>
       <arg  type="java.lang.String"  value="jmx-
console"/>
   </constructor>
<attribute
name="KeyStoreURL">resource:localhost.keystore</
attribute>
    <attribute  name="KeyStorePass">unit-tests-
server</attribute>
</mbean>
```

This creates a security domain with the name jmx-console whose SecurityDomain implementation is available via JNDI under the namejava:/jaas/jmx-console following the JBossSX security domain naming pattern. To secure a web application such as the jmx-console.war using client certs and role based authorization, one would first modify the web.xml to declare the resources to be secured, along with the allowed roles and security domain to be used for authentication and authorization.

```
<?xml version="1.0"?>
<!DOCTYPE web-app PUBLIC
          "-//Sun Microsystems, Inc.//DTD Web
Application 2.3//EN"
             "http://java.sun.com/dtd/web-
app_2_3.dtd">
```

```
<web-app>
  ...
   <security-constraint>
     <web-resource-collection>
          <web-resource-name>HtmlAdaptor</web-
resource-name>
        <description>An example security config
that only allows users with
    the role JBossAdmin to access the HTML JMX
console web
    application </description>
      <url-pattern>/*</url-pattern>
      <http-method>GET</http-method>
       <http-method>POST</http-method>
     </web-resource-collection>
     <auth-constraint>
       <role-name>JBossAdmin</role-name>
     </auth-constraint>
   </security-constraint>
   <login-config>
     <auth-method>CLIENT-CERT</auth-method>
     <realm-name>JBoss JMX Console</realm-name>
   </login-config>
   <security-role>
     <role-name>JBossAdmin</role-name>
   </security-role>
</web-app>
```

Next we, need to specify the JBoss security domain in jboss-web.xml:

```
<application-policy name="jmx-console">
  <authentication>
<login-module code="org.jboss.security.
auth.spi.BaseCertLoginModule"
       flag="required">
          <module-option name="password-
stacking">useFirstPass</module-option>
    <module-option name="securityDomain">java:/
jaas/jmx-console</module-option>
```

```
    </login-module>
<login-module
code="org.jboss.security.auth.spi.UsersRolesLoginModule"
        flag="required">
          <module-option name="password-
stacking">useFirstPass</module-option>
    <module-option
name="usersProperties">jmx-console
users.properties</module-option>
       <module-option
name="rolesProperties">jmx-console
roles.properties</module-option>
     </login-module>
  </authentication>
</application-policy>
```

Here the BaseCertLoginModule is used for authentication of the client cert, and the UsersRolesLoginModule is only used for authorization due to the password-stacking=useFirstPass option. Both the localhost.keystore and the jmx-console-roles.properties need an entry that maps to the principal associated with the client cert. By default, the principal is created using the client certificate distinguished name.

Consider the following certificate:

```
[starksm@banshee9100 conf]$ keytool -printcert -
file unit-tests-client.export
Owner: CN=unit-tests-client, OU=JBoss Inc.,
O=JBoss Inc., ST=Washington, C=US
Issuer: CN=jboss.com, C=US, ST=Washington,
L=Snoqualmie Pass, E-MAILADDRESS=admin
@jboss.com, OU=QA, O=JBoss Inc.
Serial number: 100103
Valid from: Wed May 26 07:34:34 PDT 2004 until:
Thu May 26 07:34:34 PDT 2005
Certificate fingerprints:
MD5:
4A:9C:2B:CD:1B:50:AA:85:DD:89:F6:1D:F5:AF:9E:AB
SHA1:
DE:DE:86:59:05:6C:00:E8:CC:C0:16:D3:C2:68:BF:95:B8:83:E9:58
```

The localhost.keystore would need this cert stored with an alias of CN=unit-tests-client, OU=JBoss Inc., O=JBoss Inc., ST=Washington, C=US and the jmx-console-roles.properties would also need an entry for the same entry. Since the DN contains many characters that are normally treated as delimiters, you will need to escape the problem characters using a backslash ('\') as shown here:

```
# A sample roles.properties file for use with
the UsersRolesLoginModule
CN\=unit-tests-client,\ OU\=JBoss\ Inc.,\
O\=JBoss\ Inc.,\ ST\=Washington,\ C\=US=JBossAdmin
admin=JBossAdmin
```

org.jboss.security.auth.spi.RunAsLoginModule

JBoss has a helper login module called RunAsLogin Module that pushes a run as role for the duration of the login phase of authentication, and pops the run as role in either the commit or abort phase. The purpose of this login module is to provide a role for other login modules that need to access secured resources in order to perform their authentication. An example would be a login module that accesses an secured EJB. This login module must be configured ahead of the login module(s) that need a run as role established.

The only login module configuration option is:

- *RoleName*: the name of the role to use as the run as role during login phase. If not specified a default of nobody is used.

org.jboss.security.ClientLoginModule

The ClientLoginModule is an implementation of LoginModule for use by JBoss clients for the establishment of the caller identity and credentials. This simply sets the org.jboss.security.SecurityAssociation.principal to the value of the NameCallback filled in by the callbackhandler, and theorg.jboss.security.SecurityAssociation.credential to the value of the PasswordCallback filled in by the callbackhandler. This is the only supported mechanism for a client to establish the current thread's caller. Both stand-alone client applications and server environments, acting as JBoss EJB clients where the security environment has not been configured to use JBossSX transparently, need to use the ClientLoginModule. Of course, you could always set the org.jboss.security.SecurityAssociation information directly, but this is considered an internal API that is subject to change without notice.

Note that this login module does not perform any authentication. It merely copies the login information provided to it into the JBoss server EJB invocation layer for subsequent authentication on the server. If you need to perform client-side authentication of users you would need to configure another login module in addition to the ClientLoginModule.

The supported login module configuration options include the following:

- *Multi-threaded*: When the multi-threaded option is set to true, each login thread has its own principal and credential storage. This is useful in client environments where multiple user identities are active in separate threads. When true, each separate thread must perform its own login. When set to false the login identity and credentials are global variables that apply to all threads in the VM. The default for this option is false.
- *Password-stacking*: When password-stacking option is set to useFirstPass, this module first looks for a shared username and password using javax.security. auth.login.name and javax.security. auth.login. password respectively in the login module shared state map. This allows a module configured prior to this one to establish a valid username and password that should be passed to JBoss. You would use this option if you want to perform client-side authentication of clients using some other login module such as theLdapLogin Module.
- *Restore-login-identity*: When restore-login-identity is true, the SecurityAssociation principal and credential seen on entry to the login()method are saved and restored on either abort or logout. When false (the

default), the abort and logout simply clear the SecurityAssociation. A restore-login-identity of true is needed if one need to change identities and then restore the original caller identity.

A sample login configuration for ClientLoginModule is the default configuration entry found in the JBoss distribution client/auth.conf file.

The configuration is:

```
other {
// Put your login modules that work without
jBoss here

// jBoss LoginModule
  org.jboss.security.ClientLoginModule required;

// Put your login modules that need jBoss here
};
```

WRITING CUSTOM LOGIN MODULES

If the login modules bundled with the JBossSX framework do not work with your security environment, you can write your own custom login module implementation that does.

Recall from the section on the JaasSecurityManager architecture that the JaasSecurityManager expected a particular usage pattern of theSubject principals set. You need to understand the JAAS Subject class's information storage features and the expected usage of these features to be able to write a login module that works with the JaasSecurityManager. This section examines this requirement and introduces two abstract base LoginModule implementations that can help you implement your own custom login modules.

You can obtain security information associated with a Subject in six ways in JBoss using the following methods:

```
java.util.Set getPrincipals()
java.util.Set getPrincipals(java.lang.Class c)
java.util.Set getPrivateCredentials()
java.util.Set
getPrivateCredentials(java.lang.Class c)
```

```
java.util.Set getPublicCredentials()
java.util.Set getPublicCredentials(java.lang.Class
c)
```

For Subject identities and roles, JBossSX has selected the most natural choice: the principals sets obtained via getPrincipals() andgetPrincipals(java.lang.Class). The usage pattern is as follows:

- User identities (username, social security number, employee ID, and so on) are stored as java.security. Principal objects in the SubjectPrincipals set. The Principal implementation that represents the user identity must base comparisons and equality on the name of the principal. A suitable implementation is available as the org.jboss.security.SimplePrincipal class. Other Principal instances may be added to the Subject Principals set as needed.
- The assigned user roles are also stored in the Principals set, but they are grouped in named role sets using java.security.acl.Groupinstances. The Group interface defines a collection of Principals and/ or Groups, and is a subinterface of java.security. Principal. Any number of role sets can be assigned to a Subject. Currently, the JBossSX framework uses two well-known role sets with the namesRoles and CallerPrincipal. The Roles Group is the collection of Principals for the named roles as known in the application domain under which the Subject has been authenticated. This role set is used by methods like the EJBContext.isCallerInRole(String), which EJBs can use to see if the current caller belongs to the named application domain role. The security interceptor logic that performs method permission checks also uses this role set. The CallerPrincipal Group consists of the single Principal identity assigned to the user in the application domain. The EJBContext. getCallerPrincipal() method uses the CallerPrincipal to allow the application domain to map from the operation environment identity to a user identity

suitable for the application. If a Subject does not have a CallerPrincipal Group, the application identity is the same as operational environment identity.

Support for the Subject Usage Pattern

To simplify correct implementation of the Subject usage patterns described in the preceding section, JBossSX includes two abstract login modules that handle the population of the authenticated Subject with a template pattern that enforces correct Subject usage. The most generic of the two is the org.jboss.security.auth.spi.AbstractServerLoginModule class. It provides a concrete implementation of thejavax. security.auth.spi.LoginModule interface and offers abstract methods for the key tasks specific to an operation environment security infrastructure. The key details of the class are highlighted in the following class fragment. The JavaDoc comments detail the responsibilities of subclasses.

```
package org.jboss.security.auth.spi;
/**
* This class implements the common functionality
required for a JAAS
* server-side LoginModule and implements the
JBossSX standard
* Subject usage pattern of storing identities
and roles. Subclass
* this module to create your own custom LoginModule
and override the
* login(), getRoleSets(), and getIdentity()
methods.
*/
public abstract class AbstractServerLoginModule
implements javax.security.auth.spi.LoginModule
{
protected Subject subject;
protected CallbackHandler callbackHandler;
protected Map sharedState;
protected Map options;
protected Logger log;
```

```
/** Flag indicating if the shared credential should
be used */
protected boolean useFirstPass;
/**
* Flag indicating if the login phase succeeded.
Subclasses that
* override the login method must set this to
true on successful
* completion of login
*/
protected boolean loginOk;

//...
/**
* Initialize the login module. This stores the
subject,
* callbackHandler and sharedState and options for
the login
* session. Subclasses should override if they
need to process
* their own options. A call to
super.initialize(...) must be
* made in the case of an override.
*
* <p>
* The options are checked for the <em>password-
stacking</em> parameter.
* If this is set to "useFirstPass", the login
identity will be taken from the
* <code>javax.security.auth.login.name</code>
value of the sharedState map,
* and the proof of identity from the
* <code>javax.security.auth.login.password</code>
value of the sharedState map.
*
* @param subject the Subject to update after a
successful login.
* @param callbackHandler the CallbackHandler that
```

```
will be used to obtain the
* the user identity and credentials.
* @param sharedState a Map shared between all
configured login module instances
* @param options the parameters passed to the
login module.
*/
public void initialize(Subject subject,
 CallbackHandler callbackHandler,
 Map sharedState,
 Map options)
{
//...
}

/**
* Looks for javax.security.auth.login.name and
* javax.security.auth.login.password values in the
sharedState
* map if the useFirstPass option was true and
returns true if
* they exist. If they do not or are null this
method returns
* false.
* Note that subclasses that override the login
method
* must set the loginOk ivar to true if the login
succeeds in
* order for the commit phase to populate the
Subject. This
* implementation sets loginOk to true if the
login() method
* returns true, otherwise, it sets loginOk to
false.
*/
public boolean login()
throws LoginException
{
```

```
//...
}

/**
* Overridden by subclasses to return the Principal
that
* corresponds to the user primary identity.
*/
abstract protected Principal getIdentity();

/**
* Overridden by subclasses to return the Groups
that correspond
* to the role sets assigned to the user. Subclasses
should
* create at least a Group named "Roles" that
contains the roles
* assigned to the user. A second common group is
* "CallerPrincipal," which provides the
application identity of
* the user rather than the security domain
identity.
*
* @return Group[] containing the sets of roles
*/
abstract protected Group[] getRoleSets() throws
LoginException;
}
```

You'll need to pay attention to the loginOk instance variable. This must be set to true if the login succeeds, false otherwise by any subclasses that override the login method. Failure to set this variable correctly will result in the commit method either not updating the subject when it should, or updating the subject when it should not. Tracking the outcome of the login phase was added to allow login modules to be chained together with control flags that do not require that the login module succeed in order for the overall login to succeed.

The second abstract base login module suitable for custom login modules is the org.jboss.security. auth.spi. Username PasswordLoginModule. This login module further simplifies custom login module implementation by enforcing a string-based username as the user identity and achar[] password as the authentication credentials. It also supports the mapping of anonymous users (indicated by a null username and password) to a principal with no roles. The key details of the class are highlighted in the following class fragment. The JavaDoc comments detail the responsibilities of subclasses.

```
package org.jboss.security.auth.spi;
/**
* An abstract subclass of
AbstractServerLoginModule that imposes a
* an identity == String username, credentials ==
String password
* view on the login process. Subclasses override
the
* getUsersPassword() and getUsersRoles() methods
to return the
* expected password and roles for the user.
*/
public abstract class UsernamePasswordLoginModule
extends AbstractServerLoginModule
{
/** The login identity */
private Principal identity;
/** The proof of login identity */
private char[] credential;
/** The principal to use when a null username
and password are seen */
private Principal unauthenticatedIdentity;
/**
* The message digest algorithm used to hash
passwords. If null then
* plain passwords will be used. */
private String hashAlgorithm = null;
/**
```

```
* The name of the charset/encoding to use when
converting the
* password String to a byte array. Default is
the platform's
* default encoding.
*/
private String hashCharset = null;
/** The string encoding format to use. Defaults
to base64. */
private String hashEncoding = null;

//...

/**
* Override the superclass method to look for an
* unauthenticatedIdentity property. This method
first invokes
* the super version.
*
* @param options,
* @option unauthenticatedIdentity: the name of
the principal to
* assign and authenticate when a null username
and password are
* seen.
*/
public void initialize(Subject subject,
 CallbackHandler callbackHandler,
 Map sharedState,
 Map options)
{
super.initialize(subject, callbackHandler,
sharedState,
 options);
// Check for unauthenticatedIdentity option.
Object                    option              =
options.get("unauthenticatedIdentity");
String name = (String) option;
```

```
if (name != null) {
unauthenticatedIdentity = new
SimplePrincipal(name);
}
}

//...

/**
* A hook that allows subclasses to change the
validation of the
* input password against the expected password.
This version
* checks that neither inputPassword or
expectedPassword are null
* and that inputPassword.equals(expectedPassword)
is true;
*
* @return true if the inputPassword is valid,
false otherwise.
*/
protected boolean validatePassword(String
inputPassword,
   String expectedPassword)
{
if (inputPassword == null || expectedPassword ==
null) {
return false;
}
return inputPassword.equals(expectedPassword);
}

/**
* Get the expected password for the current
username available
* via the getUsername() method. This is called
from within the
* login() method after the CallbackHandler has
```

```
returned the
* username and candidate password.
*
* @return the valid password String
*/
abstract protected String getUsersPassword()
throws LoginException;
}
```

The choice of subclassing the AbstractServerLoginModule versus UsernamePasswordLoginModule is simply based on whether a string-based username and credentials are usable for the authentication technology you are writing the login module for. If the string-based semantic is valid, then subclass UsernamePasswordLoginModule, otherwise subclass Abstract ServerLoginModule. The steps you are required to perform when writing a custom login module are summarized in the following depending on which base login module class you choose. When writing a custom login module that integrates with your security infrastructure, you should start by subclassing AbstractServerLoginModule or Username Password Login Module to ensure that your login module provides the authenticated Principalinformation in the form expected by the JBossSX security manager.

When subclassing the AbstractServerLoginModule, you need to override the following:

- *Void initialize(Subject, CallbackHandler, Map, Map)*: If you have custom options to parse.
- *Boolean login()*: To perform the authentication activity. Be sure to set the loginOk instance variable to true if login succeeds, false if it fails.
- *Principal getIdentity()*: To return the Principal object for the user authenticated by the log() step.
- *Group[] getRoleSets()*: To return at least one Group named Roles that contains the roles assigned to the Principal authenticated duringlogin(). A second common Group is named CallerPrincipal and provides the user's application identity rather than the security domain identity.

When subclassing the UsernamePasswordLoginModule, you need to override the following:

- *Void initialize(Subject, CallbackHandler, Map, Map)*: If you have custom options to parse.
- *Group[] getRoleSets()*: to return at least one Group named Roles that contains the roles assigned to the Principal authenticated duringlogin(). A second common Group is named CallerPrincipal and provides the user's application identity rather than the security domain identity.
- *String getUsersPassword()*: to return the expected password for the current username available via the getUsername() method. ThegetUsersPassword() method is called from within login() after the callbackhandler returns the username and candidate password.

A Custom LoginModule Example

In this section we will develop a custom login module example. It will extend the UsernamePasswordLoginModule and obtains a user's password and role names from a JNDI lookup. The idea is that there is a JNDI context that will return a user's password if you perform a lookup on the context using a name of the form password/<username> where <username> is the current user being authenticated. Similarly, a lookup of the form roles/<username> returns the requested user's roles.

```
package org.jboss.chap8.ex2;

import java.security.acl.Group;
import java.util.Map;
import javax.naming.InitialContext;
import javax.naming.NamingException;
import javax.security.auth.Subject;
import
javax.security.auth.callback.CallbackHandler;
import javax.security.auth.login.LoginException;

import org.jboss.security.SimpleGroup;
```

```
import org.jboss.security.SimplePrincipal;
import
org.jboss.security.auth.spi.UsernamePasswordLoginModule;

/**
 * An example custom login module that obtains
passwords and roles
 * for a user from a JNDI lookup.
 *
 * @author Scott.Stark@jboss.org
 * @version $Revision: 1.5 $
*/
public class JndiUserAndPass
  extends UsernamePasswordLoginModule

{
/** The JNDI name to the context that handles
the password/username lookup */
  private String userPathPrefix;
/** The JNDI name to the context that handles
the roles/ username lookup */
  private String rolesPathPrefix;

/**
    * Override to obtain the userPathPrefix and
rolesPathPrefix options.
    */
    public void initialize(Subject subject,
CallbackHandler callbackHandler,
                  Map sharedState, Map options)
   {
      super.initialize(subject, callbackHandler,
sharedState, options);
            userPathPrefix = (String)
options.get("userPathPrefix");
            rolesPathPrefix = (String)
options.get("rolesPathPrefix");
   }
```

```
/**
    * Get the roles the current user belongs to
by querying the
   * rolesPathPrefix + '/' + super.getUsername()
JNDI location.
    */
   protected Group[] getRoleSets() throws
LoginException
  {
     try {
       InitialContext ctx = new InitialContext();
        String rolesPath = rolesPathPrefix + '/'
+ super.getUsername();
            String[] roles = (String[])
ctx.lookup(rolesPath);
                Group[] groups = {new
SimpleGroup("Roles")};
            log.info("Getting roles for
user="+super.getUsername());
       for(int r = 0; r < roles.length; r ++) {
            SimplePrincipal role = new
SimplePrincipal(roles[r]);
       log.info("Found role="+roles[r]);
         groups[0].addMember(role);
       }
       return groups;
     } catch(NamingException e) {
       log.error("Failed to obtain groups for
            user="+super.getUsername(), e);
     throw new LoginException(e.toString(true));
     }
  }

/**
    * Get the password of the current user by
querying the
   * userPathPrefix + '/' + super.getUsername()
```

```
JNDI location.
   */
  protected String getUsersPassword()
     throws LoginException
  {
     try {
       InitialContext ctx = new InitialContext();
        String userPath = userPathPrefix + '/' +
super.getUsername();
          log.info("Getting password for
user="+super.getUsername());
               String passwd = (String)
ctx.lookup(userPath);
        log.info("Found password="+passwd);
        return passwd;
     } catch(NamingException e) {
        log.error("Failed to obtain password for
              user="+super.getUsername(), e);
      throw new LoginException(e.toString(true));
     }
  }
}
```

The details of the JNDI store are found in the org.jboss.chap8.ex2.service.JndiStore MBean. This service binds an ObjectFactory that returns ajavax.naming.Context proxy into JNDI. The proxy handles lookup operations done against it by checking the prefix of the lookup name againstpassword and roles. When the name begins with password, a user's password is being requested. When the name begins with roles the user's roles are being requested. The example implementation always returns a password of theduke and an array of roles names equal to{"TheDuke", "Echo"} regardless of what the username is. You can experiment with other implementations as you wish.

The example code includes a simple session bean for testing the custom login module. To build, deploy and run the example, execute the following command in the examples directory.

```
[examples]$ ant -Dchap=chap8 -Dex=2 run-example
...
run-example2:
     [copy] Copying 1 file to/tmp/jboss-4.0.1/
server/default/deploy
    [echo] Waiting for 5 seconds for deploy...
     [java] [INFO,ExClient] Login with
username=jduke, password=theduke
    [java] [INFO,ExClient] Looking up EchoBean2
    [java] [INFO,ExClient] Created Echo
    [java] [INFO,ExClient] Echo.echo('Hello') =
Hello
19:06:13,266 INFO [EjbModule] Deploying EchoBean2
19:06:13,482 INFO [JndiStore] Start, bound
security/store
19:06:13,486 INFO [SecurityConfig] Using JAAS
AuthConfig: jar:file:/private/tmp/jboss-4.0.1/
server/default/tmp/deploy/tmp23012chap8-ex2.jar-
contents/chap8-ex2.sar!/META-INF/login-config.xml
19:06:13,654 INFO [EJBDeployer] Deployed: file:/
private/tmp/jboss-4.0.1/server/default/deploy/
chap8-ex2.jar
```

The choice of using the JndiUserAndPass custom login module for the server side authentication of the user is determined by the login configuration for the example security domain. The EJB JAR META-INF/jboss.xml descriptor sets the security domain

```
<?xml version="1.0"?>
<jboss>
<security-domain>java:/jaas/chap8-ex2</security-
domain>
</jboss>
```

The SAR META-INF/login-config.xml descriptor defines the login module configuration.

```
<application-policy name = "chap8-ex2">
   <authentication>
  <login-module
     code="org.jboss.chap8.ex2.JndiUserAndPass"
```

```
            flag="required">
        <module-option name = "userPathPrefix">/
security/store/password</module-option>
  <module-option name = "rolesPathPrefix">/
security/store/roles</module-option>
     </login-module>
   </authentication>
</application-policy>
```

Security domains defined in the login-config.xml file are essentially static. They are read when JBoss starts up, but there is no easy way to add a new security domain or change the definition for an existing one. The DynamicLoginConfig service allows you to dynamically deploy security domains. This allows you to specify JAAS login configuration as part of a deployment (or just as a standalone service) rather than having to edit the static login-config.xml file.

The service supports the following attributes:

- *AuthConfig*: The resource path to the JAAS login configuration file to use. This defaults to login-config.xml
- *LoginConfigService*: The XMLLoginConfig service name to use for loading. This service must support a String loadConfig(URL)operation to load the configurations.
- *SecurityManagerService*: The SecurityManagerService name used to flush the registered security domains. This service must support a flushAuthen tication Cache(String) operation to flush the case for the argument security domain. Setting this triggers the flush of the authentication caches when the service is stopped.

Here is an example MBean definition using the DynamicLoginConfig service:

```
<server>
<mbean
code="org.jboss.security.auth.login.DynamicLoginConfig"
name="...">
<attribute name="AuthConfig">login-config.xml</
```

```
attribute>

      <!-- The service which supports dynamic
processing of login-config.xml
      configurations.
     -->
           <depends  optional-attribute-
name="LoginConfigService">
        jboss.security:service=XMLLoginConfig </
depends>

 <!-- Optionally specify the security mgr service
to use when
  this service is stopped to flush the auth caches
of the domains
      registered by this service.
     -->
          <depends   optional-attribute-
name="SecurityManagerService">
    jboss.security:service=JaasSecurityManager </
depends>
   </mbean>
</server>
```

This will load the specified AuthConfig resource using the specified LoginConfigService MBean by invoking loadConfig with the appropriate resource URL. When the service is stopped the configurations are removed. The resource specified may be either an XML file, or a Sun JAAS login configuration.

SECURE REMOTE PASSWORD (SRP) PROTOCOL

The SRP protocol is an implementation of a public key exchange handshake described in the Internet standards working group request for comments 2945(RFC2945). The RFC2945 abstract states:

This document describes a cryptographically strong network authentication mechanism known as the Secure Remote Password (SRP) protocol. This mechanism is suitable for negotiating secure connections using a user-supplied password, while eliminating the security problems traditionally associated with reusable passwords. This system also performs a secure key exchange in the process of authentication, allowing security layers (privacy and/or integrity protection) to be enabled during the session. Trusted key servers and certificate infrastructures are not required, and clients are not required to store or manage any long-term keys. SRP offers both security and deployment advantages over existing challenge-response techniques, making it an ideal drop-in replacement where secure password authentication is needed.

SRP is similar in concept and security to other public key exchange algorithms, such as Diffie-Hellman and RSA. SRP is based on simple string passwords in a way that does not require a clear text password to exist on the server. This is in contrast to other public key-based algorithms that require client certificates and the corresponding certificate management infrastructure.

Algorithms like Diffie-Hellman and RSA are known as public key exchange algorithms. The concept of public key algorithms is that you have two keys, one public that is available to everyone, and one that is private and known only to you. When someone wants to send encrypted information to you, then encrpyt the information using your public key. Only you are able to decrypt the information using your private key. Contrast this with the more traditional shared password based encryption schemes that require the sender and receiver to know the shared password. Public key algorithms eliminate the need to share passwords.

The JBossSX framework includes an implementation of SRP that consists of the following elements:

- An implementation of the SRP handshake protocol that is independent of any particular client/server protocol
- An RMI implementation of the handshake protocol as the default client/server SRP implementation
- A client side JAAS LoginModule implementation that

uses the RMI implementation for use in authenticating clients in a secure fashion

- A JMX MBean for managing the RMI server implementation. The MBean allows the RMI server implementation to be plugged into a JMX framework and externalizes the configuration of the verification information store. It also establishes an authentication cache that is bound into the JBoss server JNDI namespace.
- A server side JAAS LoginModule implementation that uses the authentication cache managed by the SRP JMX MBean.

On the client side, SRP shows up as a custom JAAS LoginModule implementation that communicates to the authentication server through anorg.jboss. security.srp. SRPServerInterface proxy. A client enables authentication using SRP by creating a login configuration entry that includes the org.jboss.security.srp.jaas.SRPLoginModule. This module supports the following configuration options:

- *PrincipalClassName*: This option is no longer supported. The principal class is now always org.jboss.security.srp.jaas.SRPPrincipal.
- *SrpServerJndiName*: The JNDI name of the SRP ServerInterface object to use for communicating with the SRP authentication server. If both srpServer JndiName and srpServerRmiUrl options are specified, the srpServerJndiName is tried before srpServer RmiUrl.
- *SrpServerRmiUrl*: The RMI protocol URL string for the location of the SRPServerInterface proxy to use for communicating with the SRP authentication server.
- *ExternalRandomA*: A true/false flag indicating if the random component of the client public key A should come from the user callback. This can be used to input a strong cryptographic random number coming from a hardware token for example.
- *HasAuxChallenge*: A true/false flag indicating an that

a string will be sent to the server as an additional challenge for the server to validate. If the client session supports an encryption cipher then a temporary cipher will be created using the session private key and the challenge object sent as a javax.crypto.SealedObject.

- *MultipleSessions*: A true/false flag indicating if a given client may have multiple SRP login sessions active simultaneously.

Any other options passed in that do not match one of the previous named options is treated as a JNDI property to use for the environment passed to the InitialContext constructor. This is useful if the SRP server interface is not available from the default InitialContext. The SRPLoginModule needs to be configured along with the standard ClientLoginModule to allow the SRP authentication credentials to be used for validation of access to security J2EE components. An example login configuration entry that demonstrates such a setup is:

```
srp {
   org.jboss.security.srp.jaas.SRPLoginModule
required
  srpServerJndiName="SRPServerInterface"
  ;


  org.jboss.security.ClientLoginModule required
  password-stacking="useFirstPass"
  ;
};
```

On the JBoss server side, there are two MBeans that manage the objects that collectively make up the SRP server. The primary service is the org.jboss.security.srp.SRPService MBean, and it is responsible for exposing an RMI accessible version of the SRPServerInterface as well as updating the SRP authentication session cache.

The configurable SRPService MBean attributes include the following:

- *JndiName*: The JNDI name from which the SRP ServerInterface proxy should be available. This is the location where the SRPServicebinds the serializable dynamic proxy to the SRPServerInterface. If not specified it defaults to srp/SRPServerInterface.

- *VerifierSourceJndiName*: The JNDI name of the SRPVerifierSource implementation that should be used by the SRPService. If not set it defaults to srp/ DefaultVerifierSource.
- *AuthenticationCacheJndiName*: The JNDI name under which the authentication org.jboss.util.CachePolicy implementation to be used for caching authentication information is bound. The SRP session cache is made available for use through this binding. If not specified it defaults to srp/AuthenticationCache.
- *ServerPort*: RMI port for the SRPRemote ServerInterface. If not specified it defaults to 10099.
- *ClientSocketFactory*: An optional custom java.rmi. server.RMIClientSocketFactory implem-entation class name used during the export of the SRP Server Interface. If not specified the default RMIClient SocketFactory is used.
- *ServerSocketFactory*: An optional custom java. rmi.server.RMIServerSocketFactory implementation class name used during the export of the SRP ServerInterface. If not specified the default RMI ServerSocketFactory is used.
- *AuthenticationCacheTimeout*: Specifies the timed cache policy timeout in seconds. If not specified this defaults to 1800 seconds(30 minutes).
- *AuthenticationCacheResolution*: Specifies the timed cache policy resolution in seconds. This controls the interval between checks for timeouts. If not specified this defaults to 60 seconds(1 minute).
- *RequireAuxChallenge*: Set if the client must supply an auxiliary challenge as part of the verify phase. This gives control over whether the SRPLoginModule configuration used by the client must have the useAuxChallenge option enabled.
- *OverwriteSessions*: A flag indicating if a successful

user auth for an existing session should overwrite the current session. This controls the behaviour of the server SRP session cache when clients have not enabled the multiple session per user mode. The default is false meaning that the second attempt by a user to authentication will succeed, but the resulting SRP session will not overwrite the previous SRP session state.

The one input setting is the VerifierSourceJndiName attribute. This is the location of the SRP password information store implementation that must be provided and made available through JNDI. The org.jboss.security.srp SRP Verifier StoreService is an example MBean service that binds an implementation of the SRPVerifierStore interface that uses a file of serialized objects as the persistent store. Although not realistic for a production environment, it does allow for testing of the SRP protocol and provides an example of the requirements for an SRP Verifier Storeservice.

The configurable SRPVerifier StoreService MBean attributes include the following:

- *JndiName*: The JNDI name from which the SRPVerifierStore implementation should be available. If not specified it defaults tosrp/Default Verifier Source.
- *StoreFile*: The location of the user password verifier serialized object store file. This can be either a URL or a resource name to be found in the classpath. If not specified it defaults to SRPVerifierStore.ser.

The SRPVerifierStoreService MBean also supports addUser and delUser operations for addition and deletion of users. The signatures are:

```
public void addUser(String username, String
password) throws IOException;
public void delUser(String username) throws
IOException;
```

PROVIDING PASSWORD INFORMATION FOR SRP

The default implementation of the SRPVerifierStore

interface is not likely to be suitable for you production security environment as it requires all password hash information to be available as a file of serialized objects. You need to provide an MBean service that provides an implementation of the SRPVerifierStore interface that integrates with your existing security information stores. The SRPVerifierStore interface is shown in.

```
package org.jboss.security.srp;

import java.io.IOException;
import java.io.Serializable;
import java.security.KeyException;

public interface SRPVerifierStore
{
   public static class VerifierInfo implements
Serializable
   {
   /**
      * The username the information applies to.
Perhaps redundant
      * but it makes the object self contained.
      */
     public String username;

   /** The SRP password verifier hash */
     public byte[] verifier;
   /** The random password salt originally used
to verify the password */
     public byte[] salt;
   /** The SRP algorithm primitive generator */
     public byte[] g;
   /** The algorithm safe-prime modulus */
     public byte[] N;
   }

/**
    * Get the indicated user's password verifier
```

```
information.
    */
    public VerifierInfo getUserVerifier(String
username)
      throws KeyException, IOException;
/**
    * Set the indicated users' password verifier
information. This
    * is equivalent to changing a user's password
and should
      * generally invalidate any existing SRP
sessions and caches.
    */
   public void setUserVerifier(String username,
VerifierInfo info)
      throws IOException;

/**
    * Verify an optional auxiliary challenge sent
from the client to
     * the server. The auxChallenge object will
have been decrypted
    * if it was sent encrypted from the client.
An example of a
    * auxiliary challenge would be the validation
of a hardware token
   * (SafeWord, SecureID, iButton) that the server
validates to
   * further strengthen the SRP password exchange.
    */
      public void verifyUserChallenge(String
username, Object auxChallenge)
       throws SecurityException;
}
```

The primary function of a SRPVerifierStore impleme-ntation is to provide access to the SRPVerifier Store. VerifierInfo object for a given username. The get User Verifier(String) method is called by the SRPService at that start of a user SRP session to obtain the parameters needed by the SRP algorithm.

The elements of the VerifierInfo objects are:

- *Username*: The user's name or id used to login.
- *Verifier*: This is the one-way hash of the password or PIN the user enters as proof of their identity. The org.jboss.security.Util class has acalculateVerifier method that performs that password hashing algorithm. The output password H(salt | H(username | ':' | password)) as defined by RFC2945. Here H is the SHA secure hash function. The username is converted from a string to a byte[] using the UTF-8 encoding.
- *Salt*: This is a random number used to increase the difficulty of a brute force dictionary attack on the verifier password database in the event that the database is compromised. It is a value that should be generated from a cryptographically strong random number algorithm when the user's existing clear-text password is hashed.
- *g*: The SRP algorithm primitive generator. In general this can be a well known fixed parameter rather than a per-user setting. Theorg.jboss.security.srp.SRPConf utility class provides several settings for g including a good default which can obtained viaSRPConf. get DefaultParams().g().
- *N*: The SRP algorithm safe-prime modulus. In general this can be a well known fixed parameter rather than a per-user setting. Theorg.jboss.security.srp.SRPConf utility class provides several settings for N including a good default which can obtained viaSRP Conf.get DefaultParams().N().

So, step 1 of integrating your existing password store is the creation of a hashed version of the password information. If your passwords are already store in an irreversible hashed form, then this can only be done on a per-user basis as part of an upgrade procedure for example. Note that the setUserVerifier(String, VerifierInfo) method is not used by the current SRPSerivce and may be implemented as no-op method, or even one that throws an exception stating that the store is read-only. Step 2 is the creation of the custom SRPVerifierStore interface implementation that knows how to obtain the VerifierInfo from the store you created in step 1. The verifyUserChallenge(String, Object) method of the interface is only called if the client SRPLoginModule configuration specifies the hasAuxChallenge option. This can be used to integrate existing hardware token based schemes like SafeWord or Radius into the SRP algorithm.

Step 3 is the creation of an MBean that makes the step 2 implementation of the SRPVerifierStore interface available via JNDI, and exposes any configurable parameters you need. In addition to the default org.jboss. security. srp.SRPV erifier StoreService example, the SRP example presented later in this chapter provides a Java properties file based SRPVerifierStore implementation. Between the two examples you should have enough to integrate your security store.

INSIDE OF THE SRP ALGORITHM

The appeal of the SRP algorithm is that is allows for mutual authentication of client and server using simple text passwords without a secure communication channel. You might be wondering how this is done. If you want the complete details and theory behind the algorithm, refer to the SRP references mentioned in a note earlier.

There are six steps that are performed to complete authentication:

1. The client side SRPLoginModule retrieves the SRPServerInterface instance for the remote authentication server from the naming service.
2. The client side SRPLoginModule next requests the SRP parameters associated with the username attempting the login. There are a number of parameters involved in the SRP algorithm that must be chosen when the user password is first transformed into the verifier form used by the SRP algorithm. Rather than hard-coding the parameters (which could be done with minimal security risk),

the JBossSX implementation allows a user to retrieve this information as part of the exchange protocol. The getSRPParameters(username)call retrieves the SRP parameters for the given username.

3. The client side SRPLoginModule begins an SRP session by creating an SRPClientSession object using the login username, clear-text password, and SRP parameters obtained from step 2. The client then creates a random number A that will be used to build the private SRP session key. The client then initializes the server side of the SRP session by invoking the SRPServerInterface.init method and passes in the username and client generated random number A. The server returns its own random number B. This step corresponds to the exchange of public keys.
4. The client side SRPLoginModule obtains the private SRP session key that has been generated as a result of the previous messages exchanges. This is saved as a private credential in the login Subject. The server challenge response M2 from step 4 is verified by invoking the SRPClientSession.verify method. If this succeeds, mutual authentication of the client to server, and server to client have been completed. The client side SRPLoginModule next creates a challenge M1 to the server by invoking SRPClient Session. response method passing the server random number B as an argument. This challenge is sent to the server via the SRPServerInterface.verify method and server's response is saved as M2. This step corresponds to an exchange of challenges. At this point the server has verified that the user is who they say they are.
5. The client side SRPLoginModule saves the login username and M1 challenge into the LoginModule sharedState map. This is used as the Principal name and credentials by the standard JBoss Client Login Module. The M1 challenge is used in place of the password as proof of identity on any method invocations on J2EE components. The M1 challenge

is a cryptographically strong hash associated with the SRP session. Its interception via a third partly cannot be used to obtain the user's password.

6. At the end of this authentication protocol, the SRPServerSession has been placed into the SRP Service authentication cache for subsequent use by the SRPCacheLoginModule.

Although SRP has many interesting properties, it is still an evolving component in the JBossSX framework and has some limitations of which you should be aware.

Issues of note include the following:

- Because of how JBoss detaches the method transport protocol from the component container where authentication is performed, an unauthorized user could snoop the SRP M1 challenge and effectively use the challenge to make requests as the associated username. Custom interceptors that encrypt the challenge using the SRP session key can be used to prevent this issue.
- The SRPService maintains a cache of SRP sessions that time out after a configurable period. Once they time out, any subsequent J2EE component access will fail because there is currently no mechanism for transparently renegotiating the SRP authentication credentials. You must either set the authentication cache timeout very long (up to 2,147,483,647 seconds, or approximately 68 years), or handle re-authentication in your code on failure.
- By default there can only be one SRP session for a given username. Because the negotiated SRP session produces a private session key that can be used for encryption/decryption between the client and server, the session is effectively a stateful one. JBoss supports for multiple SRP sessions per user, but you cannot encrypt data with one session key and then decrypt it with another.

To use end-to-end SRP authentication for J2EE component calls, you need to configure the security domain under which the components are secured to use the org.jboss. security.srp.jaas.SRPCacheLoginModule. The SRPCacheLogin Module has a single configuration option namedcache JndiName that sets the JNDI location of the SRP authentication CachePolicy instance. This must correspond to the AuthenticationCacheJndiName attribute value of the SRPService MBean. The SRPCacheLoginModule authenticates user credentials by obtaining the client challenge from the SRPServerSession object in the authentication cache and comparing this to the challenge passed as the user credentials.

An SRP Example

We have covered quite a bit of material on SRP and now its time to demonstrate SRP in practice with an example. The example demonstrates client side authentication of the user via SRP as well as subsequent secured access to a simple EJB using the SRP session challenge as the user credential. The test code deploys an EJB JAR that includes a SAR for the configuration of the server side login module configuration and SRP services. As in the previous examples we will dynamically install the server side login module configuration using the SecurityConfig MBean. In this example we also use a custom implementation of the SRPVerifierStore interface that uses an in memory store that is seeded from a Java properties file rather than a serialized object store as used by the SRPVerifierStoreService. This custom service is org.jboss. chap8.ex3.service.PropertiesVerifierStore. The following shows the contents of the JAR that contains the example EJB and SRP services.

```
[examples]$ java -cp output/classes ListJar
output/chap8/chap8-ex3.jar
output/chap8/chap8-ex3.jar
+- META-INF/MANIFEST.MF
+- META-INF/ejb-jar.xml
+- META-INF/jboss.xml
+- org/jboss/chap8/ex3/Echo.class
+- org/jboss/chap8/ex3/EchoBean.class
+- org/jboss/chap8/ex3/EchoHome.class
```

```
+- roles.properties
+- users.properties
+- chap8-ex3.sar (archive)
| +- META-INF/MANIFEST.MF
| +- META-INF/jboss-service.xml
| +- META-INF/login-config.xml
|     +-     org/jboss/chap8/ex3/service/
PropertiesVerifierStore$1.class
|     +-     org/jboss/chap8/ex3/service/
PropertiesVerifierStore.class
|     +-     org/jboss/chap8/ex3/service/
PropertiesVerifierStoreMBean.class
| +- org/jboss/chap8/service/SecurityConfig.class
|       +-       org/jboss/chap8/service/
SecurityConfigMBean.class
```

Example: The client side standard JAAS configuration

```
srp {
org.jboss.security.srp.jaas.SRPLoginModule
required
srpServerJndiName="srp-test/SRPServerInterface"
;

org.jboss.security.ClientLoginModule required
password-stacking="useFirstPass"
;
};
```

Example: The server side XMLLoginConfig configuration

```
<application-policy name="chap8-ex3">
<authentication>
<login-modulecode="org.jboss.security.srp.jaas.SRP
CacheLoginModule"
 flag = "required">
<module-option  name="cacheJndiName">srp-test/
AuthenticationCache</module-option>
</login-module>
<loginmodulecode="org.jboss.security.auth.spi.Users
RolesLoginModule"
 flag = "required">
```

```
<module-option name="password-
stacking">useFirstPass</module-option>
</login-module>
</authentication>
</application-policy>
```

The example services are the ServiceConfig and the PropertiesVerifierStore and SRPService MBeans. Note that the JndiName attribute of thePropertiesVerifierStore is equal to the VerifierSourceJndiName attribute of the SRPService, and that the SRPService depends on thePropertiesVerifierStore. This is required because the SRPService needs an implementation of the SRPVerifierStore interface for accessing user password verification information.

The client side login module configuration makes use of the SRPLoginModule with a srpServerJndiName option value that corresponds to the JBoss server component SRPService JndiName attribute value(srp-test/SRPServerInterface). Also needed is the ClientLoginModule configured with the password-stacking="useFirstPass" value to propagate the user authentication credentials generated by the SRPLoginModule to the EJB invocation layer.

There are two issues to note about the server side login module configuration. First, note the cacheJndiName=srp-test/AuthenticationCacheconfiguration option tells the SRPCache LoginModule the location of the CachePolicy that contains the SRPServerSession for users who have authenticated against the SRPService. This value corresponds to the SRPService AuthenticationCacheJndiName attribute value. Second, the configuration includes a UsersRoles LoginModule with the password-stacking=use FirstPass configuration option.

It is required to use a second login module with the SRPCacheLoginModule because SRP is only an authentication technology. A second login module needs to be configured that accepts the authentication credentials validated by the SRPCacheLoginModule to set the principal's roles that determines the principal's permissions. The UsersRolesLogin Module is augmenting the SRP authentication with properties file based authorization. The user's roles are coming the roles.properties file included in the EJB JAR. Now, run the example 3 client by executing the following command from the book examples directory:

```
[examples]$ ant -Dchap=chap8 -Dex=3 run-example
...
run-example3:
[copy] Copying 1 file to/tmp/jboss-4.0.1/server/
default/deploy
[echo] Waiting for 5 seconds for deploy...
[java] Logging in using the 'srp' configuration
[java] Created Echo
[java] Echo.echo()#1 = This is call 1
[java] Echo.echo()#2 = This is call 2
```

In the examples/logs directory you will find a file called ex3-trace.log. This is a detailed trace of the client side of the SRP algorithm. The traces show step-by-step the construction of the public keys, challenges, session key and verification.

Note that the client has taken a long time to run relative to the other simple examples. The reason for this is the construction of the client's public key. This involves the creation of a cryptographically strong random number, and this process takes quite a bit of time the first time it occurs. If you were to log out and log in again within the same VM, the process would be much faster.

Also note that Echo.echo()#2 fails with an authentication exception. The client code sleeps for 15 seconds after making the first call to demonstrate the behaviour of the SRPServicecache expiration. The SRPService cache policy timeout has been set to a mere 10 seconds to force this issue. As stated earlier, you need to make the cache timeout very long, or handle re-authentication on failure.

RUNNING JBOSS WITH A JAVA 2 SECURITY MANAGER

By default the JBoss server does not start with a Java 2 security manager. If you want to restrict privileges of code using Java 2 permissions you need to configure the JBoss server to run under a security manager. This is done by configuring the Java VM options in the run.bat orrun.sh scripts in the JBoss server distribution bin directory. The two required VM options are as follows:

- *java.security.manager*: This is used without any value to specify that the default security manager should be used. This is the preferred security manager. You can also pass a value to the java.security.manager option to specify a custom security manager implementation. The value must be the fully qualified class name of a subclass of java.lang. Security Manager. This form specifies that the policy file should augment the default security policy as configured by the VM installation.
- *java.security.policy*: This is used to specify the policy file that will augment the default security policy information for the VM. This option takes two forms: java.security.policy=policyFileURL and java.security. policy==policyFileURL. The first form specifies that the policy file should augment the default security policy as configured by the VM installation. The second form specifies that only the indicated policy file should be used. The policyFileURL value can be any URL for which a protocol handler exists, or a file path specification.

Both the run.bat and run.sh start scripts reference an JAVA_OPTS variable which you can use to set the security manager properties.

Enabling Java 2 security is the easy part. The difficult part of Java 2 security is establishing the allowed permissions. If you look at theserver.policy file that is contained in the default configuration file set, you'll see that it contains the following permission grant statement:

```
grant {
// Allow everything for now
permission java.security.AllPermission;
};
```

This effectively disables security permission checking for all code as it says any code can do anything, which is not a reasonable default. What is a reasonable set of permissions is entirely up to you.

USING SSL WITH JBOSS USING JSSE

JBoss uses JSEE, the Java Secure Socket Extension (JSSE), for SSL. JSSE is bundled with JDK 1.4. To get started with JSSE you need a public key/private key pair in the form of an X509 certificate for use by the SSL server sockets. For the purpose of this example we have created a self-signed certificate using the JDK keytool and included the resulting keystore file in the chap8 source directory aschap8.keystore. It was created using the following command and input:

keytool -genkey -keystore chap8.keystore -storepass rmi+ssl -keypass rmi+ssl -keyalg RSA -alias chapter -validity 3650 -dname "cn=chapter example,ou=admin book,dc =jboss,dc=org"

This produces a keystore file called chap8.keystore. A keystore is a database of security keys.

There are two different types of entries in a keystore:

1. *Key entries*: Each entry holds very sensitive cryptographic key information, which is stored in a protected format to prevent unauthorized access. Typically, a key stored in this type of entry is a secret key, or a private key accompanied by the certificate chain for the corresponding public key. The keytool and jarsigner tools only handle the later type of entry, that is private keys and their associated certificate chains.
2. *Trusted certificate entries*: each entry contains a single public key certificate belonging to another party. It is called a trusted certificate because the keystore owner trusts that the public key in the certificate indeed belongs to the identity identified by the subject (owner) of the certificate. The issuer of the certificate vouches for this, by signing the certificate.

Listing the src/main/org/jboss/chap8/chap8.keystore examples file contents using the keytool shows one self-signed certificate:

```
[examples]$ keytool -list -v -keystore src/main/
org/jboss/chap8/chap8.keystore
Enter keystore password: rmi+ssl
Keystore type: jks
Keystore provider: SUN
Your keystore contains 1 entry
Alias name: chapter
Creation date: Dec 16, 2004
Entry type: keyEntry
Certificate chain length: 1
Certificate[1]:
Owner: CN=chapter example, OU=admin book,
DC=jboss, DC=org
Issuer: CN=chapter example, OU=admin book,
DC=jboss, DC=org
Serial number: 41c23d6c
Valid from: Thu Dec 16 19:59:08 CST 2004 until:
Sun Dec 14 19:59:08 CST 2014
Certificate fingerprints:
MD5:
36:29:FD:1C:78:44:14:5E:5A:C7:EB:E5:E8:ED:06:86
SHA1:
37:FE:BB:8A:A5:CF:D9:3D:B9:61:8C:53:CE:
19:1E:4D:BC:C9:18:F2
```

With JSSE working and a keystore with the certificate you will use for the JBoss server, your are ready to configure JBoss to use SSL for EJB access. This is done by configuring the EJB invoker RMI socket factories. The JBossSX framework includes implementations of thejava.rmi.server.RMI ServerSocket Factory and java.rmi.server.RMI Client Socket Factory interfaces that enable the use of RMI over SSL encrypted sockets. The implementation classes are org.jboss.security.ssl. RMISSL ServerSocketFactory and org.jboss.security.ssl. RMISSLClient SocketFactoryrespectively. There are two steps to enable the use of SSL for RMI access to EJBs. The first is to enable the use of a keystore as the database for the SSL server certificate, which is done by configuring an org.jboss.security. plugins. JaasSecurityDomain MBean.

Example: A sample JaasSecurityDomain config for RMI/SSL

```
<!-- The SSL domain setup -->
<mbean code="org.jboss.security.plugins.Jaas
SecurityDomain"
      name="jboss.security:service=JaasSecurity
Domain,domain=RMI+SSL">
  <constructor>
   <arg type="java.lang.String" value="RMI+SSL"/
>
  </constructor>
  <attribute
     name="KeyStoreURL">chap8.keystore</
attribute>
   <attribute name="KeyStorePass">rmi+ssl</
attribute>
</mbean>
```

The JaasSecurityDomain is a subclass of the standard JaasSecurityManager class that adds the notions of a keystore as well JSSEKeyManagerFactory and TrustManagerFactory access. It extends the basic security manager to allow support for SSL and other cryptographic operations that require security keys. This configuration simply loads the chap8.keystore from the example 4 MBean SAR using the indicated password. The second step is to define an EJB invoker configuration that uses the JBossSX RMI socket factories that support SSL. To do this you need to define a custom configuration for the JRMPInvoker we saw in Chapter, *EJBs on JBoss* as well as an EJB setup that makes use of this invoker. The top of the listing shows the jboss-service.xml descriptor that defines the custom JRMPInovker

```
<mbeancode="org.jboss.invocation.jrmp.
server.JRMPInvoker"
   name="jboss:service=invoker,type=jrmp,socket
Type=SSL">
   <attribute name="RMIObjectPort">14445</
attribute>
  <attribute name="RMIClientSocketFactory">
```

```
    org.jboss.security.ssl.RMISSLClientSocketFactory
  </attribute>
  <attribute name="RMIServerSocketFactory">
    org.jboss.security.ssl.RMISSLServerSocketFactory
  </attribute>
   <attribute name="SecurityDomain">java:/jaas/
RMI+SSL</attribute>
   <depends>jboss.security:service=JaasSecurity
Domain, domain=RMI+SSL</depends>
</mbean>
```

To set up an SSL invoker, we will create an invoker binding named stateless-ssl-invoker that uses our custom JRMPInvoker. We can declare the invoker binding and connect it to EchoBean4 as shown in the following jboss.xml file.

```
<?xml version="1.0"?>
<jboss>
  <enterprise-beans>
    <session>
      <ejb-name>EchoBean4</ejb-name>
        <configuration-name>Standard Stateless
SessionBean</configuration-name>
      <invoker-bindings>
        <invoker>
         <invoker-proxy-binding-name>stateless-
ssl-invoker</invoker-proxy-binding-name>
        </invoker>
      </invoker-bindings>
    </session>
  </enterprise-beans>

  <invoker-proxy-bindings>
    <invoker-proxy-binding>
      <name>stateless-ssl-invoker</name>
                                        <invoker
mbean>jboss:service=invoker,type=jrmp,socket
Type=SSL</invoker-mbean>
<proxy-factory>org.jboss.proxy.ejb.ProxyFactory</
proxy-factory>
```

```
        <proxy-factory-config>
        <client-interceptors>
          <home>
  <interceptor>org.jboss.proxy.ejb.Home
Interceptor</interceptor>
         <interceptor>org.jboss.proxy.Security
Interceptor</interceptor>
         <interceptor>org.jboss.proxy.Transaction
Interceptor</interceptor>
         <interceptor>org.jboss.invocation.Invoker
Interceptor</interceptor>
          </home>
          <bean>
         <interceptor>org.jboss.proxy.ejb.Stateless
SessionInterceptor</interceptor>
            <interceptor>org.jboss.proxy.Security
Interceptor</interceptor>
         <interceptor>org.jboss.proxy.Transaction
Interceptor</interceptor>
         <interceptor>org.jboss.invocation.Invoker
Interceptor</interceptor>
          </bean>
        </client-interceptors>
        </proxy-factory-config>
     </invoker-proxy-binding>
   </invoker-proxy-bindings>
</jboss>
```

The example 4 code is located under the src/main/org/jboss/chap8/ex4 directory of the book examples. This is another simple stateless session bean with an echo method that returns its input argument. It is hard to tell when SSL is in use unless it fails, so we'll run the example 4 client in two different ways to demonstrate that the EJB deployment is in fact using SSL.

Start the JBoss server using the default configuration and then run example 4b as follows:

```
[examples]$ ant -Dchap=chap8 -Dex=4b run-example
...
run-example4b:
```

```
[copy] Copying 1 file to/tmp/jboss-4.0.1/server/
default/deploy
[echo] Waiting for 15 seconds for deploy...
...
[java]  Exception  in  thread  "main"
java.rmi.ConnectIOException: error during JRMP
connection establishment; nested exception is:
[java] javax.net.ssl.SSLHandshakeException:
sun.security.validator.ValidatorException: No
trusted certificate found
...
```

The resulting exception is expected, and is the purpose of the 4b version of the example. Note that the exception stack trace has been edited to fit into the book format, so expect some difference. The key item to notice about the exception is it clearly shows you are using the Sun JSSE classes to communicate with the JBoss EJB container. The exception is saying that the self-signed certificate you are using as the JBoss server certificate cannot be validated as signed by any of the default certificate authorities. This is expected because the default certificate authority keystore that ships with the JSSE package only includes well known certificate authorities such as VeriSign, Thawte, and RSA Data Security. To get the EJB client to accept your self-signed certificate as valid, you need to tell the JSSE classes to use yourchap8.keystore as its truststore. A truststore is just a keystore that contains public key certificates used to sign other certificates. To do this, run example 4 using -Dex=4 rather than -Dex=4b to pass the location of the correct truststore using the javax.net.ssl.trustStore system property:

```
[examples]$ ant -Dchap=chap8 -Dex=4 run-example
...
run-example4:
[copy] Copying 1 file to/tmp/jboss-4.0.1/server/
default/deploy
[echo] Waiting for 5 seconds for deploy...
...
[java] Created Echo
[java] Echo.echo()#1 = This is call 1
```

This time the only indication that an SSL socket is involved is because of the SSL handshakeCompleted message. This is coming from theRMISSLClientSocketFactory class as a debug level log message. If you did not have the client configured to print out log4j debug level messages, there would be no direct indication that SSL was involved. If you note the run times and the load on your system CPU, there definitely is a difference. SSL, like SRP, involves the use of cryptographically strong random numbers that take time to seed the first time they are used. This shows up as high CPU utilization and start up times. One consequence of this is that if you are running on a system that is slower than the one used to run the examples for the book, such as when running example 4b, you may seen an exception similar to the following:

```
javax.naming.NameNotFoundException: EchoBean4 not
bound at
sun.rmi.transport.StreamRemoteCall.exception
ReceivedFromServer
...
```

The problem is that the JBoss server has not finished deploying the example EJB in the time the client allowed. This is due to the initial setup time of the secure random number generator used by the SSL server socket. If you see this issue, simply rerun the example again or increase the deployment wait time in the chap8 build.xml Ant script.

CONFIGURING JBOSS FOR USE BEHIND A FIREWALL

JBoss comes with many socket based services that open listening ports. In this section we list the services that open ports that might need to be configured to work when accessing JBoss behind a firewall. The following table shows the ports, socket type, associated service for the services in the default configuration file set.

SECURING JBOSS SERVER

JBoss comes with several admin access points that need to be secured or removed to prevent unauthorized access to admin functions in a deployment. This section describes the various admin services and how to secure them.

THE JMX-CONSOLE.WAR

The jmx-console.war found in the deploy directory provides an html view into the JMX microkernel. As such, it provides access to arbitrary admin type access like shutting down the server, stopping services, deploying new services, etc. It should either be secured like any other web application, or removed.

THE WEB-CONSOLE.WAR

The web-console.war found in the deploy/management directory is another web application view into the JMX microkernel. This uses a combination of an applet and a HTML view and provides the same level of access to admin functionality as the jmx-console.war. As such, it should either be secured or removed. The web-console.war contains commented out templates for basic security in its WEB-INF/web.xml as well as commented out setup for a security domain in WEB-INF/jboss-web.xml.

THE HTTP-INVOKER.SAR

The http-invoker.sar found in the deploy directory is a service that provides RMI/HTTP access for EJBs and the JNDI Naming service. This includes a servlet that processes posts of marshalled org.jboss.invocation.Invocation objects that represent invocations that should be dispatched onto the MBeanServer. Effectively this allows access to MBeans that support the detached invoker operation via HTTP since one could figure out how to format an appropriate HTTP post. To security this access point you would need to secure the JMXInvokerServlet servlet found in the http-invoker.sar/invoker.war/WEB-INF/web.xml descriptor. There is a secure mapping defined for the/restricted/JMXInvokerServletpath by default, one would simply have to remove the other paths and configure the http-invoker security domain setup in the http-invoker.sar/invoker.war/WEB-INF/jboss-web.xml descriptor.

6

Web Applications

TOMCAT SERVICE

Tomcat 5 is the latest release of the Apache Java servlet container. It supports the Servlet 2.4 and JSP 2.0 specifications. Tomcat is distributed as a deployable service in jbossweb-tomcat-5.0.sar in the deploy directory.

It is shipped in exploded directory form, so it's easy to inspect and update the configuration of your embedded Tomcat instance.

The main service file is META-INF/jboss-service.xml. It configures the org.jboss.web.tomcat.tc5.Tomcat5 MBean which controls Tomcat.

Its configurable attributes include:

- *DefaultSecurityDomain*: This specified the JAAS security domain to use in the absence of an explicit security-domain specification in the jboss-web.xml of a WAR file.
- *Java2ClassLoadingCompliance*: This enables the standard Java2 parent delegation class loading model rather than the servlet model which loads from the WAR first. This is true by default as loading from WARs that include client JARs with classes used by EJBs causes class loading conflicts. If you enable the servlet class loading model by setting this flag to false, you will need to organize your deployment package to avoid duplicate classes in the deployment.
- *UseJBossWebLoader*: This flag indicates that Tomcat should use a JBoss unified class loader as the web

application class loader. The default is true, which means that the classes inside of the WEB-INF/classes and WEB-INF/lib directories of the WAR file are incorporated into the default shared class loader repository described This may not be what you want as its contrary to the default servlet class loading model and can result in sharing of classes/resources between web applications. You can disable this by setting this attribute to false.

- *LenientEjbLink*: This flag indicates that ejb-link errors should be ignored in favour of trying the jndi-name in the jboss-web.xml. The default is true.
- *ManagerClass*: This is the class to use as the session manager for replicating the state of web applications marked as distributable. The only provided implementation session manager is org.jboss.web. tomcat.tc5.session.JBossCacheManager, which uses JBossCache to track the distributed state.
- *SubjectAttributeName*: If set, this represents request attribute name under which the JAAS Subject will be stored. There is no default value, meaning that the subject is not set in the request.
- *SessionIdAlphabet*: This is the set of characters used to create a session ids. It must be made up of exactly 65 unique characters.
- *SnapshotMode*: This sets the snapshot mode in a clustered environment. This must be one of instant or interval. In instant mode changes to a clustered session are instantly propagated whenever a modification is made. In interval mode all modifications are periodically propagated according to the SnapshotInterval.
- *SnapshotInterval*: This sets the snapshot interval in milliseconds for the interval snapshot mode. The default is 1000ms, which is 1 second.
- *UseLocalCache*: A flag indicating if the local HTTP session value should be used if it exists. When true, the existing local HTTP session values are used and

updates are replicated, but updates to the same session on other nodes do not update the local session value. This mode is only useful for failover. When false, the session value is obtained from the distributed cache. This mode can be used with load balancing. The default is true.

- *UseJK*: This specifies that you are using MOD_JK(2) for load balancing with sticky session combined with JvmRoute. If set to true, it will insert a JvmRouteFilter to intercept every request and replace the JvmRoute if it detects a failover. This additionally requires theJvmRoute to be set inside the engine definition in the Tomcat server.xml file. The default is false.
- *Domain*: This is the JMX domain that Tomcat will register additional MBeans under. The default is jboss.web.
- *SecurityMangerService*: This is a reference to the JAAS security manager for Tomcat to use. This defaults tojboss.security:service=JaasSecurityManager.
- *CacheName*: This is a reference to the JBossCache to be used for HTTP session replication, if session replication is being used. The default is jboss. cache:service=TomcatClusteringCache.

TOMCAT SERVER.XML FILE

While the jboss-service.xml file controls the JBoss/Tomcat integration, Tomcat has its own configuration file which guides its operation.

This is the server.xml descriptor that you will find in the jbossweb-tomcat50.sar directory. Although this file doesn't have a formal DTD or schema definition, We'll now look at some of the configuration options available in the server.xml file.

The top level element is the Server element is the root element, which should contain a Service element representing the entire web subsystem.

The only supported attribute is:

- *Name*: A unique name by which the service is known.

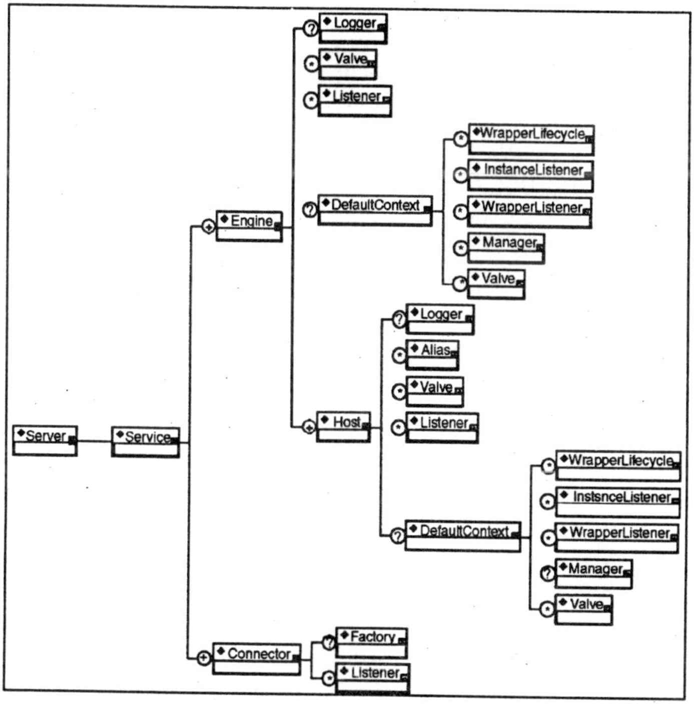

Fig. An overview of the Tomcat server.xml file.

A Connector element configures a transport mechanism that allows clients to send requests and receive responses from the Service it is associated with. Connectors forward requests to the engine and return the results to the requesting client.

Connectors support these attributes:

- *EnableLookups*: A flag that enables DNS resolution of the client hostname as accessed via the Servlet Request.getRemoteHostmethod. This flag defaults to false.
- *RedirectPort*: The port to which non-SSL requests will be redirected when a request for content secured under a transport confidentiality or integrity constraint is received. This defaults to the standard HTTPS port of 443.
- *Secure*: Sets the ServletRequest.isSecure method value flag to indicate whether or not the transport channel is secure. This flag defaults to false.

- *Scheme*: Sets the protocol name as accessed by the ServletRequest.getScheme method. The scheme defaults to http.
- *AcceptCount*: The maximum queue length for incoming connection requests when all possible request processing threads are in use. Any requests received when the queue is full will be refused. The default value is 10.
- *Address*: For servers with more than one IP address, this attribute specifies which address will be used for listening on the specified port. By default, this port will be used on all IP addresses associated with the server.
- *BufferSize*: The size (in bytes) of the buffer to be provided for input streams created by this connector. By default, buffers of 2048 bytes will be provided.
- *ConnectionTimeout*: The number of milliseconds this connector will wait, after accepting a connection, for the request URI line to be presented. The default value is 60000 (*I.e.* 60 seconds).
- *Debug*: The debugging detail level of log messages generated by this component, with higher numbers creating more detailed output. If not specified, this attribute is set to zero (0). Whether or not this shows up in the log further depends on the log4j categoryorg.jboss.web.tomcat.tc5.Tomcat5 threshold.
- *MaxThreads*: The maximum number of request processing threads to be created by this connector, which therefore determines the maximum number of simultaneous requests that can be handled. If not specified, this attribute is set to 200.
- *MaxSpareThreads*: The maximum number of unused request processing threads that will be allowed to exist until the thread pool starts stopping the unnecessary threads. The default value is 50.
- *MinSpareThreads*: The number of request processing threads that will be created when this connector is first started. The connector will also make sure it has

the specified number of idle processing threads available. This attribute should be set to a value smaller than that set for maxThreads. The default value is 4.

- *Port*: The TCP port number on which this connector will create a server socket and await incoming connections. Your operating system will allow only one server application to listen to a particular port number on a particular IP address.
- *ProxyName*: If this connector is being used in a proxy configuration, configure this attribute to specify the server name to be returned for calls to request. getServerName().
- *ProxyPort*: If this connector is being used in a proxy configuration, configure this attribute to specify the server port to be returned for calls to request. getServerPort().
- *TcpNoDelay*: If set to true, the TCP_NO_DELAY option will be set on the server socket, which improves performance under most circumstances. This is set to true by default.

ENGINE

Each Service must have a single Engine configuration. An engine handles the requests submitted to a service via the configured connectors. The child elements supported by the embedded service include Host, Logger, DefaultContext, Valve and Listener.

The supported attributes include:

- *ClassName*: The fully qualified class name of the org.apache.catalina.Engine interface implementation to use. If not specifies this defaults to org.apache. catalina.core.StandardEngine.
- *DefaultHost*: The name of a Host configured under the Engine that will handle requests with host names that do not match a Hostconfiguration.
- *Name*: A logical name to assign the Engine. It will be used in log messages produced by the Engine.

HOST

A Host element represents a virtual host configuration. It is a container for web applications with a specified DNS hostname. The child elements supported by the embedded service include Alias, Logger, DefaultContext, Valve and Listener.

The supported attributes include:

- *ClassName*: The fully qualified class name of the org.apache.catalina.Host interface implementation to use. If not specifies this defaults to org.apache. catalina.core.StandardHost.
- *Name*: The DNS name of the virtual host. At least one Host element must be configured with a name that corresponds to the defaultHostvalue of the containing Engine.

The Alias element is an optional child element of the Host element. Each Alias content specifies an alternate DNS name for the enclosing Host.

DEFAULTCONTEXT

The DefaultContext element is a configuration template for web application contexts. It may be defined at the Engine or Host level. The child elements supported by the embedded service include WrapperLifecycle, InstanceListener, Wrapper Listener, and Manager.

The supported attributes include:

- *ClassName*: The fully qualified class name of the org.apache.catalina.core.DefaultContext implementation. This defaults toorg.apache. catalina.core.DefaultContext and if overridden must be a subclass of DefaultContext.
- *Cookies*: A flag indicating if sessions will be tracked using cookies. The default is true.
- *CrossContext*: A flag indicating if the ServletContext. getContext(String path) method should return contexts for other web applications deployed in the calling web application's virtual host. The default is false.

LOGGER

The Logger element specifies a logging configuration the Tomcat instance.

The supported attributes include:

- *ClassName*: The fully qualified class name of the org.apache.catalina.Logger interface implementation. For integration with JBoss logging this should be set to org.jboss.web.tomcat.Log4jLogger.
- *Verbosity*: The default log level.
- *Category*: The default log category.

VALVE

A Valve element configures a hook into the request processing pipeline for the web container. Valves must implement theorg.apache.catalina.Valve interface.

There is only one required configuration attribute:

- *ClassName*: The fully qualified class name of the org.apache.catalina.Valve interface implementation.

The most commonly used valve is the AccessLogValve, which keeps a standard HTTP access log of incoming requests. The className for the access log value is org.jboss.web. catalina.valves.AccessLogValue.

The addition Valve attributes supported by it include:

Directory: The directory path into which the access log files will be created.

- *Pattern*: A pattern specifier that defines the format of the log messages. This defaults to common.
- *Prefix*: The prefix to add to each log file name. This defaults to access_log.
- *Suffix*: The suffix to add to each log file name. This default to an empty string, meaning that no suffix will be added.

USING SSL WITH THE JBOSS/TOMCAT BUNDLE

There are a few ways one can configure HTTP over SSL for the embedded Tomcat servlet container. The main difference is whether or not you use the JBoss specific connector socket factory that allows one to obtain the JSSE server certificate information from a JBossSXSecurityDomain. This requires establishing a SecurityDomain using the org.jboss.security.plugins.JaasSecurityDomain MBean. A server.xml configuration file that illustrates the setup of only an SSL connector via this approach is given below.

```
<Server>
            <Service      name="jboss.web"
className="org.jboss.web.tomcat.tc5.StandardService">

              <Connector      port="8080"
address="${jboss.bind.address}" maxThreads="150"
       minSpareThreads="25" maxSpareThreads="75"
enableLookups="false"
         redirectPort="443" acceptCount="100"
connectionTimeout="20000"
       disableUploadTimeout="true"/>

                   <Connector    port="443"
address="${jboss.bind.address}" maxThreads="100"
        minSpareThreads="5" maxSpareThreads="15"
scheme="https"
       secure="true" clientAuth="false"
         keystoreFile="${jboss.server.home.dir}/
conf/chap8.keystore"
       keystorePass="rmi+ssl" sslProtocol="TLS"/
>

              <Engine   name="jboss.web"
defaultHost="localhost">
       <Realm
      className="org.jboss.web.tomcat.security.JBoss
SecurityMgrRealm"
        certificatePrincipal="org.jboss.securia.
Log4jLogger"
                  verbosityLevel="WARNING"
category="org.jboss.web.localhost.Engine"/>
       <Host name="localhost" autoDeploy="false"
deployOnStartup="false"
```

```
        deployXML="false">
            <DefaultContext cookies="true"
crossContext="true" override="true"/>
        </Host>
      </Engine>
    </Service>
</Server>
```

If your running on a Unix system (Linux, Solaris, OS X) that only allows root to open ports below 1024 you will need to change the port number above to something like 8443.

Factory configuration attributes:

- *Algorithm*: The certificate encoding algorithm to be used. If not specified, the default value is SunX509.
- *ClassName*: The fully qualified class name of the SSL server socket factory implementation class. You must specify org.apache.coyote.tomcat4. CoyoteServer SocketFactory here. Using any other socket factory will not cause an error, but the server socket will not be using SSL.
- *ClientAuth*: Set to true if you want the SSL stack to require a valid certificate chain from the client before accepting a connection. A false value (which is the default) will not require a certificate chain unless the client requests a resource protected by a security constraint that uses CLIENT-CERT authentication.
- *KeystoreFile*: The pathname of the keystore file where you have stored the server certificate to be loaded. By default, the pathname is the file.keystore in the operating system home directory of the user that is running Tomcat.
- *KeystorePass*: The password used to access the server certificate from the specified keystore file. The default value is changeit.
- *KeystoreType*: The type of keystore file to be used for the server certificate. If not specified, the default value is JKS.
- *Protocol*: The version of the SSL protocol to use. If not specified, the default is "TLS".

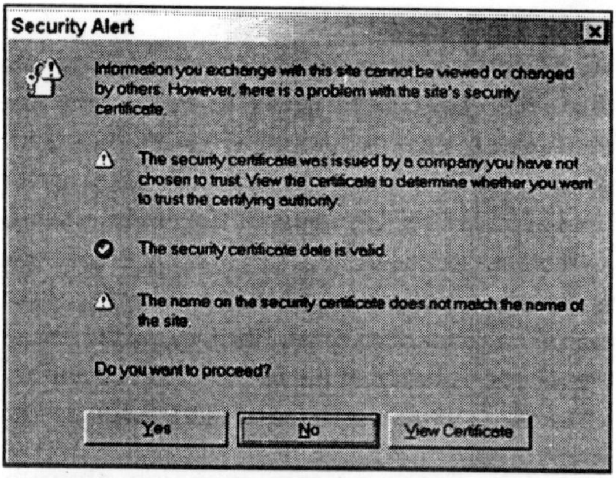

Fig. The Internet Explorer 5.5 security alert dialog.

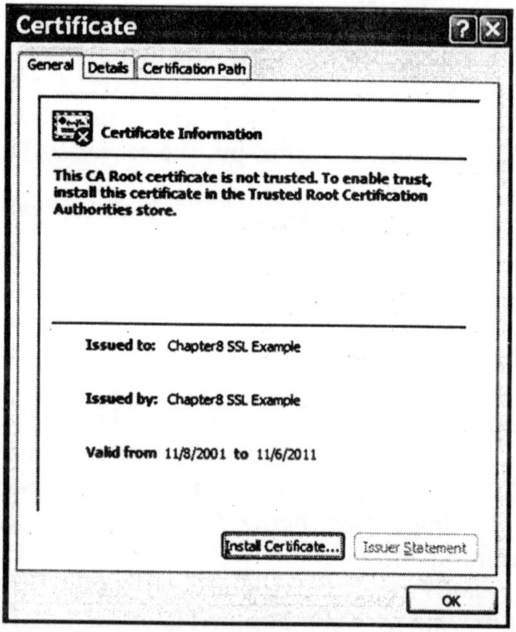

Fig. The Internet Explorer 5.5 SSL certificate details dialog.

SETTING THE CONTEXT ROOT OF A WEB APPLICATION

The context root of your web application determines

which URLs Tomcat will delegate to your web application. If your application's context root is myapp then any request for/ myapp or/myapp/* will be handled by your application unless a more specific context root exists. If a second web application were assigned the context root myapp/help then a request for/ myapp/help/help.jsp would be handled by the second web application, not the first.

This relationship also holds when the context root is set to/ , which is known as the root context. When an application is assigned to the root context, it will respond to all requests no handled by a more specific context root. The context root for an application is determined by how it is deployed. When a web application is deployed inside an EAR file, the context root is specified in the application.xml file of the EAR using a context-root element inside of a web module. In the following example, the context root of the web-client.war application is set bank.

```
<application xmlns="http://java.sun.com/xml/ns/
j2ee" version="1.4"
   xmlns:xsi="http://www.w3.org/2001/XMLSchema-
instance"
  xsi:schemaLocation="http://java.sun.com/xml/ns/
j2ee   http://java.sun.com/xml/ns/j2ee/
application_1_4.xsd">
  <display-name>JBossDukesBank</display-name>

  <module>
    <ejb>bank-ejb.jar</ejb>
  </module>
  <module>
    <web>
      <web-uri>web-client.war</web-uri>
      <context-root>bank</context-root>
    </web>
  </module>

</application>
```

For web applications that are deployed outside of an EAR file, the context root can be specified in two ways. First, the context root can be specified inside of the WEB-INF/jboss-web.xml file. The following example shows what the jboss-web.xml file would look like for the same web-client.war file if it weren't bundled inside of an EAR file.

```
<jboss-web>
<context-root>bank</context-root>
</jboss-web>
```

Finally, if no context root specification exists, the context root will be the base the name of the WAR file. For web-client.war, the context root would default to web-client. The only special case to this naming special name ROOT. To deploy your application under the root context, simply name it ROOT.war. JBoss already contains a ROOT.war web application in the jbossweb-tomcat50.sar directory. So, you will need to remove or rename that one to create your own root application.

Naming your WAR file after the context root they are intended to handle is a very good practice. Not only does it reduce the number of configuration settings to manage, but it improves the maintainability of the application by making the intended function of the web application clear.

SETTING UP VIRTUAL HOSTS

Virtual hosts allow you to group web applications according to the various DNS names by which the machine running JBoss is knownThis configuration defines a default host named vhost1.mydot.com and a second host named vhost2.mydot.com, which also has the alias www.mydot.com associated with it.

```
<Server>
  <Service name="jboss.web"
    className="org.jboss.web.tomcat.tc5.Standar
dService">

    <!-- A HTTP/1.1 Connector on port 8080 -->
                <Connector      port="8080"
address="${jboss.bind.address}"
          maxThreads="150" minSpareThreads="25"
```

```
maxSpareThreads="75"
                    enableLookups="false"
redirectPort="8443" acceptCount="100"
               connectionTimeout="20000"
disableUploadTimeout="true"/>

  <Engine name="jboss.web" defaultHost="vhost1">
                                          <Realm
className="org.jboss.web.tomcat.security.JBoss
SecurityMgrRealm"
      certificatePrincipal="org.jboss.security.auth.
certs.SubjectDNMapping"
     />
  <Logger className="org.jboss.web.tomcat.
Log4jLogger"
                verbosityLevel="WARNING"
category="org.jboss.web.localhost.Engine"/>

  <Host name="vhost1" autoDeploy="false"
    deployOnStartup="false" deployXML="false">
        <Alias>vhost1.mydot.com</Alias>
                                          <Valve
className="org.apache.catalina.valves.AccessLogValve"
                prefix="vhost1" suffix=".log"
pattern="common"
     directory="${jboss.server.home.dir}/log"/>
         <DefaultContext cookies="true"
crossContext="true" override="true"/>
      </Host>
     <Host name="vhost2" autoDeploy="false"
     deployOnStartup="false" deployXML="false">
        <Alias>vhost2.mydot.com</Alias>
        <Alias>www.mydot.com</Alias>

 <Valveclass Name="org.apache.catalina.
valves.AccessLogValve"
          prefix="vhost2" suffix=".log"
pattern="common"
```

```
            directory="${jboss.server.home.dir}/
log"/>

              <DefaultContext cookies="true"
crossContext="true" override="true"/>
        </Host>
    </Engine>
   </Service>
</Server>
```

When a WAR file is deployed, it will be by default associated with the virtual host whose name matches the defaultHost attribute of the containing Engine. To deploy a WAR to a specific virtual host you need to specify an appropriate virtual-host definition in your e jboss-web.xmldescriptor. The following jboss-web.xml descriptor demonstrates how to deploy a WAR to the virtual host www.mydot.com. Note that we can use either the virtual host name in the config file or the actual host name.

```
<jboss-web>
<context-root>/</context-root>
<virtual-host>www.mydot.com</virtual-host>
</jboss-web>
```

SERVING STATIC CONTENT

JBoss provides a default application that serves content for the *root* application context. This default context is the ROOT.war application in the jbossweb-tomcat50.sar directory. You can serve static files not associated with any other application by adding that content to theROOT.war directory. For example, if you want to have a shared image directory you could create an image subdirectory inside of ROOT.warand place the images there.

USING APACHE WITH THE TOMCAT

In some architectures, it is useful to put an Apache web server in front of the JBoss server. External web clients talk to an Apache instance, which in turn speaks to the Tomcat instance on behalf of the clients. Apache needs to be configured to use the mod_jk module which speaks the AJP protocol to an AJP connector running in Tomcat. The provided server.xml file comes with this AJP connector enabled.

```
<Connector port="8009"
address="${jboss.bind.address}"
enableLookups="false" redirectPort="8443"
debug="0"
protocol="AJP/1.3"/>
```

You'll need to consult the Apache and mod_jk documentation for complete installation instructions. Assuming you have a properly configured Apache instance, the following configuration fragment shows an example of how to connect with a WAR deployed with a context root of/jbosstest.

```
...
LoadModule jk_module libexec/mod_jk.so
AddModule mod_jk.c

<IfModule mod_jk.c>
JkWorkersFile/tmp/workers.properties
JkLogFile/tmp/mod_jk.log
JkLogLevel debug
JkMount/jbosstest/* ajp13
</IfModule>
```

The workers.properties file contains the details of how to contact the JBoss instance.

USING CLUSTERING

JBoss supports clustering in the embedded Tomcat service.

The steps to setup clustering of Tomcat embedded containers is:

- If you are using a load balancer, make sure that your setup uses sticky sessions. This means that if a user that starts a session on node A, all subsequent requests are forwarded to node A as long node A is up and running.
- If you aren't using the all configuration, make sure that cluster-service.xml is in your deploy directory. If it isn't, copy cluster-service.xml fromserver/all/

deploy into your deploy directory. You also need the jgroups.jar in your lib directory. This can be found in the server/all/libdirectory.

- Start JBoss to check if your setup works. Look at the JMX management console. Find the jboss.cache: service=TomcatClusteringCache MBean. The StateString must be Started. If it is Stopped look in the server's log file.
- To enable clustering of your web applications you must mark them as distributable in the web.xml descriptor. For example:
- <?xml version="1.0"?>
- <!DOCTYPE web-app PUBLIC
- "-//Sun Microsystems, Inc.//DTD Web Application 2.3//EN"
- "http://java.sun.com/dtd/web-app_2_3.dtd ">
- <web-app>
- <distributable/>
- <!—... —>
  </web-app>
- Deploy your WAR as usual and it should now be clustered.

If you have deployed and accessed your application, go back to the jboss.cache:service=TomcatClusteringCache MBean and invoke theprintDetails operation. You should see output resembling the following.

```
/JSESSION
/n6HywRwITbY-xvzaZ0LS5Q**
n6HywRwITbY-xvzaZ0LS5Q**:
org.jboss.invocation.MarshalledValue@9c1dddab
/R1T4Dapn7c8T-+Ynd9v9MA**
R1T4Dapn7c8T-+Ynd9v9MA**:
org.jboss.invocation.MarshalledValue@8c0f60b6
```

This output shows two separate web sessions that are being shared via JBossCache. If you don't see any output, either the application was not correctly marked as distributable or you haven't accessed the a part of application that places values in the HTTP session.

INTEGRATING THIRD PARTY SERVLET CONTAINERS

This section describes the steps for integrating a third party web container into the JBoss application server framework. A web container is a J2EE server component that enables access to servlets and JSP pages. The most widely used servlet container is Tomcat, and this is the default web container used by JBoss.

Integrating a servlet container into JBoss consists of mapping web.xml JNDI information into the JBoss JNDI namespace using an optionaljboss-web.xml descriptor as well as delegating authentication and authorization to the JBoss security layer. Theorg.jboss.web.AbstractWebContainer class exists to simplify these tasks.

THE ABSTRACTWEBCONTAINER CLASS

The org.jboss.web.AbstractWebContainer class is an implementation of a template pattern for web container integration into JBoss. Web container providers wishing to integrate their container into a JBoss server should create a subclass of AbstractWebContainer and provide the web container specific setup and WAR deployment steps.

The AbstractWebContainer provides support for parsing the standard J2EE web.xmlweb application deployment descriptor JNDI and security elements as well as support for parsing the JBoss specific jboss-web.xmldescriptor. Parsing of these deployment descriptors is performed to generate an integrated JNDI environment and security context.

Abstract Web Container Contract

The AbstractWebContainer is an abstract class that implements the org.jboss.web.AbstractWebContainerMBean interface used by the JBoss J2EE deployer to delegate the task of installing war files needing to be deployed. We'll look at some of the key methods of theAbstractWebContainer below.

```
public boolean accepts(DeploymentInfo sdi)
{
  String warFile = sdi.url.getFile();
```

```
 return warFile.endsWith("war") ||
   warFile.endsWith("war/");
}
```

The accepts method is implemented by JBoss deployers to indicate which type of deployments they accept. The AbstractWebContainerhandles the deployments of WARs as JARs or unpacked directories.

```
public synchronized void start(DeploymentInfo di)
throws DeploymentException
{
  Thread thread = Thread.currentThread();
       ClassLoader   appClassLoader   =
thread.getContextClassLoader();

  try {
  // Create a classloader for the war to ensure
a unique ENC
     URL[] empty = {};
            URLClassLoader   warLoader   =
URLClassLoader.newInstance(empty, di.ucl);
     thread.setContextClassLoader(warLoader);
      WebDescriptorParser webAppParser = new
DescriptorParser(di);

     String webContext = di.webContext;
     if (webContext != null) {
          if  (webContext.length()  >  0  &&
webContext.charAt(0) !=
         '/') {
       webContext = "/" + webContext;
       }
     }

  // Get the war URL
   URL warURL = di.localUrl != null ? di.localUrl
: di.url;
    if (log.isDebugEnabled()) {
      log.debug("webContext: " + webContext);
```

```
        log.debug("warURL: " + warURL);
      log.debug("webAppParser: " + webAppParser);
     }

     // Parse the web.xml and jboss-web.xml
descriptors
       WebMetaData metaData = (WebMetaData)
di.metaData;
        parseMetaData(webContext, warURL,
di.shortName, metaData);

           WebApplication warInfo = new
WebApplication(metaData);
     warInfo.setDeploymentInfo(di);
      performDeploy(warInfo, warURL.toString(),
webAppParser);
       deploymentMap.put(warURL.toString(),
warInfo);

    // Generate an event for the startup
     super.start(di);
   } catch(DeploymentException e) {
     throw e;
   } catch(Exception e) {
     throw new DeploymentException("Error during
deploy", e);
   } finally {
    thread.setContextClassLoader(appClassLoader);
   }
}
```

This section corresponds to the start method. This method is a template pattern method implementation. The argument to the deploy method is the WAR deployment info object. This contains the URL to the WAR, the UnifiedClassLoader for the WAR, the parent archive such as an EAR, and the J2EE application.xml context-root if the WAR is part of an EAR.

The first step of the start method is to save the current thread context class loader and then create another

URLClassCloader (warLoader) using the WAR Unified ClassLoader as its parent. This warLoader is used to ensure a unique JNDI ENC (enterprise naming context) for the WAR will be created. The warLoader ClassLoader is set as the current thread context class loader before the performDeploy call is made. Next, the web.xml and jboss-web.xml descriptors are parsed by calling parseMetaData. Next, the web container-specific subclass is asked to perform the actual deployment of the WAR through the performDeploy call. The Web Application object for this deployment is stored in the deployed application map using the warUrl as the key. The final step is to restore the thread context class loader to the one that existed at the start of the method.

STACKS

ABSTRACT DATA TYPES

The data types you have seen so far are all concrete, in the sense that we have completely specified how they are implemented. For example, the Card class represents a card using two integers. As we discussed at the time, that is not the only way to represent a card; there are many alternative implementations.

An abstract data type, or ADT, specifies a set of operations (or methods) and the semantics of the operations (what they do), but it does not specify the implementation of the operations. That's what makes it abstract.

Why is that useful?

- It simplifies the task of specifying an algorithm if you can denote the operations you need without having to think at the same time about how the operations are performed.
- Since there are usually many ways to implement an ADT, it might be useful to write an algorithm that can be used with any of the possible implementations.
- Well-known ADTs, such as the Stack ADT are often implemented in standard libraries so they can be written once and used by many programmers.

- The operations on ADTs provide a common high-level language for specifying and talking about algorithms.

When we talk about ADTs, we often distinguish the code that uses the ADT, called the client code, from the code that implements the ADT, called theprovider code.

THE STACK ADT

In this, we will look at one common ADT, the stack. A stack is a collection, meaning that it is a data structure that contains multiple elements. Other collections we have seen include dictionaries and lists. An ADT is defined by the operations that can be performed on it, which is called an interface.

The interface for a stack consists of these operations:

- __init__: Initialize a new empty stack.
- *Push*: Add a new item to the stack.
- *Pop*: Remove and return an item from the stack. The item that is returned is always the last one that was added.
- *isEmpty*: Check whether the stack is empty.

A stack is sometimes called a "last in, first out" or LIFO data structure, because the last item added is the first to be removed.

IMPLEMENTING STACKS WITH PYTHON LISTS

The list operations that Python provides are similar to the operations that define a stack. The interface isn't exactly what it is supposed to be, but we can write code to translate from the Stack ADT to the built-in operations. This code is called an implementation of the Stack ADT. In general, an implementation is a set of methods that satisfy the syntactic and semantic requirements of an interface.

Here is an implementation of the Stack ADT that uses a Python list:

```
class Stack:
 def __init__(self):
  self.items = []
def push(self, item):
```

```
 self.items.append(item)
def pop(self):
 return self.items.pop()
def isEmpty(self):
 return (self.items == [])
```

A Stack object contains an attribute named items that is a list of items in the stack. The initialization method sets items to the empty list. To push a new item onto the stack, push appends it onto items. To pop an item off the stack, pop uses the homonymous * Note list method to remove and return the last item on the list.

Finally, to check if the stack is empty, isEmpty compares items to the empty list. An implementation like this, in which the methods consist of simple invocations of existing methods, is called a veneer. In real life, veneer is a thin coating of good quality wood used in furniture-making to hide lower quality wood underneath. Computer scientists use this metaphor to describe a small piece of code that hides the details of an implementation and provides a simpler, or more standard, interface.

PUSHING AND POPPING

A stack is a generic data structure, which means that we can add any type of item to it.

The following example pushes two integers and a string onto the stack:

```
s = Stack()
s.push(54)
s.push(45)
s.push("+")
```

We can use isEmpty and pop to remove and print all of the items on the stack:

```
while not s.isEmpty():
 print s.pop(),
```

The output is + 45 54. In other words, we just used a stack to print the items backward! Granted, it's not the standard format for printing a list, but by using a stack, it was remarkably easy to do. You should compare this bit of code to the impleme-ntation of printBackward. There is a natural parallel between the recursive version ofprintBackward and the stack algorithm here. The difference is that print Back warduses the runtime stack to keep track of the nodes while it traverses the list, and then prints them on the way back from the recursion. The stack algorithm does the same thing, except that it uses a Stack object instead of the runtime stack.

USING A STACK TO EVALUATE POSTFIX

In most programming languages, mathematical expressions are written with the operator between the two operands, as in 1+2. This format is called infix. An alternative used by some calculators is called postfix. In postfix, the operator follows the operands, as in 1 2 +.

The reason postfix is sometimes useful is that there is a natural way to evaluate a postfix expression using a stack:

- Starting at the beginning of the expression, get one term (operator or operand) at a time.
  - If the term is an operand, push it on the stack.
  - If the term is an operator, pop two operands off the stack, perform the operation on them, and push the result back on the stack.
- When you get to the end of the expression, there should be exactly one operand left on the stack. That operand is the result.

*As an exercise, apply this algorithm to the expression 1 2 + 3 *.*

This example demonstrates one of the advantages of postfix there is no need to use parentheses to control the order of operations. To get the same result in infix, we would have to write (1 + 2) * 3.

*As an exercise, write a postfix expression that is equivalent to 1 + 2 * 3.*

Compared to a real tree, the B-Tree has roots at the top and leaves and nodes at the bottom. The B-Tree belongs to a group of techniques in computer science known as self-balancing search trees which attempts to automatically keep the number of levels of nodes under the root small at all times. It is the most preferred way to implement sets, associative arrays and other data structures that are used in computer

Programming languages, relationaldatabase management systems and low level data manipulations. In the B-Tree, the records are stored in the leaves. This is the location where there is nothing more beyond it. The order of the tree determines the maximum number of children per node. Depth refers to the number of required disk access. A B-Tree can have up to millions and billions of records although it is not all the time that leaves necessarily contain a record but more than half certainly do.

When decision points on the tree, which are called nodes, are on the hard disk instead of on random access memory (RAM), B-Tree is the preferred technique as hard disks could work a thousand times slower compared to RAM because processes on hard disks requires mechanical parts. On RAM, processes are done purely in electronic media. The nodes in a B-Tree can have a variable number of child nodes within a range pre-defined by the system. When a data is inserted or removed from a node, the number ofchild nodes also changes but the pre-defined ranged should be maintained so internal nodes may either be split or joined.

B-trees do not need frequent re-balancing as both the upper and lower bounds on the number of child nodes are typically fixed. As an example, a 2-3 B-Tree implementation has internal nodes that can only have 2 or 3 child nodes.

To keep the B-tree well balanced, all leaf nodes are required to be of the same depth. The depth only increases very slowly and infrequently. Searching in a B-Tree structure starts from the root and traversed from top to bottom. Insertion is done by looking for a node where a new leaf or element should be. If there is still room or the maximum legal number of elements is not exceeded, insertion takes place. Otherwise, the leaf node splits into another tow nodes. Deletion in a B-Tree has two strategies. The first involves locating the item to be deleted and immediately doing the action then restructuring the tree. The second involves doing a traversing down the tree and laying out the restructure before deleting.

In a file system, a file may contain any number of B-Trees and each B-Tree must have a unique name composed of any string of characters. Each B-Tree names is saved in the file an item containing the number of the rood node of the B-Tree. Searching, inserting and deleting through the B-Tree starts from the root node. The B-Tree was created by Rudolf Bayer and Ed McCreight. The B in the B-Tree has ambiguous meaning. Some say it stands for Bayer while others say it stands for Balanced and still there are other who consider it to stand for Boeing where both men were working for Boeing Scientific Research Labs at the time they created the B-tree.

B-Tree structures support various basic dynamic set operations including *Search, Predecessor, Successor, Minimum, Maximum, Insert,* and *Delete* in time proporticnal to the height of the tree. Ideally, a tree will be balanced and the height will be *log n* where *n* is the number of nodes in the tree. To ensure that the height of the tree is as small as possible and therefore provide the best running time, a balanced tree structure like a red-black tree, AVL tree, or b-tree must be used.

When working with large sets of data, it is often not possible or desirable to maintain the entire structure in primary storage (RAM). Instead, a relatively small portion of the data structure is maintained in primary storage, and additional data is read from secondary storage as needed. Unfortunately, a magnetic disk, the most common form of secondary storage, is significantly slower than random access memory (RAM). In fact, the system often spends more time retrieving data than actually processing data. B-trees are balanced trees that are optimized for situations when part or all of the tree must be maintained in secondary storage such as a magnetic disk. Since disk accesses are expensive (time consuming) operations, a b-tree tries to minimize the number of disk accesses. For example, a b-tree with a height of 2 and a branching factor of 1001 can store over one billion keys but requires at most two disk accesses to search for any node.

The methods must be integrated with the in-house design and manufacturing data bases, the 3-D CAD/CAMsystems, and also be easy to use. Suppliers and partners will have access to the resulting design information via Technical Data Interchange (TDI). This will ensure consistency with an up-to-date knowledge of the requirements for loads, interfaces and the space envelopes available for their products. The immediate dissemination to suppliers of information on design changes will help diminish subsequent redesign activity and the time and cost penalties incurred for rework.

The preliminary structural design will often use detailed Finite Element Methods (FEM) for analysis, coupled with constrained optimization, and the process must be highly automated for rapid creation of FEM meshing for models. In order to achieve shortened design cycle time, the loads and dynamics stiffness requirements must become available much sooner than at present.

This will require early development of MDO models for overall aerodynamic and structural optimization that will define the static and dynamic loads for flight and ground operations. Trade-off studies must rapidly search for the best designs and arrive at realistic structural sizes, providing space envelopes and accurate weights to minimize subsequent redesign.

Bibliography

Alur Deepak: *Core J2EE Patterns: Best Practices and Design Strategies*, New York: Prentice-Hall Press, 2002.

Andrew W.: *Modern Compiler Implementation in Java*, Cambridge University Press, 2001.

Barclay: *Object-Oriented Design with UML and Java*, London: Academic Press, 2005.

Bauer Christian: *Java Persistence with Hibernate*, New York: Manning Publications, 2005.

Bergsten Hans: *Java Server Pages*, USA: O'Reilly Media Press, 2003.

Bloch Joshua: *Effective Java*, London: Sun Microsystems Press, 2000.

Brittain Jason: *Title: Tomcat: The Definitive Guide*, New York: Addison-Wesley Press, 2003.

Brown Larry: *Core Servlets and JavaServer*, London: Prentice-Hall Press, 2001.

Croft: *Advanced Java Game Programming*, New York: John Wiley & Sons Publication, 2001.

Darwin: *Java Cookbook*, London: Prentice-Hall, 2002.

Dewsbury Ryan: *Google Web Toolkit Applications*, New York: Prentice-Hall Press, 2003.

Elliotte: *Java Network Programming*, London: Manning Publications, 2003.

Farley Jim: *Java Enterprise in a Nutshell*, New York: O'Reilly Media, Press, 2003.

Fisher Maydene: *JDBC API Tutorial and Reference*: Londin: Addison-Wesley, Press, 2001.

Geary: *Core JavaServer Faces*, London: Manning Publications, 2004.

Goetz Brian: *Java Concurrency in Practice*, London: Addison-Wesley Press, 2001.

Goodrich T.: *Data Structures and Algorithms in Java*, London: John Wiley & Sons Publication, 200.

Kalin Martin: *Java Web Services: Up and Running*, London: CRC Press, 2006.

Lindholm: *The Java Virtual Machine Specification*, London: Cambridge University Press, 2001.

Linwood: *Building Portals with the Java Portlet API*, New York: Beedle & Associates, 2001.

Mark D.: *SOA Using Java Web Services*, London: Cambridge University, 2003.

Martin C.: *UML for Java Programmers*, London: Prentice-Hall Press, 2001.

Monson-Haefel: *J2EE Web Services*, New York: John Wiley & Sons Publication, 2001.

Neward Ted: *Effective Enterprise Java*, New York: Digital Systems Research Center Research Report, 2001.

Sedgewick Robert: *Algorithms in Java*, New York: O'Reilly Media Press, 2003.

Shirazi Jack: *Java Performance Tuning*, London: Sun Microsystems Press. 2000.

Walrath Kathy: *The JFC Swing Tutorial: A Guide to Constructing GUIs*, London: Addison-Wesley Press, 2001.

Watt: *Programming Language Processors in Java: Compilers and Interpreters*, New York: Beedle & Associates, 2001.

Index

A

Abruptly 74, 144
Accessible 32, 152, 196, 230
Aliasesfriend 67
API 8, 9, 16, 23, 26, 27, 28, 29, 30, 31, 43, 51, 52, 53, 54, 56, 57, 58, 59, 76, 105, 114, 116, 119, 134, 168, 169, 178, 219
Appletviewer 12, 13
Architecture 9, 18, 22, 23, 24, 25, 29, 30, 45, 65, 72, 85, 86, 87, 93, 94, 95, 99, 100, 104, 105, 107, 108, 109, 161, 169, 170, 171, 178, 211, 267
Augmenting 239
Authentication 2, 4, 9, 21, 22, 52, 53, 56, 57, 58, 59, 65, 146, 157, 159, 160, 161, 162, 163, 164, 165, 166, 167, 169, 175, 176, 177, 178, 180, 181, 182, 183, 184, 185, 187, 188, 190, 191, 192, 194, 195, 197, 198, 199, 200, 201, 202, 203, 204, 205, 206, 207, 208, 209, 215, 218, 223, 224, 225, 226, 227, 228, 229, 230, 234, 235, 236, 237, 239, 240, 241, 259, 267

B

Binary 34, 39, 41, 86, 92, 93, 107, 109, 110, 111, 112, 113
Brazenly 30
Bytecodes 16, 33, 34, 35, 36, 37, 38, 41, 42, 43, 93, 108, 113, 114, 129, 132, 133, 134, 136, 138, 141, 144

C

Capabilities 1, 52, 59, 86, 95, 98, 159
Compatibility 23, 39, 40, 41, 48, 50, 93
Consequence 33, 86, 103, 248
Corba 103
Credentials 58, 160, 161, 164, 165, 166, 167, 178, 183, 195, 200, 207, 208, 209, 210, 213, 215, 218, 228, 235, 236, 237, 239
Customizable 21, 23, 45

D

DCOM 103
DTD 252
Duringlogin 218, 219

E

EJB Method 149, 151, 152, 178, 179, 180, 193
Encapsulated 48, 67, 68, 75
Encryption 2, 4, 9, 53, 226, 228, 236

F

Finalization 144
Forbidden 31, 32, 45, 46, 74

I

Importantly 1, 43
Infrastructure 23, 24, 51, 65, 66, 99, 159, 175, 190, 211, 218, 226
Initialization 97, 107, 108, 109, 112, 114, 115, 116, 117, 119, 123, 133, 188, 192
Instantiation 126, 127, 171, 172
Intermediate 36, 128
Invokespecial 132, 136, 137, 138, 140, 141, 142

J

Jaas 173, 175, 176, 177, 180, 181, 182, 183, 184, 185, 186, 187, 188, 190, 192, 204, 205, 209, 223, 225, 227, 228, 237, 238
JAR File 21, 26, 52, 53, 54, 55, 56, 57, 62, 63, 64, 66, 72, 94
JSSE 242, 243, 247, 257

M

Magnitude 3
Malicious 20, 22, 24, 25, 29, 31, 43, 45, 55, 65, 83, 105
Manipulation 43, 185

P

Periodically 251
Pluggable 159, 175
Preventing 3, 9, 29, 55, 157
Primordial 26, 27
Prohibitively 54
Propagated 149, 251
Putstaticinstruction 108

R

RMI 16, 97, 98, 100, 103, 105, 226, 227, 228, 229, 243, 244, 245, 249
Robustness 1, 33, 42, 43, 106

S

Sandbox 5, 6, 7, 8, 9, 10, 11, 12, 16, 17, 18, 21, 22, 23, 24, 29, 43, 44, 45, 52, 56, 57, 59, 65, 72, 96
Serialization 97, 98, 105
Spontaneous 20
SRP 225, 226, 227, 228, 229, 230, 231, 232, 233, 234, 235, 236, 237, 239, 240, 248
Subinterface 109, 123, 161, 167,
Superinterfaces 109, 113, 117

U

Ubiquitous 1
Ultimately 4
Utilize 1

V

Volcano 24, 25, 28, 29, 39, 40, 41